DIVINE
REVERSAL

DIVINE
REVERSAL

THE TRANSFORMING

ETHICS OF JESUS

— RABBI —

RUSSELL RESNIK

Lederer Books
a division of
Messianic Jewish Publishers
Clarksville, Maryland

Printed in the United States of America

Cover Design by
Josh Huhn, Design Point, Inc.
Layout Design by
Transcontinental Media

13 12 11 10   4 3 2 1

ISBN 978-1-880226-80-3

Library of Congress Catalog Control Number: 2009931816

Lederer Books
A division of
MESSIANIC JEWISH PUBLISHERS
6120 Day Long Lane
Clarksville, MD 21029

Distributed by
Messianic Jewish Resources International
Order line: (800) 410-7367
Lederer@messianicjewish.net
www.messianicjewish.net

I thank my wife, Jane, for her support and insights throughout the whole writing process, my friends at Lederer/Messianic Jewish Publishers for shepherding this work from broad concept to printed text, and my colleagues in the Union of Messianic Jewish Congregations for years of conversation, debate, and mutual refinement in what it means to follow Yeshua as Jews.

To my UMJC colleagues, this book is dedicated.

Shavuot 5769
Pentecost 2009

OTHER BOOKS BY AUTHOR

Gateways to Torah
Joining the Ancient Conversation on the Weekly Portion

Creation to Completion
A Guide to Life's Journey from the Five Books of Moses

CONTENTS

INTRODUCTION
THE JEWISH JESUS AND HIS MESSAGE

Not long ago, I attended services at a megachurch in Texas with some friends. As we were making our way out, my friends introduced me to a nationally known motivational speaker who was a member there. When he found out that I was Jewish, he said, "Oh, some of my favorite authors are Jewish." I thought, *Sure, Matthew, Mark, John...* but he said, "You know, Moses, Isaiah, David...." Apparently, for my new acquaintance, some wonderful Jews wrote the Old Testament, but the New Testament authors were not in that category. I'm sure he would have acknowledged that Matthew was Jewish and that the one of whom Matthew wrote was Jewish, too, but he didn't seem to have really absorbed the fact that the Gospels were originally Jewish books. Among writers and academics, both Christian and Jewish, the situation is quite different. Not only do they recognize that Jesus was Jewish, but many claim that he cannot really be understood apart from his Jewishness.

Orthodox Jewish scholar Pinchas Lapide writes, "[E]verything Jesus said and accomplished, did and did not do, on earth discloses its full meaning only when seen against his profound Jewishness."[1] Christian scholars have made a similar point:

> [W]e forget what the New Testament writers and above all Jesus himself never forgot: that salvation is of the Jews, not in some trivial sense, but in the rich sense that in order to save the world the creator God chose Abraham and said "in your seed all the families of the earth will he blessed." It is precisely because Jesus of Nazareth is the fulfillment of this promise that he is relevant in all times and places. It is precisely because he is The Jew par excellence that he is relevant to all Gentiles as well as Jews.[2]

The Jewishness of Jesus, however, is not just a matter of his descent from Abraham, but also of his deep connection with the Jewish people and their whole story. This connection is an essential key to understanding him. Brad Young in his popular work, *Jesus the Jewish*

1

Theologian, writes, "We must not 'kill' Jesus by destroying his links to his people and his faith. For Jesus, Judaism was a vibrant belief in the true God.... He sought to reform and revitalize, not to destroy and replace.... The Jewish roots of Jesus' teachings lead to a fresh hearing of the ancient text."[3]

Jesus, the Jewish Teacher

This book does not need to prove the Jewishness of Jesus. Instead it asks, if we start with the premise that Jesus is a Jewish teacher—and there is plenty of evidence that we should—how does this help us understand more fully his life and teachings? We will listen to Jewish voices, from the Mishnah and Talmud to more modern works, not to demonstrate the Jewishness of Jesus, but to better grasp the authentic ethical message of Jesus. If Jesus speaks from a Jewish context, it may be that other Jewish sources, even though many are from a later era, will help us properly understand his words. This approach is relevant to both those who acknowledge Jesus as Messiah and those who do not. Indeed, the answers we discover may help some decide whether to acknowledge him as Messiah.

As a Jewish teacher, Jesus doesn't separate matters of theology from practice. His teaching is consistently practical, ethical, and applicable to real life, even two thousand years after it was originally given, since "for Jews, love of God without deeds pleasing to God is hypocrisy, empty blather. In Jesus' words, 'By their fruits you will know them!' (Matt. 7:16)."[4] In this book, therefore, we will explore Jesus' teachings as they apply to our own deeds today, as well as how they might have applied in their original setting.

As a Jewish teacher, furthermore, Jesus personally represents and exemplifies everything he teaches. He never hides behind theory or abstraction. Hence, his life and character—who he is—help us understand his message, and conversely his message helps us understand who he really is. But be warned; Jesus' message, like Jesus' identity itself, will take us by surprise if we understand it correctly. "What he signified is always more challenging than we expect, more outrageous, more egregious."[5]

In contrast, the contemporary Christian world, at least in the West, tends to prefer an abstract, idealized sense of truth and, therefore, adopts that view of Jesus as well. It wants a Jesus who is clearly defined, incorporated into its creeds, and set up as a boundary marker between the insiders and the outsiders. One Christian author recognizes this tendency and its dangers:

> The desire to find, declare, and propagate a simple and univocal Jesus who "matches" an individual

believer (or some group of believers) perfectly—and without remainder—is ... idolatrous, since it exchanges difficult and challenging truth for a counterfeit version that is more comfortable. But by "truth" I do not mean some other single image of Jesus that is better than those being proposed. I mean instead the truth of the process of personal and intersubjective learning.[6]

It is just such a process of personal and intersubjective learning that this book will pursue. And it will pursue it by focusing on ethics— right behavior toward other people—because Jesus placed so much emphasis upon ethics in his teaching. The Sermon on the Mount is central to Jesus' ethical teaching, but the entire gospel account—not just his specific teachings, but his whole story—conveys the ethic of Jesus. Therefore, we will spend a good amount of time with the Sermon on the Mount, but we will consider the entire Jesus story as well. Because it is a Jewish story starring a Jewish Messiah, we will generally use his Hebrew name, rather than an English translation of his Greek name, and call him from here on Yeshua.

The Key to Scripture

Once, a scribe who had become impressed with Yeshua's teaching asked him what was the most important commandment of all.

Yeshua answered, "The first is, 'Hear, O Israel: the Lord our God, the Lord is one; you shall love the Lord your God with all your heart, and with all your soul, and with all your mind, and with all your strength.' The second is this, 'You shall love your neighbor as yourself.' There is no other commandment greater than these." (Mark 12:29–31)

Matthew adds an additional comment of Yeshua's, "On these two commandments hang all the Torah and the Prophets" (Matt. 22:40).[7] The whole message of Scripture, which Yeshua fully upheld in his life and ministry, hangs upon love for God and love for our neighbor. This love for neighbor, of course, is not a matter of mere sentiment, but of treating our neighbor the way we would want to be treated. Or as Yeshua said elsewhere, "In everything do to others as you would have them do to you; for this is the Torah and the Prophets" (Matt. 7:12).

    In contrast, some expressions of Christianity, particularly in the modern era, tend to view the ethical dimension as secondary to the theological dimension. They tend to emphasize Yeshua's person and the nature of his atoning work over his teaching and example. I don't want to minimize either aspect, but Yeshua himself says that the whole of Scripture—or at least the whole of Scripture that he and the rest of the Jewish people possessed in his day—depends not upon proper definitions of God and his nature but on two *commandments*. And these commandments focus on our relationships with God and our fellow human beings. Yeshua seems more intent on teaching a way of life than on defining theological truths. As we study this way of life, however, we will see that it is far more than adherence to a set of rules or ethical guidelines; rather Yeshua's ethics reveal his character as God in our midst, and adopting them transforms our character from within.

In emphasizing the ethical dimension, Yeshua is accurately reflecting the Hebrew Scriptures. In the first chapter of *A Code of Jewish Ethics*, entitled, "What Matters Most to God,"[8] Rabbi Joseph Telushkin argues that ethical behavior is the essence of Judaism and shows how this emphasis stems directly from the Hebrew Scriptures. For example, the foundational Ten Commandments "obligate Jews to affirm God … and to observe the Sabbath … and ban idolatry." They also deal with strictly ethical issues because they "prohibit murder, adultery, stealing, bearing false witness, taking God's Name in vain [which has ethical implications] and covetousness." Telushkin concludes that the testimony of the Ten Commandments "seems overwhelming: Moral rules regulating relations between human beings are primary. Morality is the essence of Judaism."[9]

Telushkin traces this emphasis through the rest of Torah and the Prophets, citing examples such as Micah 6:8—"And what does the Lord require of you? To do justice, love mercy, and walk humbly with God"[10]—and Zechariah 7:9–10—"This is what the God of Hosts said: 'Render true justice, be kind and merciful to one another. Do not oppress the widow, the orphan, the convert or the poor; and not plot evil in your hearts against one another.'" Telushkin comments, "As the prophet makes clear, it was the Israelites' refusal to obey these injunctions (Zechariah does not mention ritual violations) that prompted God's great anger at them (7:11–12)."[11]

Rabbi Telushkin, of course, doesn't believe in Yeshua as Messiah, but his words support Yeshua's claim that the whole of Scripture hangs on the two commandments to love God and our neighbor. The second commandment at least brings us into the realm of ethics, and it cannot at all be separated from the first because loving our neighbor arises out of and is dependent upon our love of God. The ethical and theological are intimately related. Furthermore, Yeshua does not just give ethical instruction; he offers transformative ethnics, ethics entailing a change of character that will inevitably become embodied in our behavior.

Ethics always have to do with how we live and behave—how we treat those around us in ways that can be seen and experienced; therefore, my emphasis throughout the book will be practical. Sometimes I will spend time laying a theological or interpretive foundation, but the goal is always to more accurately understand the practical implications of Yeshua's teachings. Because of this emphasis, this book won't explore every theological question inherent in the Jewish ethical pathway of Yeshua. But of course, "Of making many books there is no end" (Ecc. 12:12), and we will have to leave some questions for the next one.

Divine Reversal: A Jewish Theme

At the core of Yeshua's ethical teaching is the theme of divine reversal. Indeed, we will be considering divine reversal as a dominant theme of the entire gospel story. The kingdom of God is announced as a reign that overturns and reverses the priorities of the kingdoms of man. It is a kingdom based on self-giving love and true justice between human beings rather than on the quest for power and self-aggrandizement, which characterizes the kingdoms of this world. The king of this kingdom arrives on the scene in simplicity, even in weakness, reversing the way that we would expect the Son of God to step onto the stage of history. As he lays out the standards and values of his kingdom—which is the subject matter of this book—he continues this theme of reversal. Those who are great in the kingdom are the lowest of all and the servants of all. This king models servanthood in all that he does, ultimately laying down his life for his subjects. This final act of apparent weakness is in fact the pinnacle of divine reversal, overturning the powers and values of the kingdom of man to lay the foundation of the kingdom of God.

The theme of divine reversal comes to fulfillment in the Gospels but it is not foreign to Jewish thinking. Indeed, it is deeply rooted in the Hebrew Scriptures, beginning in the Torah with the narratives of Genesis. For example, God chooses Abraham to become the father of the Chosen People and a blessing to all humankind, but Abraham is without an heir and married to a woman who apparently is barren. In accord with an ancient custom, Abraham sires a son through his wife's slave, Hagar, but God makes it clear that Ishmael, the firstborn, will not be Abraham's heir. Instead, God allows Abraham's wife to finally conceive and give him a son. The son of the barren wife, the younger Isaac, will carry on Abraham's legacy (Gen. 17:15–21). Here is a double reversal: An elderly couple produces a son after many years of barrenness, and this younger son will inherit in place of his older brother. This reversal was undoubtedly even more striking to those who first heard the story. Ancient Hebrew practice clearly gave the inheritance rights and privileges to the firstborn, as was expressed later in the Torah:

> If a man has two wives, one of them loved and the other disliked, and if both the loved and the disliked have borne him sons, the firstborn being the son of the one who is disliked, then on the day when he wills his possessions to his sons, he is not permitted to treat the son of the loved as the firstborn in preference to the son of the disliked, who is the firstborn. He must acknowledge as firstborn the son of the one who is disliked, giving him a double portion of all that he has; since he is the first issue of his virility, the right of the firstborn is his. (Deut. 21:15–17)

The right of the firstborn is not explained or rationalized here. It is assumed as a foundation of the social order that is not to be overturned by mere human preference. But the line of the patriarchs displays a divine reversal of this practice: Isaac, not Ishmael; Jacob, not Esau; and Judah (or Joseph), not Reuben. Thus, the Jewish people as a whole are a product of divine reversal, displaying this dynamic on the stage of human history.

Later, the story of David echoes the same reversal. Samuel comes to the house of Jesse to anoint a new king for Israel, and Eliab, the firstborn,[12] is presented to him. "But the LORD said to Samuel, 'Do not look on his appearance or on the height of his stature, because I have rejected him; for the LORD does not see as mortals see; they look on the outward appearance, but the LORD looks on the heart'" (1 Sam. 16:7). God not only has Samuel pass over the firstborn son, but he chooses David, whom his father had mentioned as an afterthought, "There remains yet the youngest, but he is keeping the sheep" (1 Sam. 16:11). Everyone is taken by surprise, but they shouldn't have been because this simply repeated the pattern set in the patriarchs' lives, which elevates the wisdom of God over the wisdom of humankind. Significantly, when the God of Israel takes on human form, he comes as the Son of David, an afterthought in the minds of humankind—"he had no form or majesty that we should look at him, nothing in his appearance that we should desire him" (Isa. 53:2b)—but the essential player in the drama directed by God.

Divine reversal not only characterizes Yeshua and his ethical teaching, but it also holds a promise for those who seek to follow him. We are not on our own on this spiritual journey, but when we are faithful in pursuing the Master's pathway, he will change us on a personal level through a process of divine reversal. This book does not lay out a code of behavior but serves as a guide on a journey of trans-formation designed by the Master himself.

A Jewish Reading of Scripture

Our emphasis on the Jewishness of Jesus leads us to read the Gospels in ways that Jewish students have read the Torah for mil-lennia. This approach to reading will become clear as we go, but we can consider some aspects before we begin.[13]

First, the Scripture is divinely inspired, the very Word of God.[14] Hence, every phrase and word, even the smallest parts of words, which Yeshua termed "one jot or one tittle" (in the King James Version), are packed with meaning. The art of Jewish interpretation is to discover and unpack the meaning that lies within the details of the text, sometimes in rather imaginative ways. Therefore, Jewish interpretation doesn't always look for a text's one true and final meaning but often discovers, and lives quite happily with, multiple meanings. Furthermore, to the bafflement of more modern and lin-ear readers, Jewish interpretation can live happily even with appar-ently contradictory meanings. Because Scripture is the Word of God, its possibilities are boundless—although, of course, there are read-ings that violate the clear message of Scripture as a whole and can't be accepted.

Openness to multiple implications of the biblical text leads to a conversational approach to study because there is always something new to learn and consider through interaction with other students, both past and present. In this book, we extend the ancient Jewish conversation about Scripture into our reading of the Gospels to dis-cover new and deeper meaning there.

Another aspect of a Jewish reading of Scripture is its attention to narrative—the storyline of the Bible—as a means of conveying theological truth. Jewish students traditionally expect that the story's details, and the way that it's told, will have as much to teach as the more explicit doctrinal portions of Scripture.

Attention to the narrative flow of Scripture reveals an underlying unity within it. Not only is there continuity within the biblical narra-tive as a whole, but also the individual stories are often interconnect-ed in ways that carry tremendous meaning. Torah translator Robert Alter notes "… a general biblical pattern in which history is seen as a cycle of approximate and significant recurrences."[15] Thus, as an example from the earliest chapters of Genesis, God's interrogation of Cain (Gen. 4:9–12) echoes his interrogation of Adam (Gen. 3:9–12), both beginning with the question "Where?" In the next chapter, the description of Seth's birth to Adam, "in his likeness after his image"

(Gen. 5:3, NJPS), echoes God's decision to make humankind "in our image, after our likeness" (Gen. 1:26, NJPS).

As another example, after Abraham arrives in the land promised to him by God, he goes down to Egypt to escape a famine. Later he goes forth from Egypt with many possessions after God afflicts the pharaoh with plagues (Gen. 12:10–20). This story, of course, is retold in Exodus with the children of Israel re-enacting the part of Abraham. Later, it will be retold again in Matthew when Yeshua and his family flee for their lives to Egypt and then re-enter the land of Israel. The stories of Torah are repeated and expanded in Torah itself and throughout the Hebrew Scriptures to reveal new theological truth. We will encounter the same echoing and retelling of the ancient stories as we hear the Gospels with Jewish ears.

Gospel and *Midrash*

It may seem odd, however, to speak of hearing the Gospels with Jewish ears because the word *Gospel* itself is a quintessentially Christian term. But like so much surrounding the figure of Yeshua, it is thoroughly rooted in the Jewish world of his day. Gospel is a translation of the Greek word *evangelion*, which is not a specifically religious term but means good news, a glad announcement, or perhaps a declaration of victory. It parallels the Hebrew word *besorah*, which we will sometimes use in place of gospel.

Another term that is essential to our study is *midrash*, based on a Hebrew root meaning "to explore or search out." "It is a search for solutions from the text of the Bible to questions that the text does not directly address. *Midrash* is born out of problems that exist in the text as well as the contemporary needs of the believing community. … "[16] Midrash explores the rich and sometimes mysterious layers of the ancient biblical text to discover messages for our lives today. Modern readers might argue whether these messages are really *in* the text or are just read *into* it by creative interpreters. In Jewish tradition, however, discovering new and unexpected meanings—as long as there is some connection to the text—is seen as a way to honor Scripture as the Word of God and to unlock another portion of its infinite meaning. Through story and metaphor, midrash brings together the varying challenges of life and the eternal truths of Scripture. Through midrash, Scripture informs our imaginations and our common sense, and often reveals itself in new and striking ways.

Both Yeshua and the writers who tell his story utilize midrash continually. They use it to explore the meaning of Scripture in light of the new reality introduced by the besorah of Messiah and to show how that new reality emerges from all that has come before in Scripture.

Occasionally you will see the word Midrash, spelled with a capital "M." This refers to a specific rabbinic collection of *midrashim* (the plural of midrash), called Midrash Rabbah, commentaries on the Five Books of Moses, and the five scrolls of the Song of Solomon, Ruth, Lamentations, Ecclesiastes, and Esther.

Finally, I have used the term Torah several times already without explaining its meaning. Torah is one of the central concepts of Judaism, which has found its way into the vocabulary of Christian students of Scripture as well. Often translated as "law," Torah is better defined as instruction. In its simplest use it refers to the Five Books of Moses and especially to the legal and ethical instruction within those books, but it can also be applied to the whole of the Hebrew Scriptures and to Jewish writings commenting on Scripture, especially on the Five Books of Moses. Torah can even mean "teaching" when it is distinct from the Word of God. For example, we can speak of Yeshua's torah (teaching), which reflects or, as he claims, fulfills Torah (God's teachings in Scripture).

Throughout this book, we will emphasize ethics, the pathway of right behavior. But this emphasis doesn't eliminate our need for the Holy Spirit's leading. Yeshua didn't say, "Follow my instructions," or "Follow the ethical pathway that I will describe." Rather he said, "Follow me." As Eugene Peterson notes:

> When we follow Jesus, it means that we don't know exactly what it means, at least in detail. We follow him, letting him pick the roads, set the timetables, tell us what we need to know but only when we need to know it. ... When Jesus says, "Follow me," and we follow, we don't know where we will go next or what we will do next. That is why we follow the one who does know.[17]

Overview

Prologue: Creation Renewed

The *besorah* presents the life and ministry of Yeshua as a new beginning—a new creation—that restores us to the relationship with God revealed in the original creation. This new creation is the proper backdrop for understanding and applying Yeshua's ethical teachings.

Section One: *Hesed*, the Ethic of Reversal

Hesed is the Hebrew word translated as "loving-kindness," "covenant faithfulness," "mercy," or various other terms. It lies at the heart of Yeshua's ethics.

Chapter 1: "Follow Me"

Yeshua is unique among the prophets and teachers in Israel in not only calling his disciples to follow him, but also in placing this act of following as the highest value. Following Yeshua requires *t'shuvah* (repentance—turning from sinful behavior and turning to God), so that our behavior is guided, as Yeshua's was, by hesed.

Chapter 2: Mercy, Not Sacrifice

We will discover in depth the meaning of hesed by comparing it, as Yeshua did, with sacrifice, in accordance with Hosea 6:6—"I desire mercy and not sacrifice."

Section Two: Torah from the Mount

The details of Yeshua's ethical teaching are spelled out in the Sermon on the Mount, Matthew 5–7. We will consider in detail Matthew 5, which constitutes Yeshua's major commentary on Torah and on the theme of divine reversal.

Chapter 3: Introduction (Matt. 5:1–20)

Yeshua outlines the true components of happiness, which are a reversal of most of the qualities generally assumed to make people happy. He notes that this happiness doesn't come by being freed from Torah but through true obedience.

Chapter 4: Reconciliation (Matt. 5:21–26)

A genuine walk with God requires us to be at peace with our fellow human beings. Yeshua teaches on the importance of forgiveness, and this chapter outlines the steps to attain forgiveness.

Chapter 5: Faithfulness (Matt. 5:27–32)

Yeshua upholds the highest standards of sexual purity and marital faithfulness. We explore some practical ramifications of these standards.

Chapter 6: True Speech (Matt. 5:33–37)
Why is truth in our words so vital to Yeshua's ethics?
Are there any situations where we may need to compromise honesty for the sake of something else? If so, what lessons does this teach us?

Chapter 7: Resistance (Matt. 5:38–42)
One of the messages of the Sermon on the Mount that is hardest to accept is Yeshua's instruction to turn the other cheek. What exactly does Yeshua mean by this saying and how do we apply it in the midst of our current very real evils?

Chapter 8: Love (Matt. 5:43–48)
Non-resistance to evil is transformed into something even more challenging: love for our enemy. Again, we will consider what Yeshua meant by this teaching and how we can practice it today.

Section Three: The Great Reversal

Divine reversal is not only the theme of Yeshua's ethical teaching, but also of his own actions, which embody his ethical teaching.

Chapter 9: Cleansing the Leper
Immediately after Yeshua gives his Torah from the Mount, he miraculously cleanses a leper, thus demonstrating that the fulfillment of Torah means not only "teaching" its true inward meaning, but also accomplishing what the Torah is seeking and restoring the ideal that it envisions. Cleansing the leper is a paradigm of Yeshua's entire redemptive work among human beings.

Chapter 10: The Messianic Secret
Yeshua seems intent on hiding his identity, even from his disciples, until they reach the turning point at Caesarea Philippi. From that time on, Yeshua reveals who he really is and three core teachings on discipleship that come from that revelation.

Chapter 11: Triumphal Entry

Messiah's entry into Jerusalem inaugurates the week leading up to his crucifixion, a week of loneliness and alienation that he undertakes to release us from our loneliness and alienation.

Chapter 12: The Last Passover

Yeshua enacts his final Passover meal with his disciples to picture true community based on the divine reversal that he has taught and exemplified and is about to initiate with his death.

Epilogue: The Ultimate Reversal

The crucifixion and resurrection of Yeshua are the ultimate divine reversal. If we understand them correctly and apply them to our lives, they provide hope from God in a world that holds little real hope apart from him.

Even though we will study the ethics of Yeshua in a systematic fashion, I don't believe it's possible to reduce this way of life to a list of dos and don'ts. Indeed, my hope is that our exploration of the teachings of Messiah will in the end reveal more fully the person of Messiah. He intends for us to actually put his teachings into practice, and we can only do so through his power, as we desire to know him more fully. May this book move us in that direction!

PROLOGUE

Creation Renewed

This is My servant, whom I uphold,
My chosen one, in whom I delight.
I have put My spirit upon him,
He shall teach the true way to the nations.
He shall not cry out or shout aloud,
Or make his voice heard in the streets.
He shall not break even a bruised reed,
Or snuff out even a dim wick.
He shall bring forth the true way. . . .
And the coastlands shall await his teaching.

(Isaiah 42:1–4, NJPS; applied to Jesus in Matthew 12:18–21)

On a recent backpacking trip, my two grown sons and I spent several days on the Lost Coast of northern California, a remote stretch of coastline where we hiked for miles along rugged beaches without seeing more than one or two other hikers all day long. On our final day I took off ahead of my sons because they walk faster than I do and I figured they would soon catch up with me. The weather had been clear and sunny, but now the clouds rolled in and I walked through a fine mist, somewhere between a fog and a drizzle. The cool weather and the hard sand near the waterline aided me in a good walking pace, and it seemed like hours before my sons caught up.

I walked alone along stretches of black sand beside white breakers, absorbing the silence and the absence of anything human—alone at the edge of the world. It reminded me of the silence of creation, of "In the beginning," before God spoke and brought the world into being. Such silence underlies all authentic speech for, as in the beginning, creative speaking arises out of silence, silence that is so rare in our increasingly voice–filled world.

The shoreline and the lapping waves also reminded me of Yeshua walking the shores of that microcosmic sea, Lake Kinneret,[1] at the beginning of his earthly sojourn. This was another "In the beginning." Creation arises out of water—out of the deep in the first chapter of Genesis, and out of the waters of the Kinneret or the Jordan River in the first chapter of the *besorah*.

Mark's Portrayal of a New Creation

> The beginning of the besorah of Yeshua the Messiah,
> the Son of God. As it is written in the Prophets:
>
> "Behold, I send my messenger before your face, who
> will prepare your way before You." (Mal. 3:1, cf. Exod.
> 23:20)
>
> "A voice crying in the wilderness: 'Prepare the way of
> Adonai; make his paths straight.'" (Isa. 40:3)
>
> Yochanan came immersing in the wilderness and
> preaching an immersion of t'shuvah—return to God
> for the forgiveness of sins. (Mark 1:1–4, author's
> translation)

The first word in the original Greek of Mark's account is *arche* ("beginning"), which is an echo of the first word in the Hebrew Scriptures, *b'reisheet*, ("in the beginning"). Thus, Mark signals that his account of Yeshua's ministry will involve a midrash on Genesis. This does not mean that Mark is writing historical fiction or writing a script based on a true event as we sometimes see in films; instead Mark provides an accurate narration of the early chapters of Yeshua's story in phrases that reflect the early chapters of Torah. As Moses does in much of the continuous story of Genesis and Exodus, Mark employs narrative theology, that is, he tells the story with a careful choice of words and phrases to highlight connections and implications that carry a theological message. Thus, in his opening words—"the beginning of the besorah of Yeshua the Messiah"—Mark portrays the appearance of Messiah as a re–creation, a new beginning, and goes on to reinforce this idea in the following verses.

When Mark uses creation terminology to describe this more recent act of divine intervention, he is following a pattern set in Exodus, which portrays the deliverance from Egypt as a new creation. In Genesis, God creates humankind as the culmination of his work of creation. In Exodus, God creates a new humankind, Israel, to be his chosen people among all the peoples of the earth. In Genesis, God promises the patriarchs that he will make of them a great people; in Exodus he fulfills that promise. In Genesis, when God creates humankind, he blesses them: "be fruitful and multiply and fill the land" (Genesis 1:28). Later, this blessing passes on through Abraham and his offspring (Gen. 17:6–8, 28:3–4, 48:4), to reappear at the opening of Exodus: "the children of Israel were fruitful and increased abundantly, multiplied and became very numerous; and the land was filled with them" (Ex. 1:7).

The drama of "In the beginning" continues to shape the Exodus story as the Israelites leave the bondage of Egypt and arrive at the shore of the Red Sea. In Genesis, the sea was the primordial chaos out of which God brought order and beauty. On the second day of Creation, the Lord made a "firmament" to divide the waters above from the waters below. On the third day he said, "Let the waters under the heavens be gathered together into one place, and let the dry land appear" (Gen. 1:9). Now, in Exodus, the Lord divides the waters again, this time to bring salvation to the Israelites. The waters are divided by a *ruach*, a "strong east wind" (Exod. 14:21), just as the *ruach*, or spirit, of the Lord had hovered over the waters in the beginning. As during Creation, the waters are tamed to reveal dry land, and in Exodus the dry land emerges as the scene of divine rescue.[2]

Exodus employs these echoes of the Genesis account to reveal that redemption is a new creation. The same God who spoke all things into being will now speak salvation into being for his people. Hundreds of years later, Isaiah takes up this Genesis–Exodus imagery and applies it to the return from Babylon.

A voice rings out:

"Clear in the desert
A road for the LORD!
Level in the wilderness
A highway for our God!
Let every valley be raised,
Every hill and mount made low.
Let the rugged ground become level
And the ridges become a plain.
The Presence of the LORD shall appear,
And all flesh, as one, shall behold—
For the LORD Himself has spoken." (Isa. 40:3–5, NJPS)

As God did in the Exodus from Egypt, Isaiah declares, he will again prepare a way in the wilderness. Just as the Lord parted the Red Sea, he will remove all barriers to create a path of return from Babylon. Just as Exodus echoes the language of Creation to tell its story, Isaiah echoes both Exodus and Genesis.

And the LORD will utterly destroy the tongue of the sea of Egypt; and will wave his hand over the River with his scorching wind; and will split it into seven channels, and make a way to cross on foot; so there shall be a highway from Assyria for the remnant that is left

of his people, as there was for Israel when they came
up from the land of Egypt.

You will say in that day: I will give thanks to you, O
Lᴏʀᴅ, for though you were angry with me, your anger
turned away, and you comforted me. Surely God is my
salvation; I will trust, and will not be afraid, for the
Lᴏʀᴅ Gᴏᴅ is my strength and my might; he has become
my salvation. (Isa. 11:15–12:2)

The final two lines here are the key to interpreting this whole passage
in Isaiah because they first appear in the song that Moses and the
children of Israel sing at the crossing of the Red Sea. "The Lord is my
strength and my might; he has become my salvation." At the creation,
the Lord brings forth the dry land from the waters. In the new creation of the Exodus, he parts the waters to reveal dry land again. And
now, Isaiah declares, he will do the same to bring about a new Exodus,
out of the exile imposed by the Assyrians and Babylonians, to restore
his people to the Promised Land. "Thus there shall be a highway for
the other part of His people out of Assyria, such as there was for
Israel when it left the land of Egypt" (Isa. 11:16).

The Waters of New Creation

Exodus was a new creation; the return from exile was a new exodus.
Now, Mark takes up the language of Isaiah to show that the coming of
Messiah is also a new creation, a new exodus, and a new return from
exile. "A voice crying in the wilderness: 'Prepare the way of *Adonai*;
make his paths straight'" (Mark 1:3).

After Mark establishes this prophetic setting he introduces
Yochanan, John the Baptizer, and recounts the details of his story
(Mark 1:4–8). Baptism, or immersion in water, was a familiar ritual of
cleansing and consecration in first-century Judaism, but Mark will
lend additional meaning to immersion as he tells the story of
Yochanan's ministry, meaning that is new, but based on the ancient
text of the Hebrew Scriptures.

Mark employs midrash to show that within the concrete events of
his day, an apocalyptic new creation has already begun. The key text
of his opening verses, Isaiah 40, was a favored passage of the Qumran
community, the keepers of the Dead Sea Scrolls. Yochanan immersed
in the wilderness of Judea (Matt. 3:1), a location in the southern
Jordan Valley. Qumran is located by the Dead Sea, not far from this
same area. It is striking that the Qumran community took the same
words, Isaiah 40:3, with which Mark introduces Yochanan, as their
theme verse.

In Jewish tradition, Isaiah 40 is the first of seven sections from Isaiah read in the weeks leading up to *Rosh Hashanah* (Jewish New Year) and called "the portions of consolation." This section begins with the words, "Comfort, oh comfort My people, says your God," and then continues:

> Speak tenderly to Jerusalem,
> And declare to her
> That her term of service is over,
> That her iniquity is expiated;
> For she has received at the hand of the LORD
> Double for all her sins.
> A voice rings out:
> "Clear in the desert
> A road for the LORD!" (Isa. 40:1–3, NJPS)

In applying Isaiah 40 to Yochanan, Mark casts his message as one of consolation. Israel is living under Roman occupation and oppression, and there is an even more difficult time of judgment to come, but the result will be restoration to God. Yochanan's ministry is clearing a pathway of return for all of Israel who will heed his words and respond by receiving immersion for the forgiveness of sins. All of this— the cleared roadway and the multitudes cleansed of sin—is in preparation for the appearing of the promised Messiah, who brings a new creation to the faithful in Israel and the world.

After quoting from Isaiah, Mark tells of the multitudes that come from Jerusalem and all Judea to be immersed. Then he continues:

> In those days Yeshua came from Nazareth of Galilee and was immersed by Yochanan in the Jordan. And just as he was coming up out of the water, he saw the heavens torn apart and the Spirit descending like a dove on him. And a voice came from heaven, "You are my Son, the Beloved; with you I am well pleased." (Mark 1:9–11)

Again, Mark invokes the language of Creation to tell his story. Commentator William L. Lane notes, "The cosmic significance of this event is indicated by the vision of the rending of the heavens, the descent of the Spirit and the testimony of the voice from heaven."[3] The dramatic impact is heightened by Mark's choice of words. "Torn apart" is from the Greek verb *schizo*, a dramatic word that appears only in Mark's account of Yeshua's immersion, and hints at the Creation itself. Likewise, the Spirit descending like a dove and a voice speaking from heaven remind us of Genesis.

> In the beginning God created the heavens and the earth. The earth was without form, and void; and darkness was on the face of the deep. And the Spirit of God was hovering over the face of the waters. Then God said, "Let there be light"; and there was light. (Gen. 1:1–3, NKJV)

Lane continues, "The descent of the Spirit signifies new creation, corresponding to the cosmic overtones in the rending [schizo] of the heavens."[4] When Yeshua came from Galilee to be immersed by Yochanan, he was not just following an obscure ritual practiced by some religious first-century Jews; rather his immersion marked a new beginning, a re–creation that would have significance for the whole human race, including each of us. When we consider following the Jewish Jesus, we are not just choosing one way of life or one set of ethical teachings over another; rather following Yeshua means a new start in life, a personal re–creation that restores us to the original purpose for which we were made.

New Creation in the Wilderness

Before we study this way of Yeshua in more detail, there is one final connection between the opening verses of Mark and the early chapters of Genesis. Mark writes:

> And the Spirit immediately drove him out into the wilderness. He was in the wilderness forty days, tempted by Satan; and he was with the wild beasts; and the angels waited on him. (Mark 1:12–13)

As in the previous passage, Mark employs a word here that is unique to him. In the other Gospels, after Yeshua's immersion by Yochanan, Yeshua is *led* by the Spirit into the wilderness (Matt. 4:1; Luke 4:1). Here he is *driven* out. Mark's word is *ekballo*, which also appears in the Greek translation of Genesis, when Adam and Eve were "driven out" of the Garden of Eden after they sinned (Gen. 3:24). Mark is again echoing Genesis, but this time he deliberately reverses the order of the story: In Genesis, Adam first names the wild animals; later, he is tempted and falls; and then he is driven out of the Garden. Yeshua is first driven out into the wilderness; then he is tempted but doesn't fall. Then he is with the wild animals. At the end of Yeshua's sojourn in the wilderness, the angels "took care of him" in contrast with Adam's sojourn when the angels (or cherubim) "took care of him" by closing the way back to Eden with a flaming sword (Gen. 3:24).

In Mark the wilderness (or desert; both the Hebrew and Greek terms can be translated either way) is the place of restoration. It is the opposite of Eden, the well-watered garden, yet it paradoxically becomes a new Eden where the new humanity represented by Yeshua can again meet with the Lord who walked "in the garden in the cool of the day" (Gen. 3:8, AV). In the wilderness, Yeshua is tempted but prevails and is cared for by the angels. Even earlier in Mark, the wilderness is the place of encounter with God. Yochanan appears in the wilderness, and everyone goes out to him there, just as Israel had to go out of Egypt and into the wilderness to be redeemed from bondage. Yeshua also goes out to the wilderness to be immersed and then, in direct allusion to Exodus, spends forty days in the wilderness, just as Israel spent forty years in "the great and awesome desert, in which were fiery serpents and scorpions and thirsty land where there was no water" (Deut. 8:15). In Exodus, the journey through the wilderness first brings Israel to Mount Sinai, the place of revelation. In the besorah, likewise, the wilderness is the place of encounter with God—not just at the beginning of the story but throughout. (See, for example, Mark 1:35, 45; 6:31; 9:2; Luke 5:16.) Both stories are told against the backdrop of Creation, revealing the encounter in the wilderness as a new creative act of God that will change everything.

What does all this mean for our theme of following the transformative ethics of Yeshua? Our Jewish reading of the gospel story provides not just an interesting accessory to the narrative, but unlocks meaning and implications for us today. It helps us see that following Yeshua is not a course correction or an embellishment for our already full lives, but a radical redirection that changes the whole nature of our lives. Following Yeshua is not just adherence to a body of ethical teaching, although that is undeniably involved, but also a transformation from above that empowers us to obey. Just as Yeshua himself embodies a new creation as he appears in the wilderness and rises up from the waters of immersion, so his followers become new creations as they walk in the pathway that he has opened up for them.

SECTION

1

Hesed, the Ethic of Reversal

CHAPTER

1

"FOLLOW ME"

Mark's account of the good news of Messiah opens in the desert, but it does not remain there for long; soon it traces Yeshua's steps back to Galilee, the densely populated homeland of his youth, where he will begin his public ministry.

> Now after Yochanan was arrested, Yeshua came to Galilee, proclaiming the good news of God, and saying, "The time is fulfilled, and the kingdom of God has come near; repent, and believe in the good news." (Mark 1:14–15)

As we have seen, the Hebrew equivalent for "good news" is besorah. It appears in Isaiah 40, a few verses after the "voice in the wilderness" passage we considered in our last chapter. "Get you up to a high mountain, O Zion, herald of good tidings; lift up your voice with strength, O Jerusalem, herald of good tidings, lift it up, do not fear; say to the cities of Judah, 'Here is your God!'" (Isaiah 40:9).

"Herald of good tidings" is one word in Hebrew, based on the same root as besorah. A herald is one who brings a royal proclamation, most often of good things. The word appears twice in 40:9 and twice again in 52:7, "How beautiful upon the mountains are the feet of the messenger who announces shalom, who brings good news, who announces salvation, who says to Zion, 'Your God reigns.'" In Samuel, the root word appears repeatedly to describe a report, usually positive, fresh from the field of battle (1 Sam. 31:9; 2 Sam. 1:20; 4:10; 18:19). We can picture the herald running to the king's encampment, or to a beleaguered city, telling them that victory has just been won, announcing salvation, and declaring that the king reigns, as in Isaiah 52:7. The word appears again in Isaiah 61 in the passage that Yeshua reads in his home synagogue in Nazareth, announcing his own ministry, "The spirit of the Lord GOD is upon me, because the LORD has anointed me; he has sent me to bring good news to the oppressed, to bind up the brokenhearted, to proclaim liberty to the captives, and release to the prisoners … " (Isaiah 61:1).

Commentator William Lane writes that the content of besorah is "an historical event which introduces a new situation for the world." He continues:

> Especially in Isaiah the Hebrew terms signifying "good news" concern the announcement of future salvation, or of the time of salvation. In this context, to proclaim salvation on God's authority is itself a creative act; in a sense it inaugurates the reality of which it speaks.[1]

The Good News of Repentance

An announcement like this requires a response, of course, and this element of the besorah becomes an essential part of its meaning. Thus, Yeshua combines his announcement of good news with a call to repentance, "The time is fulfilled, and the kingdom of God has come near; repent, and believe in the good news." This call to repentance, however, does not stand alone but leads to another challenge. Immediately after he cries out, "Repent!" Yeshua encounters two brothers, Simon and Andrew, laboring over their fishing nets. He says to them, "Follow me and I will make you fish for people" (Mark 1:15–17). In his parallel account, Matthew captures the same sequence of repent and follow, as Yeshua returns to Galilee from the desert to launch his ministry:

> From that time Yeshua began to proclaim, "Repent, for the kingdom of heaven has come near." As he walked by the Sea of Galilee, he saw two brothers, Simon, who is called Peter, and Andrew his brother, casting a net into the sea—for they were fishermen. And he said to them, "Follow me, and I will make you fish for people." (Matt. 4:17–19)

The call to repentance goes forth to all, and Yeshua will proclaim it "from that time on." "Follow me!" is a specific personal call, which he will repeat to each individual. The call to repentance reiterates the message of the Hebrew prophets, who spoke extensively of repentance, or return as it is called in Hebrew. For example, consider the words of Hosea, to whom we will return in our next chapter:

> Come, let us return to the LORD; for it is he who has torn, and he will heal us; he has struck down, and he will bind us up. (Hos. 6:1)

> But as for you, return to your God, hold fast to love and justice, and wait continually for your God. (Hos. 12:7 [Hos. 12:6 in Christian Bibles[2]])

Return, O Israel, to the LORD your God, for you have stumbled because of your iniquity. Take words with you and return to the LORD; say to him, "Take away all guilt; accept that which is good, and we will offer the fruit of our lips." (Hos. 14:2–3 [Hos. 14:1–2])

To return is an essential Jewish message and essential to the good news that Yeshua proclaims. There can be no real faith and no genuine response to God that does not include turning away from our old behavior and taking on new behavior. The Greek term for repentance is *metanoia*, which can be translated literally as "change of mind." Bible students sometimes think of it as a change of mind that leads to a change of behavior. But in the Hebrew text and in the Jewish outlook that comes from it, repentance focuses on the change of behavior itself. If we want to follow the Jewish Jesus, we need to be ready for an overhaul of our behavior and not just a modification of our beliefs.

The Transforming Ethics of Jesus form a way of life that we are not just to discuss but to follow. Yeshua continuously distinguishes between followers and adherents—those who profess faith in Yeshua but give little indication of seeking to follow in his footsteps. Indeed, the difference between adherents and followers unfolds throughout history since the days of Messiah. One of the main Jewish objections against Yeshua as Messiah is, "The prophets say that when the Messiah comes there will be peace on earth, justice will reign, and all of humankind will worship the true God. None of this has happened, so obviously the Messiah hasn't come yet, and, therefore, Jesus can't be the Messiah." To echo the title of this book, we might paraphrase this objection, "The prophets say that when Messiah comes, he will bring a divine reversal of the conditions of this age to establish true peace and justice."

If we examine this traditional Jewish argument more closely, we can see another strand of reasoning. Not only have peace and justice not arrived, but the adherents of Jesus contribute to strife and injustice as much as anyone. One of the greatest figures in medieval Judaism, Nachmanides, made this argument nearly seven hundred and fifty years ago. "From the days of Jesus until now, the whole world has been full of violence and plundering, and the Christians are greater spillers of blood than all the rest ... "[3]

I still hear the argument today, as evidenced in a recent email dialogue:[4]

When I was eight, I was beaten up and mocked for killing Christ. Years later, I read the New Testament and found it to be full of anti–Semitic attitudes that put down Judaism and threw away the Ten

Commandments. Maybe this is why the Christian world has such a horrible history of persecution and butchery of Jews.

Notice that it isn't just the evil and injustice in the world that makes it so hard for these Jewish people to imagine that Jesus could be the Messiah; rather it is the injustice perpetrated by those who claim to follow Jesus that is the stumbling block. If the world were as evil as it is but included a band of people faithfully following the teachings of Jesus of Nazareth in a divine reversal of the corruption around them, doubtless more Jewish people could consider the possibility that this Jesus is the Messiah. If the world remained evil but those who professed faith in Jesus had truly turned away from sin and turned to God—repenting and becoming followers rather than adherents—the overall Jewish response to Jesus might have been far different.

Yochanan is alert to the need for genuine repentance. Thus, when people come to him to be immersed, he warns them that immersion itself won't suffice; they must bear fruit worthy of repentance. The people respond, "So then, what should we do?" and Yochanan answers:

> "Whoever has two coats must share with anyone who has none; and whoever has food must do likewise."
>
> Even tax collectors came to be immersed, and they asked him, "Teacher, what should we do?"
>
> He said to them, "Collect no more than the amount prescribed for you."
>
> Soldiers also asked him, "And we, what should we do?"
>
> He said to them, "Do not extort money from anyone by threats or false accusation, and be satisfied with your wages." (Luke 3:10–14)

Yochanan clearly understands repentance to involve action, not just a revised state of mind. It means turning to God and turning away from sin—not as an abstract condition but as the specific ugly, wrong things we do in real life. His answer to the question, "What should we do?" places us squarely in Jewish space. Centuries later, one of the sages of the Talmud taught, "When man is led in for Judgment he is asked, did you deal faithfully . . .?" (Shab. 31a). Rabbi Telushkin explains, "The Talmud proposes that the first question the Heavenly Court puts to someone who has died is "Did you conduct your business affairs honestly?"[5] Likewise, what Yochanan seems to require of many who come to him for immersion is that they "deal faithfully" in their financial and professional dealings. The tax collectors remain tax collectors, and the soldiers remain soldiers. Repentance means they must become honest tax collectors and soldiers, which, of course, is difficult enough. In contrast today, we sometimes hear the good news of Messiah proclaimed as if it has nothing to do with our behavior at all: "Only believe," we are told with the implication that believing is an entirely inward matter.

Both of my daughters attended college in the Bible Belt and worked part of their way through school at a local Mexican restaurant. They told me that all of the wait staff hated to work on Sunday because the after-church crowd included the worst tippers of the week. I am sure there were generous tippers among the church folk, but some of them came in straight from services with their kids in tow and asked for a lot of lemon slices with their water. Then, they'd squeeze the lemons into the water, add sugar, and make their own lemonade right at the table. After leaving a big mess at their table, they left some loose change for a tip. Even worse, others left a witnessing tract instead of a tip. One tract looked on the outside like a five-dollar bill but inside gave a "tip" on how to get to heaven when you die. I don't know if such behavior was inspired by the idea that only what you believe—and not how you behave—really counts. But it was clearly the opposite of what John the Baptist expected repentance to produce, a not-so-divine reversal of the message of the besorah.

In a recent email correspondence with a Jewish woman attracted to Yeshua but still doubting, she spoke about some of the claims about him that "still don't compute," including "Jesus died for my sins (this has always appeared to me to be the grand cop-out for Christians)." I have to agree in part: Believing that Jesus died on my behalf can be a cop-out if I use such belief to avoid real repentance, but that wouldn't be the belief promoted in the Scriptures. In the Jewish worldview, belief is vitally important, but it is always evident in the way we behave. One of the great contrasts between the Jewish and Christian religious outlooks is that Christians are concerned first with what you believe—whether you are sound in doctrine— and Jews are concerned with how you act—whether you're a *mensch* (a real human being) in your behavior. The Jewish Jesus doesn't let us get away with using "Jesus died for my sins" to avoid responsibility for our behavior. When we consider following him, we must think about changing not just our religious behavior, but everyday behaviors, including those within our business and professional worlds.

Yeshua's Brand of Repentance

This call to repentance reflects the teaching of the Hebrew prophets, but no prophet ever called his listeners to follow him. (Indeed, Elijah even tells Elisha *not* to follow him [2 Kings 2:1–6].) Rather, when the prophets call people to repentance, they expect them to follow, or walk after, God, as in Deut. 13:5 (Deut. 13:4 in Christian Bibles). When Yeshua says, "Follow me!" therefore, he is issuing a radical command that puts feet—very particular feet—to the call for repentance. Repentance is familiar terrain in a Jewish context, but now the besorah takes us into new terrain: Repentance means following Yeshua. Within his Jewish context, when Yeshua says, "Follow me!" he is hinting at a claim to deity, asking for an allegiance that only God can demand.

A talmudic discussion of the command to "walk after" God in Deuteronomy 13:5 will illuminate what it means to follow Yeshua and how following Yeshua fits within the Jewish perspective on Scripture.

> What does it mean, "You shall walk after the Lord your God"? Is it possible for a person to walk and follow in God's presence? Does not the Torah also say, "For the Lord your God is a consuming fire" (Deut. 4:24)? But it means to walk after the attributes of the Holy One, Blessed be He. Just as He clothed the naked, so you too clothe the naked, as it says, "And the Lord made the man and his wife leather coverings and clothed them" (Gen. 3:21). The Holy One, Blessed be He, visits the ill, as it says, "And God visited him in Elonei Mamreh (Gen. 18:1); so you shall visit the ill. The Holy One, Blessed be He, comforts the bereaved, as it says, "And it was after Abraham died that God blessed his son Isaac… " (Gen. 25:11), so too shall you comfort the bereaved. The Holy One, Blessed be He, buries the dead, as it says, "And He buried him in the valley" (Deut. 34:6), so you too bury the dead.[6]

This interpretation makes two points that are vital to following Yeshua: First, acts of kindness, such as visiting the sick and burying the dead, are the heart of Torah and were established even before the more formalized laws and rituals given at Sinai. Remember the instructions that Yochanan gives, "Whoever has two coats must share with anyone who has none; and whoever has food must do likewise. … Collect no more than the amount prescribed for you. … Do not extort money from anyone by threats or false accusation, and be satisfied with your wages." These are all measurable behaviors, which are linked to specific precepts given in Torah. To practice such behaviors is a worthy beginning, but the sages teach that there is a walk with God that goes beyond. The walk begins with repentance, as Yochanan preached, and then progresses through the continual practice of compassion that Yeshua exemplified as he embodied the core teachings of Torah.

Second, by picturing God as the first one to exemplify such acts of kindness, the sages understand that Torah reveals a God who is not remote and inaccessible but who is intimately connected with human beings. We should not be surprised then that this revelation reaches its climax as God comes fully onto the human scene in human form as Yeshua the Messiah, nor should we be surprised that Messiah is constantly among the sick and needy embodying acts of kindness, and bids us to follow him in these same acts.

Jewish tradition has a name for such acts, *gemilut hasadim* (bestowals of loving-kindness), which are considered to be foundational to Jewish life. "Simon the Righteous was one of the last of the Great Assembly. His motto was: 'The world stands on three things – the Torah, the [Temple] service, and loving acts of kindness' [gemilut hasadim]"[7]

This saying is part of *Pirke Avot* (Ethics of the Fathers), an important and well-known portion of the Mishnah, a body of Jewish law put into writing in about 200 CE but reflecting older Jewish teachings. When Simon the Righteous speaks of "Torah" in this context, he refers not only to the Five Books of Moses and their teachings, but also to the discussions and traditions that seek to put these teachings into practice. We might paraphrase Torah here as "communal obedience to the Word of God." "The [Temple] service" in this context means "worship," as in the traditional synagogue service. We can apply it broadly as referring to all true worship in general. The third pillar is gemilut hasadim. Hasadim is the plural form of the word hesed, an important term in the Hebrew Scriptures. By linking its practice with Torah and worship, the Jewish sages recognized the tremendous importance that the Scriptures themselves place on hesed. Yeshua, in turn, makes hesed the centerpiece of the way of life that he seeks to impart to his followers, reflecting his Jewish understanding of the singular importance of compassionate behavior. Such behavior is a divine reversal of the values of power, acquisition, and domination that normally shape human society, including religious human society. It entails a transformation of the human personality that is at the heart of the besorah.

This realization leads to a third lesson from the passage above. Gemilut hasadim is the *imitatio dei* (imitation of God), within Judaism. Yeshua follows the Lord in the practice of gemilut hasadim and then calls us to follow him in the same manner. The Jewish Jesus is deeply concerned with our ethical behavior, but he does not teach an ethical system as much as he embodies ethics. Following Yeshua in the practice of hesed is not a matter of checking off good deeds on our ethical master list but a personal pursuit that leads us to God in new and unimagined ways. "When Jesus says, 'Follow me,' and we follow, we don't know where we will go next or what we will do next. That is why we follow the one who does know."[8]

Hesed: The Fruit of Repentance

Before examining Yeshua's example of hesed and how we are to follow it, let's explore the background of the term in the earliest chapters of Scripture. The first person called upon to practice hesed in Scripture is a woman, who is in a state of great vulnerability. Sarah goes into exile with her husband, Abraham, who tells the locals that Sarah is his sister, so that she is taken into the king's household. Before the king can touch her, however, God reveals to him in a dream that Sarah is really Abraham's wife. When the king demands an explanation from Abraham, he claims that Sarah is actually his half-sister and says, "And when God caused me to wander from my father's house, I said to her, 'This is the hesed you must do me: at every place to which we come, say of me, 'He is my brother'" (Gen. 20:13). Abraham's request is highly questionable, of course, but he correctly understands that Sarah, even in her position of weakness, still has the powerful option of practicing hesed.

A few chapters later Abraham sends his servant back to his homeland to find a bride for his son, Isaac. When the servant arrives at the well in Abraham's hometown of Haran, he decides to seek the chosen bride by asking for a drink (Gen. 24:14, 17). He begins this quest with a prayer, "O Lord, God of my master Abraham, please grant me success today and show hesed to my master Abraham" (Gen. 24:12). God is the source of hesed, but hesed will be revealed in a simple act of human kindness. "Let the girl to whom I shall say, 'Please offer your jar that I may drink,' and who shall say, 'Drink, and I will water your camels'—let her be the one whom you have appointed for your servant Isaac. By this I shall know that you have shown hesed to my master" (Gen. 24:14). It turns out just as the servant prayed; a young woman named Rebecca offers a drink to him and his camels. Once again, it is a woman—in this case a young unmarried woman in a patriarchal society, assigned to the mundane task of drawing water for the household—who exercises her limited freedom to become the instrument of hesed. As she does so, God reverses her marginality to give her tremendous power as the channel of divine choice that shapes the destiny of Abraham's entire line.

When the servant learns that this girl is of the household of Bethuel, the kinsman of Sarah and Abraham, he says, "Blessed be the Lord, the God of my master Abraham, who has not forsaken his steadfast love and his faithfulness [*hesed v'emet*] toward my master" (Gen. 24:27). To underline the divine origin of *hesed*, the Torah links it with *emet* (meaning truth) here and again in Genesis 24:49. Later, the Lord will again link these two words when he describes his nature to Moses in Exodus 34, "The Lord, the Lord, a God merciful and gracious, slow to anger, and abounding in hesed v'emet [grace and truth]." Hesed is a divine attribute, and yet human beings display it, particularly by those living on society's margins. It lies at the heart of the divine reversal ethic that characterizes Yeshua's entire moral teaching. We might expect the strong and well-positioned to be the surest source of mercy, but Scripture often portrays the weak in this role. We look to the firstborn, the richest, the most gifted to be the instruments of God's purpose, but Scripture often portrays number two as the man or woman of the hour. Later in his own life, Yeshua carries this divine reversal to its ultimate expression.

Perhaps the prime example in the Hebrew Scriptures of hesed as the ethic of reversal appears in the book of Ruth. One ancient rabbinic commentary asks, "This scroll tells us nothing either of cleanliness or of unseemliness, either of prohibition or permission. For what purpose then was it written? To teach how great is the reward of those who do deeds of kindness [gemilut hasadim]."[9]

The story of Ruth is full of these deeds of kindness. At the beginning of the book, Naomi attributes hesed to Ruth, along with her sister-in-law Orpah, "Naomi said to her two daughters-in-law, 'Go back each of you to your mother's house. May the Lord deal with you in hesed, as you have dealt with the dead and with me" (Ruth 1:8). Later, when Ruth presents herself as a marriage partner to Boaz, he says, "May you be blessed by the Lord, my daughter; this last instance of your hesed is better than the first; you have not gone after young men, whether poor or rich" (Ruth 3:10). Boaz characterizes Ruth's whole pattern of behavior since returning with Naomi as hesed from beginning to end. When Christians read Ruth, they don't tend to ask why it is in the Scriptures but why Ruth appears in the genealogy of Yeshua (Matt. 1:5), generally follows normal usage and traces Yeshua's descent through the males. Perhaps Ruth appears in the genealogy for the same reason that her book is included in the Hebrew Scriptures— because she exemplifies gemilut hasadim. From her position of weakness as a foreigner, a woman, and a widow, Ruth exercises her limited freedom to practice hesed and thus becomes its foremost example in the Hebrew Scriptures.

Yeshua develops this theme of hesed as a virtue of outsiders, as we will discuss in the next chapter. Yeshua calls upon the insiders to learn hesed from his work among the outsiders. Furthermore, Yeshua often practices hesed in ways that make him an outsider. When we remember that God is the first one in Torah to practice these acts of hesed, this quality of hesed as the ethic of the marginalized is even more striking. What a reversal of institutional religion, which so often is the defender of the status quo! Eugene Peterson writes:

> North-American Christians are conspicuous for going along with whatever the culture decides is charismatic, successful, influential—whatever gets things done, whatever can gather a crowd of followers—hardly noticing that these ways and means are at odds with the clearly marked way that Jesus walked and called us to follow. Doesn't anyone notice that the ways and means taken up, often enthusiastically, are blasphemously at odds with the way Jesus leads his followers? Why doesn't anyone notice?[10]

Followers of Yeshua, whether North American Christians, Third-World Christians, or Messianic Jews, are supposed to be countercultural—not in the 1960s sense of dropping out but as a prophetic community that lives the Torah's message, particularly as embodied in Yeshua and particularly as it is at cross-currents with contemporary trends. Peterson cites the example of Elijah, who demonstrated the "way of marginality" long before Yeshua brought it to fulfillment.[11]

> He held no position, lived a solitary life in obscurity, appeared from time to time without fanfare and disappeared from public view without notice. His formative impact on how we as a people of God understand responsibility and witness in society is inescapable and irreversible. ... The essence of the Elijah way is that it counters the world's way, the culture's way.[12]

A Radical Call

Yeshua's call to "Follow me!" is always a radical call. Something is gravely amiss when the professed followers of Yeshua become the institutional or cultural mainstream, especially when, as in North America, the institutions and culture don't appear to have become redirected toward the way of Yeshua as a result. Following the ethical pathway of Yeshua has tremendous implications for our contemporary religious culture, which has been shaped by material-ism and consumerism far more than we care to recognize.

Two common misinterpretations can divert our steps from this pathway. First, we might see following Yeshua as optional, a mere accessory to the central act of accepting him into our hearts and getting saved. We have seen the corrective to this misinterpretation in our discussion of repentance. The distinction between faith in Yeshua and obedience to Yeshua is a false distinction, and can only be made outside of a biblical frame of reference.

The other misinterpretation takes Yeshua's teachings seriously enough but writes off the more mysterious and supernatural aspects of the besorah. I came to faith in Yeshua as a hippie in the mountains of northern New Mexico in the early 1970s. Many of my hippie com-patriots found Messiah (or actually Messiah found them) in the space of a couple of years. But there were holdouts, and one of the toughest was Terry, a hard working, pragmatically minded hippie, which was an unusual combination in itself. Terry felt that the Sermon on the Mount and the Book of James were all you needed in the entire Bible. Just live according to their teachings and you'll be in good shape. Don't worry about all the rest, including the cross, the resurrection, and our need for salvation.[13]

According to this view, Yeshua was a great teacher and a rabbi, perhaps the greatest of our rabbis, but not the divine Messiah. Mark records Yeshua being called rabbi by both followers and detractors, but Matthew makes a careful distinction, with rabbi being used by outsiders and Lord by the true followers. "For those Jews (and all others) who do not accept Jesus as risen Messiah, he is simply an-other teacher, like the rabbis of formative Judaism. For those who confess him as crucified and raised Messiah, while Jesus is a teacher … he is also much more: he is the Lord who [teaches] with 'all author-ity' (28:18) … "[14]

Following Yeshua then is different in kind from any other follow-ing. It is not simply following his instructions or even following his instructions as embodied in his example, but it is following the Living One who empowers us to follow throughout our entire lives. "What we learn *about* him must therefore include what we continue to learn *from* him … [and] since faith is a response to the living Lord who presses upon us at every moment, there is no time at which we can quit without betraying the entire process in which we have been engaged."[15]

The Jewish Jesus remains our rabbi, and like every rabbi, he teaches by example and presence—but because he is also the resur-rected Lord, his example is transcendent and his presence is every-where. We are seeking to follow Yeshua, who not only is the exalted

Son of God, but also is deeply concerned with the ethical and practical dimension of life. He expects us to encounter God with him, in eating and drinking, tending to the sick, serving, and meeting human needs. In the Gospels, however, after Yeshua calls his first disciples, he does not spend much time explaining all this; rather he demonstrates this teaching in various settings right away, including an early incident at his home base of Capernaum. Let us meet Yeshua there and learn more of what it means to follow him.

MERCY, NOT SACRIFICE
Matthew 9:1–13

A simple house in the town of Capernaum, not far from the shore of Lake Kinneret, is packed with guests, ordinary folk like fishermen and merchants plus some guests who are not so ordinary in a gathering like this—tax collectors and women of questionable repute. And, as if that weren't unusual enough, several Pharisees are gathered in the house as well, sitting around the perimeter of the room. In the middle of it all, Yeshua, the new teacher with amazing healing powers, is reclining at the table, which is loaded with the best food this household can assemble: fish, freshly baked loaves, and wine in abundance. But before Yeshua can chant the blessing, he overhears some of the Pharisees challenging his disciples, "Why does your rabbi eat with tax collectors and sinners?" Yeshua looks up at them, and the crowd grows silent as he opens his mouth to respond (Matt. 9:10–11).

Before criticizing the Pharisees in this story, note that they have made the effort to draw close to Yeshua. They're engaging with him on a level that is rare in our modern world, where religious figures are either put on a pedestal or placed safely on the margins. But these Pharisees are noting Yeshua's mighty acts, hearing his teachings, arguing with him on various points, and still listening. Moreover, they may be acting as self-appointed gatekeepers, but all they are trying to do is to maintain clear boundaries between the devout and the sinful. In the Jewish world of their time, a gathering likes this had meaning beyond ordinary eating and drinking because those who reclined at the same table and ate of the same loaf became part of the same group.

Commentator Marcus Borg writes, "There were two reasons why eating together had symbolic significance. First, in the ancient Mediterranean world in general and the Jewish homeland, sharing a meal was a form of social inclusion, and refusing to share a meal was a form of social exclusion. Meals reflected the social boundaries of a group."[1]

To put this more simply and in more Jewish terms, hospitality is one of the gemilut hasadim, the acts of hesed that underlie Yeshua's entire ethical approach. When Yeshua eats and drinks with sinners, he is reversing their social rejection into social inclusion, wrapping them in the mantle of hospitality, which has tremendous power in the Jewish world even to this day. Yeshua is in the role of host, and he models a radical hospitality that welcomes both the pious and the polluted. Indeed, Yeshua's hospitality here is the defining essence of the hesed that we have been discussing. He doesn't just provide for the poor and outcast, but he sits down and eats with them. Yeshua doesn't base his "ministry to the poor" on advocacy for social programs, raising awareness, or gathering funds for the disadvantaged. He sits down and eats with them—and this is the lesson for us.

My home city has a rescue mission that serves breakfast and dinner to homeless people every day. The mission has been successful in garnering support from the surrounding community, including local congregations. It has an abundant supply of volunteers. Some come at 5:30 A.M. to prepare for breakfast. Volunteers greet the homeless folks who drift in after spending a night on the street and trying to stay warm until morning when they can make their way to the rescue mission. The volunteers are starting their day with an act of sacrifice and service that reflects following Yeshua. But imagine that one morning the mission director asks the volunteers to come out from behind the counter where they have been pouring cups of coffee and dishing out scrambled eggs and sit down at the tables with the street people to drink coffee and eat scrambled eggs. Less efficient—and some supporters might ask why their donations are going to feed middle class church folk—but what a signal that might send to the homeless! The move from behind the counter to a seat beside the man in an old sweatshirt with three days' stubble and bleary eyes is the heart of hesed as Yeshua practices it.

> In one respect more than any other he differed from both his contemporaries and even his prophetic predecessors. The prophets spoke on behalf of the honest poor, and defended the widows and the fatherless, those oppressed and exploited by the wicked, rich and powerful. Jesus went further. In addition to proclaiming these blessed, he actually took his stand among the pariahs of his world, those despised by the respectable. Sinners were his table–companions and the ostracized tax–collectors and prostitutes his friends.[2]

Borg continues, "Meals had a second significance within the Jewish homeland. For at least two groups, the Pharisees and the Essenes, meal practice had become a symbol of what God wanted Israel to be. Both practiced 'closed commensality' grounded in an understanding of God's command in Leviticus 19.2: 'You shall be holy, for I the Lord your God am holy.' They understood holiness to be purity."[3]

This helps us to understand the criticism continually brought against Yeshua for eating with tax collectors and sinners. "The accusation is that Jesus' meal practice included people whose presence discredited him. ... [T]he meal practice of Jesus was sufficiently central and public that it became a source of controversy and conflict."[4] The Pharisees objected to Yeshua's eating with certifiable sinners not only because that was something that just was not done, but also because they might have liked to join the feast, too, but now they could not. In the Jewish world of Yeshua's day, people don't have the opportunity to recline at a full table every day.

Moreover, in the mind of the Pharisees, they are the ones who should be sitting with this controversial but fascinating teacher and discussing Torah. They are bound to have some lively and memorable debates, but sitting at the table as Yeshua has organized it means joining a group of people who have neglected and despised the very Torah that they want to discuss. Moreover, one of the Pharisees' biggest issues is maintenance of purity laws, and who knows what kinds of impurities these folk are carrying with them? So by inviting sinners and tax collectors, Yeshua has excluded them, and they protest.

Yeshua responds aloud to the Pharisees' whispered objections, "Those who are well have no need of a physician, but those who are sick. *Go and learn what this means*, 'I desire mercy, not sacrifice.' For I have come to call not the righteous but sinners" (Matt. 9:12–13, emphasis added).

Whatever this might mean, it is clear that Yeshua expects us to learn it. We need to start by considering the possibility that the Pharisees are *us*: the solid, committed, serious-about-God folk who read books about Jesus. The Pharisees are not so prominent in the Gospels because they were a huge movement in Yeshua's day—scholars tell us that they were influential but numbered only in the thousands—nor are they so prominent because they represent rabbinic Judaism in all times and places, as readers of the Gospels often seem to assume. The Gospel accounts pay so much attention to the Pharisees because they typify religious folk in general. They are already engaged in the very things that Yeshua is discussing: God, righteousness, faith, and obedience to Scripture. Whatever Yeshua is trying to tell the Pharisees, he is trying to tell us.

Why Not Sacrifice?

We, then, are the ones who need to learn what this means, "I desire mercy and not sacrifice." But what's wrong with sacrifice? We are proud of the sacrifices we make to reach a worthy goal, and we commend others who make sacrifices. The Scriptures initiate a whole system of sacrifices that culminates in the sacrifice of Yeshua himself. What is wrong with that?

Remember that this phrase is a quote from Hosea where it is paired with another phrase, "For I desire mercy and not sacrifice, the knowledge of God rather [or more] than burnt offerings" (Hos. 6:6). God's desire for mercy and not sacrifice is not absolute but comparative. The Hebrew word translated as "I desire" can also be understood as "I delight in." God ordains sacrifices, but he *delights* in mercy. This comparative reading is reinforced by the second phrase, "I desire the knowledge of God *more than* burnt offerings." He isn't doing away with sacrifice in the first line or burnt offerings in the second but stating that they are secondary to mercy and the knowledge of God. When we read this verse today, we shouldn't interpret it as doing away with ritual and tradition, just as it didn't bring an end to sacrifices in Hosea's day; instead it establishes the priority of hesed above sacrifice and ritual.

To understand Hosea's point more fully, consider how he uses the term hesed throughout his prophecy. You may be familiar with the Jewish tradition of *tefillin* (phylacteries), based on the words of the *Sh'ma* in Deuteronomy 6:8, "Bind [these words] as a sign on your hand and let them serve as a symbol on your forehead" (NJPS). Tefillin are leather cases containing a small parchment with the words of the Sh'ma handwritten in Hebrew. The cases have straps attached to them, so that one can be worn on the forehead and one bound to the arm in accordance with Deuteronomy 6:8. Traditional Jewish men put these on each morning (except Shabbat) at the beginning of the daily prayers, reciting the words of Hosea:

> I will betroth you to me forever;
> And I will betroth you to me in righteousness and in justice,
> And in hesed and in compassion;
> I will betroth you to me in faithfulness,
> And you will know the LORD. (Hos. 2:21–22, author's translation)

Hosea is recording God's promise to renew his covenant with unfaithful Israel, a promise that he expresses in the metaphor of marriage, estrangement, and reconciliation. Israel is the unfaithful bride of the LORD, who has wandered off to other lovers. But the LORD will restore her in the end.

> And in that day—declares the LORD—
> You will call [Me] Ishi,
> And no more will you call Me Baali,
> For I will remove the names of the Baalim from her mouth,
> And they shall nevermore be mentioned by name.
> (Hos. 2:16–17 [Hos. 2:18–19]

Ishi and *Baali* both mean "my husband" in ordinary Hebrew usage, but Baali can also mean "my Baal," referring to a false god. God will be the true husband, and Israel will be joined to no other. This promise precedes and provides the context for the statement of betrothal, in which God says to Israel three times, "I will betroth you." The phrase, "I will betroth you to me forever" (Hos. 2:21), introduces the whole vow, and the phrase, "I will betroth you in faithfulness," summarizes it with the result that "you will know the LORD." In biblical Hebrew, "to know" often refers to marital intimacy, so the whole promise here leads to a restored and active love relationship between God and Israel. Every morning, those who lay tefillin, as it is termed in Jewish practice, affirm this relationship and commit to being faithful to it.

Those who are betrothed to the Lord are expected to behave in harmony with his attributes—righteousness, justice, hesed, and compassion—which the prophet lists in the middle section:

> And I will betroth you to me in righteousness and in justice,
> And in hesed and in compassion.

These attributes are listed as two pairs, righteousness–justice and hesed–compassion. Modern commentators might be tempted to contrast these pairs, but Scripture sees them as a mutually reinforcing. We can't have true righteousness–justice without hesed–compassion, nor true hesed–compassion without righteousness–justice. Thus, the Lord tells Israel, "Sow for yourselves righteousness; reap hesed; break up your fallow ground; for it is time to seek the LORD, that he may come and rain righteousness upon you" (Hos. 10:12). This metaphor is from the old-fashioned world of agriculture, but the thought is always up to date. As we long for and pursue righteousness, it will bear fruit in the form of hesed—loving-kindness freely given to those around us, as well as compassionate outpouring to those in need.

To change the metaphor, the qualities in Hosea 2:21–22, which we pair as righteousness–justice and hesed–compassion, represent the full adornment of the bride. These are the qualities she must have to maintain her eternal partnership with the Lord. And he himself will provide these qualities to Israel. "As the bride-price which the bridegroom will pay, He will confer these qualities on her, so that she will never offend again."[5] Sacrifices have their place within the marriage between the Lord and Israel, but hesed maintains the intimacy that lies at the heart of it. God has promised to provide hesed, and now he exhorts Israel to practice it, so that she might have the knowledge of God, which is the goal of the whole marriage.

"Go and Learn What This Means"

Nearly eight hundred years after Hosea first spoke these words to Israel, Yeshua repeated them to the Israel of his day, and ultimately to anyone who would follow him—"Go and learn what this means, 'I desire mercy and not sacrifice.'" To learn what this means we need to consider three ways that hesed contrasts with sacrifice:

> 1. *Sacrifice is directed toward God; hesed toward our fellow human beings.*

If you are a parent, imagine one of your children throwing a big bash for your birthday and then saying, "But, of course, my brother John won't be there because we aren't on speaking terms." You would probably say, "Forget the big bash. What I want for my birthday is for you and John to be reconciled."

Sacrifices are something we direct toward God. Some sacrifices are means of atonement, and others simply express worship or thanksgiving, but they are all directed toward God, not toward other human beings. Hesed, on the other hand, is normally expressed toward other humans. The Lord is setting a clear priority for us. Before we attempt to worship him, in whatever way we are called to worship him, we must first practice hesed and right relationship toward others. The ethical must precede—or provide a foundation for—the practice of spirituality.

Hosea is saying that you can't enter the sacred terrain of sacrifice to God without hesed, which is always practiced toward someone other than God. This truth counters the narcissism of our day, which often pictures spirituality as another commodity among others. This sort of spirituality is intensely personal and generally disembodied from ethics and relationships. This narcissistic spirituality is a distinctive condition of our times, which following Yeshua will reverse.

Yeshua addresses this question of sequence or priority of worship in Matthew 5:23–24:

> So when you are offering your gift at the altar,
> if you remember that your brother or sister
> has something against you, leave your gift

> there before the altar and go; first be recon-
> ciled to your brother or sister, and then come
> and offer your gift.

"Your gift" is a sacrifice, but before you can bring it, you must practice hesed toward your brother, who has something against you. Broken relationships always affect both parties, always entail the opposite of hesed, and can most often be restored through hesed. An ancient rabbinic commentary has the Lord saying, "The acts of kindness that you do for each other are more precious to Me than all the sacrifices offered to Me by King Solomon."[6]

2. Sacrifice fulfills the rules; hesed transcends the rules.

Hosea considers sacrifice and burnt offerings, as the Prophets often do, as simply outward, but he takes it one step further by criticizing those sacrifices and burnt offerings that are only outward acts without the foundation of faithfulness and hesed. In the same manner, Yeshua says to those concerned with outward conformity to religious practice (such as maintaining a high level of purity in table fellowship), that mercy is a much higher requirement of Torah.

Sacrifice applies to outward religious acts in general, including a religious sense of playing by the rules, which leads us to demand the same of others around us. *I have sacrificed to get where I am,* we think, *and so must you.* Hesed, in contrast, freely grants forgiveness and spiritual respect to others even if they don't match up to all of our requirements.

Years ago, my wife and I worked at a Bible-centered residential drug treatment program. Many of our residents, or "students" as we called them, were there on parole after serving some time in prison. We held a worship service every Friday night, and some of the students sang or played with the worship team. One of the students, a particularly troubled soul whom I'll call Johnny, had a good sense of rhythm, and I invited him up to play the tambourine. It did wonders for his self-esteem and wasn't bad for the band either, but some of the other staff members felt it was inappropriate to have him onstage because he still had so many problems and hadn't shown much spiritual growth since joining the program. I accepted their opinion and asked Johnny to bow out of the worship team as gently as I could, but I wondered if I had done the right thing. Perhaps we took our role as gatekeepers too seriously and our role as bestowers of hesed not seriously enough.

Sacrifice in this context describes the outlook of the legally upright, who often take it upon themselves to categorize others, such as tax collectors and sinners. Yeshua, however, says that God is not nearly as interested in proper religious labeling as he is in compassion to the marginalized. Sacrifice is concerned with the rules; hesed is willing to stretch the rules to deliver compassion. Did Yeshua break Torah by eating with sinners? No—but to the Pharisees who set themselves up as the gatekeepers, he was on a slippery slope. *It might not break the rules to eat with sinners,* they might have thought, *but there is no rule that says you* have to *eat with them and it's safer not to.* Religious folk sometimes take the stand that you should do what is clearly required and not mess with the rest, but Yeshua goes beyond maintaining the norms to seek out and save what is lost.

3. Sacrifice is quantifiable; hesed is without limit.

The daily Jewish prayers include this quote from the Mishnah:

> These are the precepts that have no prescribed measure: the corner of a field [which must be left for the poor], the first-fruit offering, the pilgrimage, acts of kindness [*gemilut hasadim* in the original], and Torah study.[7]

The prayer book notes, "The Torah does not prescribe how much is involved in the performance of [these] commandments."[8] With sacrifice we can satisfy the requirements; with hesed there is always room for more. Thus, our practice of hesed is to reflect, however dimly, God's hesed, which is always without limit, as the Psalmist says, *"Ki l'olam hasdo!"* (For his hesed is forever!). Indeed, the Psalmist repeats this phrase twenty-six times in Psalm 136. During the Passover seder, Psalm 136 is recited after the festive meal at the culmination of the second-to-last section of the seder, which is called *Hallel* (Praise). When our children were growing up, we found this psalm to be a great way to keep them engaged in the seder until the end. I read the first verse, "Give thanks to the Lord, for he is good," and everyone responded as loudly and raucously as they could, *"Ki l'olam hasdo!"* And so we went through all twenty-six verses. It was a great way to stay awake and a great way to remind ourselves that God's hesed isn't just something that happened long ago for our ancestors in Egypt, but is a quality of God that endures forever.

So Scripture prescribes no limits to our practice of hesed. Furthermore, hesed is without limit because it is directed toward other human beings, and the worth of human beings, who are created in the image of God, is also without limit. We tend to emphasize that Yeshua has compassion on sinners because we are so helpless and he is so merciful. This is true, but there is another aspect, which Luke Timothy Johnson highlights:

> Jesus' outreach to sinners shows God's desire to form a people from among those whom the world finds unworthy. Jesus declares, 'Healthy people don't need a doctor, sick people do. I have not come to invite righteous people to repentance, but sinners' *(Luke 5:31–32)* ..."[9]

Johnson goes on to cite the three parables in Luke 15 of "ministry to the outcast—the lost sheep (15:3–7), the lost coin (15:8–10), and the lost son (15:11–32)." These parables imply that the motive for Yeshua's outreach is not only compassion for the lost, but also recognition of the value of the lost. The shepherd goes after the lost sheep because he values it and wants it restored to the flock—not just for its own sake but to preserve its value and the wholeness of the flock. The lost coin has intrinsic value. Yeshua tells these stories in response to his critics who say, "This fellow welcomes sinners and eats with them" (Luke 15:2). Yeshua probably makes matters worse in his critics' eyes when he explains that he welcomes sinners not only because they are lost and he has compassion on them, but also because they are of incomparable value and so must be sought out and restored.

When Yeshua practices hesed, he doesn't just hand a loaf of bread to the hungry man, but he sits down with him, breaks the loaf, and eats it with him. This sort of hesed contrasts with sacrifice in three ways:

1. Sacrifice is directed toward God; hesed toward our fellow human beings.
2. Sacrifice fulfills the rules; hesed transcends the rules.
3. Sacrifice is quantifiable; hesed is without limit.

I recently visited Israel with my friend Michael, who works with a ministry providing aid to elderly Holocaust survivors living in poverty in Israel. We accompanied a team on their first visit to the apartment of an old couple that had survived the Holocaust and decades of life under communism in the Soviet Union before coming to Israel in

1997. They had been surviving on about 3000 shekels, or $750 dollars, a month for food, medicine, rent ($320) and everything else. Now, the husband's health had declined, and his medicine was taking a larger share of the budget. He slept on a child's bed in the sitting room because there was no money for a larger bed. We expressed a lot of love and support and were able to tell them that help—including a new bed—was on the way. As we were starting to leave, I saw Michael take the woman aside to talk with her, and then she broke out in a big, tearful smile and gave him a hug.

After we left, Michael told me that he had taken the woman aside and asked her if she spoke Yiddish, the mother tongue of generations of Jewish people. He went on in Yiddish to tell her that friends in America had given him some money to share with her. It wasn't *his* money, he emphasized, but friends wanted her to have it. She had received it with the smile that I had observed in the apartment. "I don't like to visit anyone in need without leaving money with them," Michael explained. "It's not enough to smile and hug someone and promise to help. You need to bring help with you." This exemplifies the hesed that Messiah instructs us to learn.

Yeshua wants his audience to learn the meaning of hesed, not sacrifice, but as his story continues, it seems doubtful that Yeshua's audience is really learning. As Yeshua continues to visit the outsiders, his critics treat him more and more like an outsider, even accusing him of being a glutton and a drunkard (Matt. 11:19). Then when the Pharisees accuse Yeshua's followers of violating the Shabbat on a technicality, Yeshua responds, "If you had known what this means, 'I desire mercy and not sacrifice,' you would not have condemned the guiltless" (Matt. 12:7)—indicating that they have not learned it at all. But, of course, Matthew doesn't record all of this to fuel criticism of the Pharisees. The Pharisees could be us, and Yeshua's words are for us today as well as Yeshua's detractors long ago:

> "I desire mercy and not sacrifice."
> Are we learning what that means?

Torah from the Mount

CHAPTER 3

TORAH FROM THE MOUNT, INTRODUCTION
Matthew 5:1–20

Most teachers would love to draw the crowds, but Yeshua seems to avoid them. "When Yeshua saw the crowds, he went up the mountain; and after he sat down, his disciples came to him. Then he began to speak, and taught them, saying … " (Matt 5:1–2). Note how his actions remind us of Moses, who also left behind the crowds to ascend a mountain—Mount Sinai. Like Moses, Yeshua climbs "*the* mount to let the God-given teaching resound from the heights. … Jesus leaves the multitude behind him, just like Moses who was commanded, 'not to allow the people to go up with him' (Exod. 24:2)."[1] Unlike Moses, however, Yeshua will not be alone on the heights because his disciples join him there and receive instruction from him. Indeed, Yeshua's instruction is not only designed for his disciples, but actually serves to make them into disciples. Bible scholars for centuries have debated the relevance and applicability of what they call the Sermon on the Mount, but its place within the story makes it clear that to follow Yeshua means following the ways that he teaches us from this mountain.

The well-known opening of the Sermon on the Mount expresses the theme of divine reversal in poetic form: In Messiah God reverses, or overturns, the ways of this age to reveal among the faithful the ways of the age to come. This passage also expresses the besorah of the kingdom that Yeshua has announced from the beginning. This good news is a royal announcement, as in Isaiah or 1 and 2 Samuel, and its full meaning and impact only become clear in the presence of the King himself. Therefore, it isn't primarily an announcement of some distant future but of life here and now in the presence of Messiah. Just as the good news is not only future but also present, so it is not only the story of how I "get saved," but also the announcement of a way of life that is at hand and which we are now invited to enter through repentance and faith. In the Sermon on the Mount, the good news includes a description of this way of life, beginning with the series of reversals commonly called the Beatitudes. They open, "Happy are the poor in spirit, for theirs is the kingdom of heaven."

These Beatitudes offer neither congratulations, nor consolations with promises for the next world; they are the good news that the God of our forebears, who demands a reversal of our own thinking, will reassess all earthly values.[2]

The True Happiness

As so often in Scripture, the opening word of these Beatitudes un-locks the meaning of the entire passage. Most translations into English begin with the word *blessed*, from which we get the name Beatitudes, based on the Latin. Rabbi Lapide, however, considers "how to translate the key initial word with an equivalent that will do justice to the meaning intended ... by the teacher on the mount." He concludes that "happy" "quite surprisingly ... comes closest to the original sense."[3] I agree, for several reasons:

- The opening word in Matthew's original Greek is *makarios*. When Jewish scholars in ancient times translated the Hebrew Scriptures into Greek, they employed this word as the equivalent of the Hebrew word *ashrei*.[4] Thus, Psalm 1 opens with ashrei in the original and makarios in the Greek translation. As the first word in Psalm 1, ashrei introduces the entire book of Psalms:

> Ashrei—Happy is the man who has not followed the counsel of the wicked,
> or taken the path of sinners,
> or joined the company of the insolent;
> rather, the teaching of the Lord is his delight,
> and he studies that teaching day and night.
> (Psalm 1:1–2, NJPS)

Ashrei not only introduces Psalms, but it also appears throughout Psalms to describe the one who fully trusts in God,[5] in God's Word,[6] or in his ways.[7] Psalm 1 is a springboard for Yeshua's message in his Sermon on the Mount. The first psalm describes the happiness of the one who doesn't follow sinful ways but trusts in God; Yeshua describes the happiness of one who doesn't follow the normal values of this world but trusts in God, whose kingdom reverses the ways of this world. In both cases, Scripture isn't speaking so much of a blessed future in the life to come or the ethereal blessedness of the super-pious but of concrete happiness here and now through an active relationship with God.

• "Happy" captures the sense of congratulation that is tied in with the word ashrei and with Yeshua's message in his sermon. We need to think of happiness, however, not as just a good feeling, but as a good condition or a happy state of being. Those who are happy in Yeshua's description don't just feel good but are in a good, prosperous condition—"in good shape" as we might say in today's English.

• Finally, "happy" is a good translation for Yeshua's opening word simply because it sounds less religious than "blessed." Yeshua isn't describing some ideal state of sainthood or future reward but the conditions under God's authority today, which we can experience if we have the faith and vision to follow him. Yeshua repeatedly expresses the happiness of God's realm as a reversal of the happiness of man's realm.

Of course, this discussion means that we won't want to speak of these ten verses as the Beatitudes, either, because that term is based on the Latin word for "blessed." We already have a good alternate name for these verses in the opening word ashrei. This is the name of a major Jewish prayer, mostly made up of Psalm 145 and recited three times each day, so we might rename the Beatitudes with the good Jewish title, the Ashrei of Messiah.

Nine-fold Happiness

The Ashrei of Messiah includes nine sayings, eight spoken in the third person (Happy are those…), and a final one in the second person (Happy are you…). Because we have already noted echoes of Moses and Mount Sinai, the number nine might remind us of the Ten Commandments that Moses received there. Here, however, there are ten minus one, almost as though Yeshua is anticipating the words he will speak a little later, "Do not think that I have come to abolish the Torah … " (Matt. 5:17). Yeshua insists that the Ten Commandments that summarize Torah retain their unique significance, but he is doing something new here as well.

Lapide reminds us that when Yeshua originally gave this message, he "did not say 'law' but 'Torah,' which means 'directive' or 'teaching.' The word has more a sense of promise, fulfillment, salvation history, and ethos about it than of actual law or rule, which supposedly leads to 'arid legalism' or 'sterile formalism,' as many Christian biblical commentaries assert even today."[8] Thus, just as we rename the Beatitudes the Ashrei of Messiah, we can rename the Sermon itself Torah from the Mount. Notice I used the preposition "from" instead of "on" as in the usual title, Sermon on the Mount. Yeshua is, of course, *on* the mount when he gives his torah, but his teaching goes forth to us *from* the mount to reach us in our own time and place. The title Torah from the Mount means that this section of Matthew's Gospel is instruction for life today. It is a sermon if we understand sermon not as a lofty religious discourse, but as an encounter with God's Word and a call to respond in concrete and specific ways.

Yeshua is giving a new torah, then, but to make sure no one thinks it is meant to replace the old Torah, he opens with nine sayings rather than ten. Furthermore, these nine sayings are not commandments like the opening ten sayings in Exodus 20, but descriptions of the true happiness hidden in the divine reversal. We can consider the number of sayings in another way, which unlocks additional meaning. Eight of the Ashrei are given in the third person—"Happy are those … " The first and last of the eight end with the same description, " … for theirs is the kingdom of heaven." The ninth is really an application of all eight to the followers of Yeshua, "Happy are *you* when people insult you and persecute you and speak all kinds of evil against you … " In this interpretation, there are eight items in the Ashrei of Messiah. What is the significance of eight? Eight is seven, the number of completion, plus one. Eight signifies a new beginning, a new spiritual creation. Thus, a Jewish male baby is circumcised on the eighth day to show that he is a new creation as a member of the covenant people of Israel and not just a human being created in the image of God on his day of birth. The Ashrei of Messiah, then, describe the conditions of a new creation in Messiah:

> Happy—in good shape—are the poor in spirit, for theirs is the kingdom of heaven.
> Happy are the mourners, for they will be comforted.
> Happy are the gentle, for they will inherit the earth.
> Happy are those hungering and thirsting for justice, for they will be filled.
> Happy are the merciful, for they will receive mercy.
> Happy are the pure in heart, for they will see God.
> Happy are the peacemakers, for they will be called children of God.
> Happy are those persecuted for the sake of righteousness, for theirs is the kingdom of heaven.
> Happy are you when people insult you and persecute you and speak all kinds of evil against you falsely on my account. Rejoice and be glad, for your reward is great in heaven, for in the same way they persecuted the prophets who were before you. (Matt. 5:3–12, author's translation)

Before we consider some of these verses in more depth, we can summarize them all:

- Each saying reverses a common idea of happiness to reveal the source of true happiness.
- Each saying develops an idea already stated by the Hebrew Prophets.
- Each saying references the ideal future and sees that future as already present among the faithful.
- The final saying reveals that this realized future comes in response to Yeshua, who speaks of what his followers will experience "on my account."

Year of Jubilee

The biblical theme of jubilee will help us understand the Ashrei of Messiah more fully. This theme runs throughout Scripture and reaches its fulfillment in Yeshua's ministry. Back in the Torah, Moses instructed the Israelites to keep a sabbatical year after each cycle of six ordinary years. During the sabbatical year, they gave the land a complete rest by not sowing crops or pruning vineyards and eating only what had been stored up during the six ordinary years and what the land yielded on its own (Lev. 25:4–7). At the end of seven cycles of seven years, the Torah instructs:

> You shall have the shofar[9] sounded loud; on the tenth day of the seventh month—on the day of atonement— you shall have the shofar sounded throughout all your land. And you shall hallow the fiftieth year and you shall proclaim liberty throughout the land to all its inhabitants. It shall be a jubilee for you: you shall return, every one of you, to your property and every one of you to your family. (Lev. 25:9–10)

Every fiftieth year, God reverses the normal social process in which the rich get richer and the poor get poorer, restoring the original equity among the people of Israel. Those who have had to lease out their land or even their own bodies just to survive are restored to their property and to their family. Every fiftieth year is a time of restoration that pictures the final restoration—the divine reversal—of the age to come. Isaiah develops the imagery of jubilee to describe the ministry of the anointed one—the Messiah—who will inaugurate that age:

> The spirit of the Lord *Adonai* is upon me, because *Adonai* has anointed [mashach] me; he has sent me to bring good news to the oppressed, to bind up the brokenhearted, to proclaim liberty to the captives, and

> release to the prisoners; to proclaim the year of the
> Lord's favor, and the day of vengeance of our God; to
> comfort all who mourn … (Isa. 61:1–2)

Two verbal clues link this passage in Isaiah to the jubilee described in
Leviticus. First, the phrase "to proclaim liberty" is a direct quote of
Leviticus 25:10, in which "liberty" is the Hebrew word *dror*. This is a
technical term that appears only eight times in the Hebrew Bible, with
every instance but one describing the liberty mandated for the seventh
year and fiftieth year.[10] Proclaiming liberty, therefore, means proclaiming the jubilee. Second, the anointed one proclaims "the year of the
Lord's favor." The word *proclaim* again echoes Leviticus 25, and the
year that the Lord favors above all others is the jubilee, in which the
prisoners and oppressed mentioned in Isaiah 61:1 are restored to freedom and wholeness.

Yeshua reads this passage from Isaiah when he visits his home
synagogue in Nazareth at the beginning of his ministry, saying, "Today
this scripture has been fulfilled in your hearing" (Luke 4:21). Thus,
Yeshua launches his ministry in terms of jubilee. Yeshua's torah, his
ethical instruction, is ancient and yet brand new. It will pick up and
carry forward themes already established in Torah and discussed in
similar ways by the Jewish sages, but these themes must now be understood in the context of Yeshua's proclamation of jubilee. His torah
is a foretaste of the age to come—and a sign that it is at hand—when
all things will be restored to God's original order.

Bible commentators point out the parallels between the
Beatitudes—the Ashrei of Messiah—and Isaiah 61:

> "Blessed are those who mourn, for they shall be com-
> forted" borrows from Isa. 61:2. "Blessed are the poor
> in spirit, for theirs is the kingdom of God" is inspired
> by Isa. 61:1. And "Rejoice and be glad" recalls Isa.
> 61:10 ("I will greatly rejoice in the Lord, and my whole
> being shall exult in my God").[11]

> A look at Isaiah 61 in Greek shows that the poor, the
> mourners, the meek, the brokenhearted, and those
> who rejoice all are noted in the first eleven verses. In
> addition, the idea of righteousness is prevalent.[12]

The connection to Isaiah 61 sheds light not only on Yeshua's message, but also on Yeshua himself because Isaiah 61 "affirms a time
when a herald of God's good news will be anointed and present. If the
promises of Isa. 61 are at work, then the figure of Isa. 61 must be present."[13] As always, the ethical teachings of Yeshua point beyond themselves to the teacher himself. As one commentator says about the
Isaiah 61 connection:

> But what does all this mean for the interpretation of the Sermon on the Mount? It means above all that the authority who speaks the Sermon belongs to a history. Jesus is not an isolated novum [something brand new] on history's religious landscape. He is rather the goal of a story, the history told in the Jewish Bible. [14]

Isaiah 61 also unlocks the meaning of some of the specific phrases in the Ashrei of Messiah, such as the "poor in spirit," who are termed in the Hebrew Scriptures the *anavim*.

> These are people who suffer because they have walked in humility with their God, so they are meek, mourning, brokenhearted now. Mercy, purity of heart, and a desire for righteousness and peacemaking drive them. Jesus promises that God will recognize and reward that pursuit ... because they have sought to walk in his steps and reflect his character as his children. [15]

We opened this chapter saying that the Sermon focuses on life in this world here and now rather than on the world to come. Thus, Yeshua is telling us that the poor, meek, and brokenhearted, those whom the dominant culture considers to be in the worst shape, are happy, in good shape from God's perspective. But now we see that these teachings do indeed point to the world to come as well. Yeshua's instructions provide a picture and first installment of the age to come, in which God's righteousness will be fully restored over all the earth. They apply here and now because the kingdom of God is already present in the person of God's anointed King, particularly among those who are on the margins of the earthly kingdom. They apply to the future because God's rule in Messiah will someday be established over all the earth. The Ashrei of Messiah invite us into his kingdom today.

One of the traditional criticisms of Yeshua's teachings, and indeed of the Scriptures as a whole, is the notion that he is promising "pie in the sky," as in the old protest song written by Joe Hill to the tune "Sweet Bye and Bye":

> Long-haired preachers come out every night
> To tell you what's wrong and what's right
> But when asked how about something to eat
> They will answer in voices so sweet:
> You will eat, bye and bye
> In that glorious land above the sky
> Work and pray, live on hay
> You'll get pie in the sky when you die.
> That's a lie. [16]

Karl Marx stated this position more simply and famously, saying that religion "is the opium of the people."[17] So we might ask, when Yeshua pronounces the poor and meek to be the truly happy, is he telling them to be content with their lot and not to complain against the oppressive system—or worse, is he telling the representatives of the system that they need not consider changing? Certainly Yeshua's teaching could be distorted into such a message, but there are several factors arguing against it:

- The same accounts that record these sayings of Yeshua have already recorded the call to repentance sounded by Yeshua and his predecessor Yochanan. As we have seen, this call defines repentance in terms of social justice. Remember that the whole body of Yeshua's Torah from the Mount is introduced in terms taken from the biblical jubilee, which was a matter of public policy. It is foreign to the text to argue that following Yeshua is strictly a private matter that has no bearing on public policy or behavior.

- One corollary of Yeshua's message is that those who appear to be in good shape in this world are *not* in such good shape, or happy, in the sight of God—and, therefore, need to do something about it. That response may take various forms, but it will be shaped by Yeshua's entire ethical teaching, which repeatedly targets the established and complacent.

- Still, Joe Hill and Karl Marx might argue that Yeshua's individual followers might claim to have clean hands because their hearts are pure and they long for the kingdom to come, even though they participate in a corrupt or oppressive governing system. This criticism is not without some basis in reality, but it doesn't reflect Yeshua's example or teaching. Consider Yeshua's example of driving the moneychangers out of the Temple (Matt. 21:12ff and parallels). On the one hand, this is a strictly individual matter. Yeshua does it by himself and doesn't call his followers to do the same. We can't imagine him organizing a committee to preserve the purity of the Temple. At the same time, it is a visible, public action with undeniable social and political implications. The same pattern occurs during the Triumphal Entry (see Chapter 11), another one-time individual, prophetic action that makes an undeniable socio-political statement.

This question will come up again in the Torah from the Mount: Are Yeshua's instructions strictly personal—and, therefore, compatible with participation in corrupt social and political systems—or do they have implications for those systems themselves? The answer is that individual transformation inevitably shapes our response to public policy. Yeshua doesn't seem to call his followers to take over the system, or even to fix it, but to maintain a corrective prophetic stance toward it. Those who do so, he says in his Ashrei, are in good shape with God even if their circumstances do not look so great. It is a real mistake to argue from this perspective that the status quo is just fine and should be left alone.

The Evidence

Yeshua's torah embodies divine reversal by declaring the poor, the mournful, the weak, and hungry to be the ones who are really happy. And it implies a critique of the system that declares the rich and powerful to be really happy. Yeshua goes on to teach that the happiness of which he speaks isn't just an inward thing but must be visible and self-evident.

> "You are the salt of the earth; but if salt has lost its taste, how can its saltiness be restored? It is no longer good for anything, but is thrown out and trampled under foot. You are the light of the world. A city built on a hill cannot be hid. No one after lighting a lamp puts it under the bushel basket, but on the lampstand, and it gives light to all in the house. In the same way, let your light shine before others, so that they may see your good works and give glory to your Father in heaven." (Matt. 5:13–16)

Yeshua uses two metaphors here—salt and light—to describe his followers. Both speak of something tangible, concrete, and highly valued in Yeshua's world. Salt was necessary not only to flavor food, but also and even more important, to preserve it in a world without refrigeration. It was a valuable commodity, underlying the word *salary*, which originally referred to the pay a Roman soldier was "given to buy salt,"[18] because salt was so essential to his livelihood. Salt in the Jewish world had, and still has, additional value as a sign of covenant. "You shall not omit from your grain offerings the salt of the covenant with your God; with all your offerings you shall offer salt" (Lev. 2:13). At the Shabbat meal, many Jewish people sprinkle salt on the *challah* (a ceremonial loaf of bread) as a reminder of covenant after reciting the blessing.

Light was also precious in a world without electricity or even kerosene lamps. Like salt, light had value because it stood out within its context; it dispelled darkness, just as salt dispelled decay and brought out true flavor. The town built on a hill stood out in terrain that was often inhospitable. A weary traveler, still on the road as night approached, would look for such a town and feel his heart leap when its lights came into view. Salt and light also share this quality: Both are worthless if they do not manifest their essential nature.

We need to remember these metaphors as we engage with a culture that alternates between private expressions of spirituality with little relevance to the public arena, and a bumper-sticker faith that displays its convictions like so many marketing slogans. Yeshua has something else in mind. If we have the real thing, he says, it will be obvious, undeniable, and of evident value to those around us regardless of their religious perspective. The happiness of which Yeshua speaks is not just an inward, personal feeling, nor an outward affiliation that we can pin to our lapel. Rather, people will see our faith in the form of good works. Yeshua's disciple Shimon says the same thing: "Conduct yourselves honorably among the Gentiles, so that, though they malign you as evildoers, they may see your honorable deeds and glorify God when he comes to judge" (1 Pet. 2:12). On the other hand, if we do not live good lives—if we are like unsalty salt or darkened light—our faith might be in doubt altogether.

We are back in Jewish space with its emphasis on deed over creed and practical expressions of the faith over abstract pronouncements. We are also in contemporary space. Today's "digital generation"[19] has access to more information online than it can ever process. If the good news of Messiah is presented as just more information, it will have difficulty even gaining a hearing. Yeshua, however, calls his followers to display the good news through their deeds. Indeed, his metaphors point to experience—taste and sight—over theory. As the digital generation unfolds, "People will want, more and more, to see how life works in real time as opposed to the abbreviated seminar [or sermon or tract] version."[20] In particular, people will want to get beyond the surrounding consumerism of our age to experience undeniable saltiness and light.

I recently stopped in Berkeley, California, to visit my niece who was working at a shop on Telegraph Avenue, a famous counterculture hub dating back to the 1960s. I was struck by two things; first, how little Telegraph Avenue had changed since I had frequented it as a hip college student almost forty years earlier, and second, how much Telegraph Avenue seemed like just an alternative shopping venue. It expressed counterculture by offering handmade purses instead of Gucci bags, T-shirts with radical or obscene slogans instead of designer labels, and marijuana accessories instead of six packs of Bud Light. I am sure that behind the scenes there is some serious political and social thought going on, which I might be able to respect even if I disagree with it, but at face value the community appears to be just an alternative consumerism. I fear that the followers of Messiah often present the same image, consumers of positive, family-friendly commodities in place of the mainstream offerings. Yeshua is after something far different, far more radical—more radical even than Telegraph Avenue. He calls his followers to be a community visibly displaying the divine reversal and interacting with the wider community in acts of undeniable goodness, service, and self-sacrifice.

Yeshua's Torah

To demonstrate that this call is not just a lofty ideal, Yeshua lays out detailed instructions—torah—in several vital social concerns, which are covered in the following chapters: reconciliation (Chapter 4), marital faithfulness (Chapter 5), true speech (Chapter 6), resistance against evil (Chapter 7), and love of all humankind (Chapter 8). First, however, Yeshua makes it clear that his torah does not replace the Torah given by Moses.

> "Do not think that I have come to abolish the Torah or the prophets; I have come not to abolish but to fulfill. For truly I tell you, until heaven and earth pass away, not one letter, not one stroke of a letter, will pass from the Torah until all is accomplished. Therefore, whoever breaks one of the least of these commandments, and teaches others to do the same, will be called least in the kingdom of heaven; but whoever does them and teaches them will be called great in the kingdom of heaven."
> (Matt. 5:17–19)

Again, the Jewish scholar Pinchas Lapide provides the most striking comment: "In all rabbinic literature I know of no more unequivocal, fiery acknowledgement of Israel's holy scripture than this opening to the Instruction on the Mount."[21] Note that Yeshua speaks of the Torah and the Prophets, which is a term for the whole body of the Hebrew Scriptures. He isn't just speaking of the Five Books of Moses but of the entire revelation given in the Word of God.

Yeshua helps us to overcome the western, rationalist perspective, which assumes that a new torah—his new teaching—must replace the old Torah. He models a view of Scripture more in line with Jewish thinking throughout the ages than with the rationalist approach that has defined our thinking for the past few centuries. Because Torah is the Word of God, it is an inexhaustible vein of truth that we can mine throughout the generations without diminishing it. This does not mean that every interpretation is equally valid or that we should study Scripture with the overly subjective approach of "what this passage means to me." It does mean, however, that we come to Scripture humbly, knowing that God's truth is absolute, but our understanding isn't, and so there is always more to learn. Torah itself has room for Yeshua's new torah. He brings more torah than any predecessor, one that fulfills Torah, not in conflict with Moses but in concert with him. Yeshua is the ultimate guide to the "more to learn" that lies within God's word. His torah, therefore, fulfills the Torah of Moses, not by replacing it but by bringing out its full meaning, depth, and impact.

Against this background, Yeshua will unveil this fulfilled Torah, which leads to a righteousness "greater than that of the Torah–teachers and Pharisees" (Matt. 5:20). He does so by citing a verse of Torah or an accepted teaching based on Torah and then interpreting that portion to reveal God's original intention in Torah. Six times in Matthew 5:21–48 Yeshua uses the formula, "You have heard ... I say to you ..."[22] The word connecting the two phrases is a simple conjunction in the Greek, *de*, which can be translated either as "and" or "but." There is a stronger Greek word, *alla*, which can only be translated as "but." This stronger term isn't used in the six phrases in 5:21–48 but appears earlier when Yeshua says, "I have come not to abolish *but* to fulfill" (5:17). Here the only word that makes sense is *but*, and so *alla* is used. Nevertheless, even though *de* can simply mean "and," most translations render the phrase as, "You have heard ... *but* I say to you ..." leading commentators over the centuries to argue that Yeshua is replacing the teaching of Torah with his new teaching—and ignoring what he said just a few verses before! Such commentators misread Yeshua's statement that he came to "complete" or "fulfill" the Torah (5:17), arguing that *fulfill* means "to bring it to an end" or "to do all that it requires so that it no longer has any hold on anyone else."

But such a reading is impossible in the immediate context of the surrounding verses and in the wider Jewish context of Yeshua's life and teachings. David Stern provides a better understanding of Matthew 5:17, "In fact, this verse states the theme and agenda of the entire Sermon on the Mount, in which Yeshua completes, makes fuller, the understanding of his *talmidim* concerning the *Torah* and the Prophets, so that they can more fully express what being God's people is all about."[23]

Indeed, Yeshua might be using a formula the ancient rabbis employed as they taught Torah to their disciples.[24]

> "You have heard" or "It is said," followed by "And I say to you" are a complementary pair of technical expressions from the basic vocabulary of rabbinic rhetoric. The first means, "Until now you have understood this scriptural passage in the following way," whereupon either the literal sense, the current exegesis, or the opinion of one's opponent is quoted. Then follows the

second phrase, "And I say to you," presenting the pro-
ponent's new explanation.[25]

In other words, when Yeshua says, "You have heard…" he not only
quotes the word of God, but also refers to ways that it has been understood and discussed among the people. When he says, "And I say
to you…" he isn't setting aside the word of God that he so staunchly
defended in Matthew 5:17–20, nor is he even setting aside the Jewish
discussion of the word of God. He is entering the discussion to reveal
the additional truths and hidden depths of Torah that remain relevant
as guides to our community today.[26]

Yeshua, then, speaks from within the world of Jewish legal discussion,[27] but as an absolutely unique voice, so that at the end of his
Ashrei, "the crowds were astounded at his teaching, for he taught
them as one having authority, and not as their scribes" (Matt. 7:28–
29). Yeshua deliberately teaches on his own authority, not on the
authority of the unbroken chain of rabbinic discussion that preceded
him.[28] "At many points in this protracted account of Jesus' specific
teachings [the Sermon on the Mount], we now recognize that at issue
is the figure of Jesus, not the teachings at all."[29] No matter how many
similarities we may trace between Yeshua and traditional Jewish
teaching, there will always be this contrast over the issue of authority. Yeshua handles Scripture with the same creative flexibility as the
best Jewish sages, flexibility intended to preserve the deeper principles of Scripture. At the same time he lives out his teaching more
fully than any master before or after him. The final acts of Yeshua's
life establish his authority for all time:

> The moral is obvious: without the passion and the cru-
> cifixion, the Instruction on the Mount would remain
> an eloquent, though demanding, axiological sermon.
> It gets its true binding force through the exemplary
> life, sufferings, and death of the Nazarene who sealed
> its validity with his own blood. Indeed, by his fruits
> you will recognize him![30]

CHAPTER 4

TORAH FROM THE MOUNT—RECONCILIATION
Matthew 5:21–26

My wife, Jane, and I became followers of Messiah in the early 1970s, when we were living as hippies in the mountains of New Mexico. A good number of our friends came to Messiah as well in those days. One of them, Bill,[1] continued to struggle with alcohol, drugs, and a violent temper. One night, on the way back from a drinking bout, Bill became angry with another man on the commune and slammed the car he was driving into the wall of this guy's adobe house. The next morning, when he had sobered up, he said, "I don't know what came over me. Jesus was with me all night, but he jumped out of the car just before I slammed into the wall." The lesson, of course, was that if Jesus is with you, you might not want to be slamming into your brother's wall. Indeed, you might not want to get drunk and harbor rage at all. Anger can become a sort of inner murder that violates Torah even if we don't act upon it. And, as Bill learned, such anger is inconsistent with following Yeshua, who reminds us to avoid navigating our lives in a way that makes him jump out of the car.

> "You have heard that it was said to those of ancient times, 'You shall not murder'; and 'whoever murders shall be liable to judgment.' But I say to you that if you are angry with a brother or sister, you will be liable to judgment; and if you insult a brother or sister, you will be liable to the council; and if you say, 'You fool,' you will be liable to the hell of fire." (Matt. 5:21–22)

In his teaching on anger, Yeshua establishes a pattern that he will follow throughout the rest of Matthew 5; he cites an aspect of Torah and then gives his complete, or fulfilled, interpretation. "You have heard" (or similar words), introduces the passage of Torah; "and I tell you … " leads into a deeper understanding of the passage. We will hear this pattern repeated throughout Matthew 5. In this first installment, Yeshua quotes one of the Ten Commandments—"you shall not murder"—and then adds a phrase—"whoever murders shall be liable to judgment"—which is not a direct quote, but a summary of Torah's teaching on murder, perhaps based on Genesis 9:5–6:

> For your own lifeblood I will surely require a reckoning: from every animal I will require it and from human beings, each one for the blood of another, I will require a reckoning for human life. Whoever sheds the blood of a human, by a human shall that person's blood be shed; for in his own image God made humankind.

Torah forbids murder and threatens judgment upon any who commit it; Yeshua goes beyond this to warn of judgment upon the inner source of murder, which is anger. Then he goes even further to speak about dealing with anger at its root, not by suppressing or hiding it, but by seeking reconciliation with the one with whom we are angry.

> "So when you are offering your gift at the altar, if you remember that your brother or sister has something against you, leave your gift there before the altar and go; first be reconciled to your brother or sister, and then come and offer your gift. Come to terms quickly with your accuser while you are on the way to court with him, or your accuser may hand you over to the judge, and the judge to the guard, and you will be thrown into prison. Truly I tell you, you will never get out until you have paid the last penny." (Matt. 5:23–26)

Our postmodern culture emphasizes subjective and individual experience, and Yeshua sometimes seems to share this emphasis. He isn't satisfied that we refrain from murderous actions but demands that we get rid of murderous thoughts. We might think, therefore, that the battle against anger is strictly subjective, an inner struggle of the heart, but Yeshua quickly turns our attention back to how we treat others. The opposite of anger, and its remedy, isn't suppression, positive thinking, or even calm acceptance of every offense, but reconciliation.

> So what the Sermon on the Mount here envisages is not isolated individuals seeking to subdue their passions but disciples going about the often awkward task of trying to right perceived wrongs. Perhaps in this the Sermon is wisely committing us to the mean between expression and repression, between ignoring our anger and venting it. … It is when rapport and harmony are established with the objects of anger that anger disappears.[2]

Justifiable Anger

When Yeshua prohibits anger, Rabbi Lapide points out, he is following the rabbinic tradition of providing a "hedge around Torah," a protective barrier that keeps us from getting too close to breaking Torah itself.

> We all know from experience that homicide begins in the heart with hate for or disparagement of someone as a "misanthrope," a "parasite," or "vermin." … It can begin at a desk or be drafted in an office. Because every murder begins in the heart, it is there that it must be nipped in the bud.[3]

Anger in the heart is the source of murder, so it is in the heart that anger must be nipped in the bud. At the same time, however, it would be a mistake to see Yeshua's prohibition of anger as absolute. Later in Matthew's account, Yeshua certainly seems angry when he drives the moneychangers out of the Temple courts (Matt. 21:12–13), and when he issues his scathing criticism of the Pharisees in Matthew 23. Indeed, in that chapter, Yeshua calls the Pharisees fools (Matt. 23:17) and worse, in apparent contradiction of his own words in Matthew 5:22.

Rabbi Joseph Telushkin cites numerous texts in the Tanakh and the rabbinic writings that condemn anger as destructive, ungodly, and foolish and then follows this list with a section on "Justifiable Anger."[4] He tells of a pious Jewish woman who informs her therapist that she never allows herself to become angry. The therapist has her read through the Bible and mark passages in which God or a biblical hero, like Moses or Isaiah, becomes angry. The woman realizes that "there are times when anger is an appropriate response to others' cruel or otherwise wrongful behavior, and any lesser response is wrong."[5] Indeed, if Telushkin had included the Gospels in his Bible reading, he would see Yeshua, like Moses, Isaiah, and God himself, becoming angry as well.

Apparently, as dangerous as anger can be, there are times when it is appropriate. Such cases have to do with an offense against God or injustice against others. Harboring anger over an offense against ourselves does not reflect Yeshua's example of driving out the moneychangers; anger on behalf of another may. But even in such cases, anger must be temporary and lightly held. Yeshua teaches that to "love your neighbor" is one of the two great commandments upon which Torah and the Prophets depend (Matt. 22:36–40). In context, this commandment reads, "You shall not take vengeance or bear a grudge against any of your people, but you shall love your neighbor as yourself …" (Lev. 19:18). There may be occasion for anger, but Torah instructs us not to bear a grudge or seek vengeance. Yeshua goes further to reveal that bearing a grudge becomes a source of inward murder, even if we do not act upon it. "So when you are offering your gift at the altar, if you remember that your brother or sister has something against you, leave your gift there before the altar and go; first be reconciled to your brother or sister, and then come and offer your gift" (Matt. 5:23–24).

We might expect Yeshua to say here, "So when you are offering your gift at the altar, if you remember that *you have something against your brother* ..." In other words, he has just told us to deal with our inner feelings of anger, which can cause us to harbor ill will toward a brother, but instead he says, "If you remember that *your brother has something against you*," shifting the focus from our own anger to the disrupted harmony between brothers. Whether we are angry with our brother or he is angry with us—whether we need to forgive or to be forgiven—reconciliation is essential. Indeed, Yeshua's illustration tells us that a lack of reconciliation hinders our worship.

Reconciliation, of course, is not always feasible, as Paul recognizes: "If it is possible, so far as it depends on you, live peaceably with all" (Rom. 12:18).[6] We may have people in our lives that refuse to be reconciled with us, but in such cases we can still forgive. Indeed, Yeshua repeatedly commands us to forgive unilaterally—that is, whether or not the forgiven one responds—and unconditionally— that is, without requiring anything of the one we have forgiven. Later in his Torah from the Mount, Yeshua instructs us to pray, "'And forgive us our debts, *as we also have forgiven* our debtors ...'' For if you forgive others their trespasses, your heavenly Father will also forgive you; but if you do not forgive others, neither will your Father forgive your trespasses" (Matt. 6:12, 14–15 emphasis added). Apparently, reconciliation is not always possible, but forgiveness is.

Forgiveness and Its Limits

In his book, *Total Forgiveness*, the Christian writer R.T. Kendall effectively develops this idea of unilateral and unconditional forgiveness. At one point, however, he states, "The Bible teaches us to forgive—totally. It is very surprising, therefore, to learn that there is no teaching of this kind of forgiveness in Judaism. After the Holocaust, there was a consensus that the Jewish people would never forget—ever."[7] Like Kendall, I was surprised to learn that there is "no teaching" in Judaism on total forgiveness, but I wasn't sure the statement was true. Consider this Jewish commentary on a verse mentioned above, Leviticus 19:18: "You shall not take vengeance, nor bear any grudge against the children of your people, but you shall love your neighbor as yourself: I am the Lord."

The rabbis said: What is considered "vengeance" and what is "bearing a grudge?"

If you say to your neighbor, "Lend me your scythe," and he refuses, and the next day comes to you and says, "Lend me your spade," if you answer, "I won't lend it to you, just like you won't lend your tool to me"—that's vengeance. Therefore the Torah says, "You shall not take vengeance."

And what is considered bearing a grudge? If you say to your neighbor, "Lend me your scythe" and he won't lend it to you, and the next day comes to you and says, "Lend me your spade," if you answer, "Here, take it. I'm not like you, who wouldn't lend your tool to me"—that's bearing a grudge. And therefore the Torah says, "You shall not bear a grudge."[8]

As another example, Rabbi Israel Salanter, a great Torah scholar of a century ago, was once traveling by train to the city of Vilna, when a fellow passenger, who was a young Torah student, insulted him. When the young man realized whom he had insulted, he apologized profusely. Rabbi Israel not only forgave him, but also helped him complete his studies in Vilna and find a good position there. The rabbi explained to him:

When you first came to me and apologized I said that I forgave you completely and had no resentment at all against you. And I sincerely meant what I said. ... So I decided to do you a favor, to remove any possible trace of resentment from my heart and so that I would truly be your friend. For it is human nature that when you do a kindness for someone you come to love him and feel yourself his friend.[9]

Some traditional Jewish teachers promote the sort of forgiveness that Yeshua mandates for his followers. At the same time, Kendall's statement about a Jewish consensus that we would never forget the offenses of the Holocaust may be accurate. This statement points to a remarkable Jewish book on forgiveness, *The Sunflower* by Simon Wiesenthal. When Wiesenthal was an inmate in a Nazi concentration camp, he was brought into a hospital room where a young SS soldier lay dying. The soldier had asked the nurse to bring a Jew to his room so he could confess his sin of murdering other Jews and ask for forgiveness. At the end of a lengthy confession, the soldier asks Wiesenthal to forgive him. Wiesenthal, who has patiently listened to everything, gets up and walks out of the room without saying a word.

That night the soldier dies without receiving the forgiveness he wanted. At the end of the story, Wiesenthal turns to the reader and says, "You, who have just read this sad and tragic episode in my life, can mentally change places with me and ask yourself the crucial question, 'What would I have done?'"[10]

Wiesenthal invites a number of writers to respond to this question. A clear pattern emerges as they do: The Jewish writers agree that he did the right thing in walking out on the SS man while a number of Christian writers feel he should have spoken words of forgiveness. The Jewish consensus in *The Sunflower* seems to counter Yeshua's teaching on unilateral and unconditional forgiveness, but it actually highlights some factors that will help us in our own practice of forgiveness.

First, Yeshua's instruction on forgiveness has to do with sins against ourselves. His highest expression of forgiveness came upon the cross and was directed toward those who had put him there: "Father, forgive them, for they do not know what they do" (Luke 23:34). *Total forgiveness*, as Kendall terms it, not only forgives the offender, but asks *God* to forgive him, desiring to see the offender reconciled to God, which in turn means relinquishing all hope of revenge. But note that even here, Yeshua is speaking of those who sinned against *him*. Of course, through his sacrificial death Yeshua brings forgiveness to all who believe and accept it, yet it is significant that on the cross, speaking as a man, Yeshua seeks forgiveness specifically for those who had victimized him.

Several respondents in *The Sunflower* state that Wiesenthal cannot forgive sins committed against others, as the soldier wants him to do. One Catholic respondent agrees that "an individual cannot forgive what was done to *others*."[11] According to Jewish tradition, not even God does that. It teaches that Yom Kippur, the Day of Atonement, brings forgiveness only for sins against God. Sins against another human will not be forgiven unless the sinner goes to the offended one and seeks to make it right.[12] Yeshua gives us a similar instruction: "Therefore if you bring your gift to the altar, and there remember that your brother has something against you, leave your gift there before the altar, and go your way. First be reconciled to your brother, and then come and offer your gift" (Matt. 5:23–24).

The reconciliation of which Yeshua is speaking doesn't happen just in the mind of one or even both estranged parties. The person who remembers his estrangement with his brother or sister has to "go his way," and do the work of reconciliation before he can come back and offer his gift. Inward and unconditional forgiveness means that I am *willing* to be reconciled, and it initiates the process, but it does not in itself constitute reconciliation. Trust, once broken, must be rebuilt through real and observable changes in behavior. For example, after Yeshua's resurrection, he appears to his disciples and takes Shimon aside to ask three times if he, Shimon, loves him (John 21:15–19). This threefold interrogation parallels Shimon's threefold denial of Yeshua before the crucifixion (John 18:17, 25, 27). Shimon shows remorse for his denial (e.g., Matt. 26:75), and certainly had been covered by Yeshua's prayer, "Father, forgive them, for they do not know what they are doing" (Luke 23:34). Yeshua still needs to restore Shimon, however, through eliciting a new affirmation of his love and charging him to "feed my sheep" (John 21:17).

So we shouldn't think of forgiveness as a way out of dealing with the real effects of offending or being offended. I believe this is another reason why Wiesenthal will not forgive the dying Nazi. To really gain forgiveness, the Nazi has to deal with those he offended, but he cannot, for they are dead. Those who believe in the atoning work of Messiah, like the Christians in Wiesenthal's book, may hope there is still some way for him to be forgiven in the sight of God, but Wiesenthal cannot be the mediator of that forgiveness.

What if our brother is unwilling to be reconciled or is no longer alive? Forgiveness does not in itself restore a relationship, but it is the first step of restoration that we can always take regardless of the other's response. In a remarkable nonreligious book on forgiveness, *Forgive for Good*, Dr. Fred Luskin details the health and emotional benefits of forgiveness based on his work with the Stanford University Forgiveness Project. Speaking as a social scientist, he sees forgiveness as "an extremely beneficial option" that people can choose regardless of the offender's response.[13]

> Forgiveness does not change the past, but it changes the present. Forgiveness means that even though you are wounded you choose to hurt and suffer less. Forgiveness means you become part of the solution. Forgiveness is the understanding that hurt is a normal part of life. Forgiveness is for you and no one else. You can forgive and rejoin a relationship or forgive and never speak to the person again.[14]

Yeshua's picture of forgiveness goes much deeper than this description because it is founded in the character of God himself. Still, this definition captures the sense of unilateral and unconditional forgiveness. Restoration, on the other hand, is not unilateral and unconditional but must involve both parties and can be a lengthy process. Nevertheless, we don't have to wait to forgive until we have been reconciled with the offender. We can choose forgiveness without any conditions at all as a starting point, which means that we are ready to "go our way and be reconciled to our brother."

Returning to Wiesenthal's story, we learn another lesson: Forgiveness does not ignore the truth. It's not based on pretending that the offender did nothing wrong. We begin to practice authentic forgiveness as we acknowledge sin, in ourselves as well as others, instead of denying or making excuses for sin. In *The Sunflower*, Wiesenthal never extends forgiveness to the dying Nazi. We may debate the appropriateness of that result, but the book is right on target in teaching that forgiveness must come after squarely looking at reality. It isn't just a religious exercise that might be pursued in denial of reality, but a bold response to reality. Indeed, religious denial is one of the main barriers to genuine forgiveness.

Barriers to Forgiveness

Yeshua tells the story of a slave who owed an astronomical sum of money to his master:

> [A]nd, as he could not pay, his lord ordered him to be sold, together with his wife and children and all his possessions, and payment to be made. So the slave fell on his knees before him, saying, "Have patience with me, and I will pay you everything." And out of pity for him, the lord of that slave released him and forgave him the debt. But that same slave, as he went out, came upon one of his fellow slaves who owed him a hundred denarii; and seizing him by the throat, he said, "Pay what you owe." Then his fellow slave fell down and pleaded with him, "Have patience with me, and I will pay you." But he refused; then he went and threw him into prison until he would pay the debt.

> When his fellow slaves saw what had happened, they were greatly distressed, and they went and reported to their lord all that had taken place. Then his lord summoned him and said to him, "You wicked slave! I forgave you all that debt because you pleaded with me. Should you not have had mercy on your fellow slave, as I had mercy on you?" And in anger his lord handed him over to be tortured until he would pay his entire debt.

> So my heavenly Father will also do to every one of you, if you do not forgive your brother or sister from your heart. (Matt. 18:25–35)

Forgiveness, the story teaches us, doesn't mean denying the offense or making excuses for the offender; it means canceling and no longer seeking the very real debt that he owes us. It doesn't mean that we're automatically reconciled with the offender, but it is the essential first step if reconciliation is ever to take place. Those who receive such forgiveness, but are unwilling to cancel the debts that others might owe them, find themselves liable for their old debts once again. Finally, Yeshua tells us, this act of writing off debts must come from the heart. When we refuse to forgive the debts of others wholeheartedly, we bind ourselves to our own debts. Forgiveness, then, is a form of divine reversal. Rather than seeking to receive forgiveness, we give forgiveness because we already *have* received it. Even as those who have received forgiveness, however, like the unforgiving slave in Yeshua's story, we might discover barriers to forgiving lodged within ourselves. Let's consider four of these barriers:

1. Religious Denial: "There's Nothing to Forgive."

Denial means not just refusing to talk about our problems, but also actually believing that the problems aren't there or that they aren't serious enough to cause concern. Religious denial enlists pious terminology to pretend that problems don't exist. Instead of admitting pain and anger, religious denial claims that everything is already forgiven or that it doesn't really matter anyway, so there is nothing more to discuss. Luskin, again from a nonreligious viewpoint, speaks of three preconditions for forgiveness:

- Know what your feelings are about what happened.
- Be clear about the action that wronged you.
- Share your experience with at least one or two trusted people.[15]

Religious denial counters all three preconditions. Still, it is hard to break because it carries the double benefit: It provides us with a pious front at the same time as it protects us from intense feelings of pain, anger, and loss. It employs a pseudo forgiveness that glibly dismisses the offense and avoids forgiving "from the heart" as Yeshua commands. Forgiveness from the heart requires that we acknowledge our hurt and face our anger and loss rather than denying it. For this reason, we have to be careful not to turn Yeshua's teaching against anger into a prop for denial by suppressing our anger, or pretending it isn't there, rather than overcoming it from the heart.

Traditional Jewish perspectives on forgiveness, which seem narrower than Yeshua's approach, have the benefit of avoiding religious denial. Rabbi Telushkin opens his chapter on forgiveness with a Yeshua-like quote from the Talmud, "One who overcomes his natural tendencies [i.e., to hold on to a grudge] and instead forgives, all his sins are forgiven."[16] Telushkin goes on, however, to outline not only cases in which forgiveness is obligatory, but also cases in which it is optional or even forbidden under Jewish law. As we have already noted, we cannot forgive sins committed against another; Jewish law would even say that such forgiveness is forbidden. In this view, a person might forgive a murderer for the pain that his evil deed caused him, but he can't forgive the sin of murder itself because he wasn't the victim. Telushkin also questions whether it is right to forgive every inflicted offense. "Is a victim of rape obliged to forgive her rapist? And is a man falsely accused of rape supposed to forgive his accuser? I cannot think of a reason why."[17]

Luskin's research on forgiveness provides "a reason why"—because forgiving the offender helps free me from the pain and damage of the offense. Or as Telushkin himself says, "… it is sometimes worth forgiving not for the sake of the one who hurt us, but for our own. Not letting go of our rage is likely to have the effect of prolonging, not shortening, our suffering."[18] Like the servant, we could be handed over to be tortured if we don't forgive. Yeshua provides an additional and far more profound reason: We forgive because God has first forgiven us. Nevertheless, the traditional Jewish perspective reflects realism and honesty about forgiveness, which helps counter religious denial and avoids the pitfall of superficial forgiveness, which might be only a religious pretense.

2. Guilt and Shame: "Who Am I to Forgive?"

Instead of forgiving offenses, we sometimes excuse them by saying things like, "It really wasn't that bad. She really couldn't help it. It was probably my own fault anyway." Statements like these are common among those who have been hurt by parents. A child views the world as inherently fair and orderly. If something bad happens, the child feels somehow to blame. Because the world must be fair when a parent hurts a child, the child feels she must deserve it. We naturally tend to protect our parents and other important figures in our early life. We're more comfortable with excusing them or minimizing their behavior than with facing the reality that our world isn't a safe place and that those placed by God in our lives to protect and nurture us fail to do so.

This pattern is common among sexual abuse victims, who often feel they must have deserved the treatment they received. Often, their strongest feeling about the abuse is one of shame rather than anger toward the perpetrator. Some people find it easier to bear the guilt than to realize the world can be so unfair and feel the anger. As long as we excuse those who have harmed us, however, we remain bound. We cannot fully forgive until we admit that we were truly hurt, though we didn't deserve to be, and hold the offending party responsible. As we drop the shame, we may still need to face pain and loss, but we prepare the way for genuine forgiveness.

3. Fear of Weakness: "I'll Never Forgive."

This barrier to forgiveness is the opposite of shame. Shame is willing to take on all of the blame and deny that anyone else owes anything. Fear of weakness blames the other and holds him to his debt because it gives a sense of power over him. Anger and blame help some people overcome the feeling of victimization. Such anger can become a chronic condition that pervades our lives and is expressed in destructive ways.

Men especially often hold out in righteous indignation against the world at large rather than face their own hurt and disappointment. The power that accompanies this posture is illusory. Their fear of appearing or feeling weak keeps them from taking the steps that restore them to genuine strength. Underlying this chronic anger is a sense of vulnerability, "I won't cancel the debt because people will think I'm a pushover. If I forgive her, she'll just do it again." Paradoxically, holding on to our offenses keeps us stuck in the victim role. Beneath the hostile exterior of many domineering men is a tremendous fear of being hurt. The truth is that we *are* vulnerable; we can indeed get hurt again. We can't protect ourselves, however, by clinging to not forgiving, nor do we become more vulnerable when we finally do forgive. We become more powerful because we're no longer dependent on the response of the other or living out the consequences of their past behavior.

4. Self-righteousness: "I'll Forgive When ... "

Like anger, self-righteousness creates a false sense of power to compensate for deeper feelings of violation. It says, "I'll forgive if he admits he's wrong and I'm right." This stance might feel powerful, but it actually gives away power because it keeps us bound in not forgiving until someone else decides it's time to make things right. Unfortunately, that time often never comes, and the victim of sin remains a victim of a hardened heart as well. Often we prefer to be right than to have peace of mind. We hang on to our offenses in the irrational hope that we can change the past, change those who have hurt us, and set the accounts right once again. We demand justice, as the unforgiving slave did toward his fellow slave, and like him we end up getting the justice we deserve. On the other hand, when we cancel the debts of those who have hurt us, we face that we can't undo what was done or change the past. This frees us to find peace with God and ourselves and to start over in the present.

Yeshua empowers us to overcome all of these barriers when he tells us to forgive unilaterally and unconditionally. This forgiveness is empowering because we can exercise it and thereby maintain our spiritual freedom regardless of what the offender chooses to do. When we harbor a lack of forgiveness, on the other hand, we place the key to our wholeness in the offender's hand. Only when he admits his wrongdoing and makes some kind of restitution, can we be released. In contrast, Yeshua's teaching on forgiveness makes it conditional only on the fact that we have already been forgiven by God.

Steps in Forgiveness

Forgiveness lies at the heart of Yeshua's message and of the ethical pathway that he lays out for us. It is also at the heart of God's own description of himself, "The LORD, the LORD, a God merciful and gracious, slow to anger, and abounding in steadfast love and faithfulness, keeping steadfast love for the thousandth generation, forgiving iniquity and transgression and sin ... " (Exod. 34:6–7a). Yeshua models the same forgiveness from within the agony of crucifixion, "Father, forgive them; for they do not know what they are doing."

Our ability to forgive arises from our reconciliation with this forgiving God. If the offending party refuses to take responsibility for his wrongdoing, it could be impossible to fully trust him again, but we still forgive, leaving the matter in God's hands and remaining open to reconciliation if it becomes possible. Such forgiveness is a decision, not an emotion. It is a decision, however, that involves the whole person and can take considerable time and emotional investment. We have considered barriers to forgiveness. Now, we can break down the process of forgiveness into typical steps:

1. Admit the Offense.

We have seen how Yeshua's teaching on forgiveness can be distorted into a form of religious denial. Instead of facing hurt and anger, we might claim that there is nothing to forgive or that all is forgiven already, so that we don't need to deal with it any longer. The problem is that the offense, though not admitted, continues to do its work deep within. As we have seen, the Stanford University Forgiveness Project identified three preconditions for forgiveness, "They are to know what you feel, to know what was wrong, and to tell a couple of trusted people what happened."[19] All of these are part of this first step.

For example, Suzanne was raised by an angry, critical father, who rarely expressed approval or love towards her. She felt deprived of his warmth and attention, especially in her teenage years. One day, she came home from school to find her phone missing from her bedroom and an empty hole where it had been torn out of her wall (this was back when phones had cords). Suzanne's father didn't talk about it, but she gathered from her mother that he was angry because a teacher had called to inform him that Suzanne's schoolwork wasn't up to par. Because she spent too much time talking with friends, and too little time studying, the phone had to go, according to her father. As an adult, Suzanne developed that same kind of explosive anger and found it difficult to control.

This woman had struggled to forgive her father but never labeled his actions as sin. She had to see that when he tore out her phone, he was sinfully indulging his own bad temper and violating her personal dignity. Sin, intentional or not, needs to be labeled as such. The person who wronged you violated God's standards, and as a consequence you were hurt, deprived, or betrayed. When you begin to see the offense this clearly, you also see what you need to forgive.

Suzanne finally began to write a letter to her father, listing the charges that she had against him. She wasn't planning to send the letter but to use it to help her admit her feelings as the first step in forgiveness. She had a hard time getting the letter done, however. "I'm not sure I want to write all this stuff down in a list," she said. "I'd rather just forget it." I responded that she had already written the letter in her heart. She needed to get it out of her heart and down on paper, so that she could see the offenses, stop hiding them, and eventually tear up the list.

2. Give up on Changing the Past and Change Yourself Instead.

Forgiveness involves the pain of facing our losses, of realizing our utter inability to fix the past or change the offender. Rather than face this pain and the accompanying sense of powerlessness, many individuals hang on to their charges, vainly hoping someday to collect. They create a "grievance story" in which they are the victims of another's abuse in the past and blame that abuse for their problems in the present.[20] Such blaming can help delay the mourning of their losses, but it also delays the healing that normally follows mourning.

I once had a friend who lost most of his life savings to an embezzler. He kept track of that total as a debt that the embezzler owed him. Whenever he thought of his offender, my friend became angry and thought about how much he could use that money. For a long time, my friend expected to get it back and counted on it to remedy his financial problems. Eventually, he realized that he would never see that money again and that it was time to write it off. He had to go through a period of mourning his financial ruin, which he had never really faced as long as he had hoped to be paid back. He needed to take this step before he could begin to get his finances under control. By accepting the past, he gained power over his future.

We sometimes refuse to forgive in hopes that the offender will change and somehow fix what he or she has done. You take a major step in forgiveness, however, when you believe that you can change your own feelings and outlook even if no one else ever changes. The past cannot be fixed, but the present offers a new start if we'll take it.

3. Drop the Charges as Your Charges Were Dropped.

The realization that we need forgiveness ourselves doesn't minimize or excuse what another has done. It does recognize our own ongoing need for God's grace. This recognition often helps overcome the hardness of heart against those who have hurt us the most. As we recognize our need to be forgiven, we can reflect God's forgiveness toward others. Real forgiveness is like dropping a legal case against someone even when you know you can win it. The Scriptures teach that the basis for forgiving someone is not his repentance but the fact that God has already forgiven us, "… forgiving each other, just as in Messiah God forgave you" (Eph. 4:32).

Imagine walking into a courtroom with your high-powered attorney and reams of evidence. Your opponent is cowering in a corner of the courtroom. As the trial unfolds, it becomes evident that he has no real defense against you. Everything is going your way. Suddenly you jump up in the middle of the proceedings and announce to the judge, "Your Honor, never mind, I drop all charges. My opponent can go free." Your attorney looks at you as though you're crazy; the judge shrugs his shoulders; and your opponent walks away sneering.

Notice a couple of things about this scenario:

First, your decision is a choice, not an emotion; it's an act of the will, not a matter of waiting until you feel like it. Forgiveness is a process, but now you have arrived at the point of decision. Eventually, the time comes when we have to say, "I drop the charges."

Second, your decision is unilateral and unconditional. Your opponent didn't admit to his wrong, ask for mercy, or even appear grateful when you dropped your complaint against him. This is the power of forgiveness—it depends on no one else but only on the reality of being forgiven ourselves.

4. Create a Framework for Reconciliation.

Because our forgiveness is unilateral and unconditional, it doesn't depend upon any change in the offending party. When we forgive, therefore, we do not restore the damaged relationship, but we do become willing to enter a process of reconciliation, which must involve both parties.

Remember my friend who lost money to an embezzler? When he forgave the debt, he gave up the hope of collecting what he was owed. When he thought about the embezzler, he no longer became angry at how much he needed the money owed him. But he wasn't about to loan the embezzler money again. Forgiveness doesn't in itself restore the trust that sin has destroyed. This requires effort, especially from the offending party. Apologizing isn't enough; he must earn trust again. Here are some factors in the restoration process:

- Both parties must acknowledge the need for incremental rebuilding. Sometimes an offender uses the command to forgive to manipulate the person he has harmed. He says, "You're a believer, so you have to forgive me," and seeks to shift the blame on to the innocent party. Or he says in a wounded tone, "You don't trust me." Our response can be, "I forgive you. I am willing to be reconciled to you, but you have lost my trust. You'll have to make a real effort to regain it."

- Identify specific concrete ways that trust can be restored incrementally. I sometimes say to those in conflict, "What small changes in behavior could the other make that would help you trust him or her more than you do right now?" Trust isn't an either/or proposition—not 100 percent or nothing—but something that grows. Both sides need to be willing to make realistic, measurable commitments and follow through on them.

- Seek improvement rather than perfection but also set clear limits. There will be setbacks and disappointments on the way to reconciliation, so don't set perfection as the requirement. Some behaviors, however, like physical abuse or infidelity, cannot recur without derailing the whole reconciliation process. Set and maintain clear limits.

5. Keep the Case Closed.

We need to balance willingness to forgive with a realistic restoration process. One of the most common objections is, "If I forgive him, I know he will just do it again." Not forgiving, however, doesn't make the offender any less likely to offend again, but it does weigh us down with feelings of resentment, guilt, and bitterness. Whether or not we are reconciled with the offender, we can still maintain inner peace, which makes interpersonal peace more attainable.

If feelings against a person return, that doesn't mean that you didn't really forgive in the first place. You may say, *I thought I forgave so-and-so, but I guess I didn't because I found myself resenting him again.* If you have dropped the charges, however, feelings of resentment are a temptation that you can resist like any other. You can say, *because I already forgave so-and-so, I'm not going to reopen my case against him no matter how I feel.* This is true whether or not reconciliation proves to be possible. We can ask ourselves daily if there are any accounts receivable we are still holding on to, waiting for a payment that might never come. If there are, we need to write them off, so that we can benefit from peace of mind, joy, and a right relationship with God.

Forgiveness opens the way for restoration and reconciliation. Forgiveness as Yeshua teaches it, however, cannot fully be understood just in terms of relational and emotional well-being. It is at the heart of our whole response to God. Yeshua's teaching on forgiveness is part of his announcement that jubilee has arrived, the day of release and peace for Israel that God has promised all along.

> [This announcement] means "the time has come for the faithful people to abolish all the debts which bind the poor ones of Israel, for your debts toward God are also wiped away (for that is the gospel, the good news)." … Jesus was establishing a strict equation between the practice of jubilee and the grace of God. He who was not legalist at any other point, and who was ready without hesitation to pardon prostitutes and disreputable people, was nonetheless extremely strict upon one point: "only one who practices grace can receive grace."[21]

Later in his Torah from the Mount, Yeshua will teach us to follow our prayer, "your kingdom come," with the prayer, "and forgive us our debts, as we also have forgiven our debtors" (Matt. 6:10–12). Yeshua's teaching on anger provides us with the first example of the Torah fulfilled, instructing us to replace anger with forgiveness in an act of divine reversal that reflects God's own forgiveness. Thus, in our everyday relationships, we reflect the presence of his kingdom among us.

CHAPTER 5

TORAH FROM THE MOUNT—FIDELITY
Matthew 5:27–32

"You have heard that it was said, 'You shall not commit adultery.'
And I say to you that everyone who looks at a woman with lust has
already committed adultery with her in his heart." (Matt. 5:27–28)

Ex-President Jimmy Carter has been a controversial figure in recent years, but one of the earliest storms surrounding him occurred during the 1976 presidential race. Candidate Carter, known as a born-again Christian throughout the campaign, granted an interview to *Playboy* magazine. Toward the end of his interview, Carter said:

> Christ set some almost impossible standards for us.
> The Bible says, "Thou shalt not commit adultery."
> Christ said, I tell you that anyone who looks on a
> woman with lust has in his heart already committed
> adultery. I've looked on a lot of women with lust. I've
> committed adultery in my heart many times. ... [1]

Comedians had a great time with the image of this pious, church-going Baptist struggling with lustful thoughts toward "a lot of women," especially one who had appeared to be so thoroughly domesticated as Governor Carter. The interview stirred up more serious discussion at the time as well. Should a born-again Christian cooperate with *Playboy* magazine at all—or was Carter compromising his Christian values to expand his voter base? Was Carter wise to expose this side of his humanity while he was under consideration as a possible President of the United States?

Adultery of the Heart

The interview's most famous line remains, "I've committed adultery in my heart many times." Carter goes on from there to reach this conclusion:

> This is something that God recognizes, that I will do
> and have done, and God forgives me for it. But that
> doesn't mean that I condemn someone who not only

> looks on a woman with lust but who leaves his wife and
> shacks up with somebody out of wedlock... The guy
> who's loyal to his wife ought not to be condescending
> or proud because of the relative degree of sinfulness.[2]

It is hard to argue with an admonition against condescension and spiritual pride. And surely such an admonition is in line with Yeshua's general teaching in his Torah from the Mount. Carter implies that he is just a normal male and lust in the heart is inevitable. It serves as a reminder that the "righteous" need God's forgiveness as much as the "sinners" do. Not a bad application of Yeshua's teaching about adultery of the heart—and far better than another one that I have sometimes heard: "Since I've already committed adultery in my heart, there's no real reason not to commit it in the body as well."

Years ago, my wife and I worked at a Christian drug rehabilitation center. One of the excuses that paved the way to drug relapse for a number of our clients was, "I've been thinking about that next shot of heroin so much that I figured I might as well go get it—I already committed shooting up in my heart, so I might as well shoot up!" A Christian adulterer might employ a variation of this theme, "Everyone commits adultery in his heart, so you can't condemn me for doing what you really want to do yourself!"

Yeshua, on the other hand, seems to be getting at something more here, something that goes beyond reversing spiritual pride and condescension. He seems intent on actually eliminating this adultery of the heart altogether:

> "If your right eye causes you to sin, tear it out and
> throw it away; it is better for you to lose one of your
> members than for your whole body to be thrown into
> hell. And if your right hand causes you to sin, cut it off
> and throw it away; it is better for you to lose one of
> your members than for your whole body to go into
> hell." (Matt. 5:28–30)

Apparently, inner infidelity is not inevitable, but results from actions of the eye and hand that we can reverse if we are willing to pay the price. Can we deny that today's visual bombardment of sexual imagery fuels adultery of the heart? Tearing out the eye today means turning off the television, blocking the website, or closing the book or magazine ruthlessly if necessary. Film, in particular, often employs explicit sexual images in a context that is otherwise artistically compelling. But Messiah's standards require us to forgo experiences that may have a positive side for the sake of wholeness before God.

What about the hand? How does that feed adultery of the heart? Could Yeshua be hinting at the generally avoided topic of masturbation? Contrary to a common preconception, the Scriptures don't deal directly with this issue at all. In the past, masturbation was often called *onanism* after the sin of Onan, who "spilled his semen on the ground" and was put to death by the Lord (Gen. 38:9–10). But the context of Onan's story reveals that his sin was social rather than sexual. He spilled his seed because he didn't want to fulfill the ancient obligation to impregnate his dead brother's widow and thereby continue his brother's family line.

David Flusser cites "a Jewish opinion [from *Midrash Hagadol* on Exod. 20:14] that the word 'to commit adultery' in Hebrew had four letters in order to warn us that adultery could be committed by hand, foot, eye, and heart."[3] Masturbation might not be the dark and shameful act it is often portrayed to be in the religious world, but surely it involves the hand in the lustful cultivation of adultery of the heart. Yeshua is always ready to forgive, as Carter noted back in 1976. In this passage, however, he is reminding us to go after the roots of sinful behavior, even those that might appear harmless, rather than reassuring us that he will forgive us if we allow those roots to bear fruit.

Obviously, Yeshua is quoting one of the Ten Commandments in this passage, "You shall not commit adultery." Israeli Bible teacher Joseph Shulam believes that Yeshua is also citing another of the Ten Commandments, "You shall not covet" (Exod. 20:17). Yeshua combines the two commandments in a Jewish interpretive move called *hekkesh*. Shulam explains, "*Hekkesh* literally means 'to take two stones and hit them together,' which is a metaphor for comparing two verses that have similar language in order to learn something not previously known." In this case, what was not previously known is that *you shall not commit adultery* "not only means the act itself, but also the intention which arises in the heart and is committed with the eyes."[4]

Darrell Bock also notes the connection Yeshua makes with "You shall not covet." "The connection is not an accident. To lust after someone dehumanizes that person and turns that person into an object of self-indulgence."[5] Bock raises a vital point that guides us through our discussion of Yeshua's ethical pathway: *We must be concerned not just with inner purity and a sense of nearness to God, but also with the welfare of others.* Even lust, which seems like the most personal and inward of sins, affects those around us and diminishes the image of God in our fellow human beings. We can see this reality in our lust-addicted culture and the havoc it wreaks not just in the minds of the lustful but also in the actual lives of many today, particularly children and women.

Divorce and Remarriage

Within this challenging call to sexual purity, Yeshua introduces his equally challenging teaching on divorce:

> "It was also said, 'Whoever divorces his wife, let him give her a certificate of divorce,' and I say to you that anyone who divorces his wife, except on the ground of unchastity, causes her to commit adultery; and whoever marries a divorced woman commits adultery." (Matt. 5:31–32)

This teaching seems to reinforce Carter's perception that "Christ set some almost impossible standards for us." It seems particularly tough in our day of serial monogamy, with quick, easy, no-fault divorces and multiple remarriages, even among professed followers of Yeshua. In Yeshua's own day when he repeats this teaching later in the Gospel, his disciples conclude, "If such is the case of a man with his wife, it is better not to marry" (Matt. 19:10). It seems like an impossible standard, yet it was clearly one that Yeshua expected his followers to maintain. To resolve this dilemma, consider Yeshua's instructions in their original context.

To begin with, Yeshua's statement in Matthew 5:17 remains axiomatic, "I have not come to abolish, but to fulfill Torah." It is unlikely then that Yeshua means to contradict Torah by absolutely forbidding something that it allows. It permits divorce as long as the rejected wife is given a certificate of divorce, which is called a *get* in Jewish law. Yeshua is bringing out the more profound original teaching of Torah, which underlies later discussions and modifications concerning divorce. Note that the passage of Torah that Yeshua quotes, Deuteronomy 24:1ff., permits the husband to send away the wife but not vice versa. It favors the husband, but it does protect the wife by requiring the husband to provide a get, so that she is eligible to remarry. A state of permanent singleness was particularly difficult for a woman of Yeshua's time. Yeshua continues in the direction set by the Torah to provide greater protection for the woman by drastically limiting divorce. Also note that Deuteronomy 24 doesn't command divorce, or even sanction it, but only regulates it. Yeshua teaches that the ideal established in Torah is lifelong marriage. Deuteronomy 24 doesn't contradict this ideal, even though an inaccurate reading of that passage might obscure it.

Deuteronomy recognizes that without a get, which permits her to remarry, the woman would have been permanently estranged and isolated unless she returned in disgrace to her father's house. According to some of the ancient rabbis, though, as long as the husband issues the certificate, he is free to dismiss his wife on nothing more than a whim. Others disagree, and a passage from the Talmud captures the various viewpoints:

> Beth Shammai [the followers of Rabbi Shammai] say: a man should not divorce his wife unless he has found her guilty of some unseemly conduct, as it says, because he hath found some unseemly thing in her (Deut. 24:1). Beth Hillel [the followers of Rabbi Hillel], however, say [that he may divorce her] even if she has merely spoilt his food, since it says, because he hath found some unseemly thing in her. Rabbi Akiba says, [he may divorce her] even if he finds another woman more beautiful than she is, as it says, [in the same passage] it cometh to pass, if she find no favour in his eyes.[6]

Yeshua, whose teachings often resemble those of the more lenient and peace-loving Beth Hillel, agrees with the stricter Beth Shammai in this debate. He would particularly agree with Rabbi Eleazar's conclusion of the whole discussion in the Talmud:

> If a man divorces his first wife, even the altar sheds tears, as it says, And this further ye do, ye cover the altar of the Lord with tears, with weeping and with sighing, insomuch that he regardeth not the offering any more, neither receiveth it with good will at your hand. Yet ye say, Wherefore? Because the Lord hath been witness between thee and the wife of thy youth, against whom thou hast dealt treacherously, though she is thy companion and the wife of thy covenant [Mal. 2:13–14].[7]

In similar fashion, Yeshua teaches that even with the required certificate that protects the estranged wife and allows her to remarry, divorce still violates the heart of Torah. Indeed, "Whoever divorces his wife and marries another commits adultery" (Mark 10:11). The paperwork, even if executed in accord with Torah, can neither alleviate the offense to the woman nor override the man's inward motivation. Nor can it restore the original intent of Torah itself. A follower of Messiah, therefore, must never initiate divorce, except "on the ground of unchastity," as Yeshua mentions above.

Marriage from the Beginning

But what exactly is meant by unchastity here? To answer this question, we need to consider in more detail Yeshua's discussion of divorce in Matthew 19.

> Some Pharisees came to him, and to test him they
> asked, "Is it lawful for a man to divorce his wife for
> any cause?"
>
> He answered, "Have you not read that the one who
> made them at the beginning 'made them male and fe-
> male,' and said, 'For this reason a man shall leave his
> father and mother and be joined to his wife, and the
> two shall become one flesh'? So they are no longer
> two, but one flesh. Therefore what God has joined to-
> gether, let no one separate."
>
> They said to him, "Why then did Moses command us
> to give a certificate of dismissal and to divorce her?"
>
> He said to them, "It was because you were so hard-
> hearted that Moses allowed you to divorce your wives,
> but from the beginning it was not so. And I say to you,
> whoever divorces his wife, except for unchastity, and
> marries another commits adultery." (Matt. 19:3–9)

Yeshua begins his discussion by citing the Torah ideal for marriage
"from the beginning." "Jesus, like many other rabbis, finds this original will of God at the beginning of his Bible, before the original fall,"
which has "transformed the harmony of becoming-one-flesh into a
battle of the sexes, a struggle of victory and defeat, of lordship and
subjection, making the order of creation deteriorate into an order of
destruction."[8]

Yeshua fulfills Torah by interpreting the legislation of its later
chapters in light of the ideal pictured in its opening chapters. This
ideal will be restored in the kingdom of God that he has come to
announce.

> "But in the beginning it was not so." In Jesus' words
> can be heard not only sadness over all the evil since
> the deluge but also an insatiable yearning for the reign
> of God that will reestablish the conditions of primal
> time: unbetrayed love, freedom from sin, the presence
> of God, and an end to all wickedness on earth.[9]

Yeshua builds his discussion of divorce on this big vision of a restored
creation and also on the specific wording of Torah as it describes the
creation ideal: "The two shall become one flesh." Because this transformation of two into one flesh is from the beginning and is an act of
God, human beings do not have the authority to reverse it. Yeshua is
employing typical rabbinic argument here, drawing upon specific details within the text to substantiate a ruling, even an unconventional

one. It is also typical of rabbinic discussion that Yeshua seeks to protect the weaker party, the wife, by limiting the husband's right to divorce. Later rabbis also sought within Torah, or at least in constant reference to it, for ways to protect women within marriage.

Ideal and Application

A superficial reading of Torah appears to grant the husband an unrestricted right of divorce, provided only that he "give a certificate a divorce." When Yeshua teaches a far more restricted right of divorce, he doesn't set aside the Mosaic ordinance, as some interpreters claim, but applies Torah humanely to real-life conditions. Likewise, mainstream rabbinic Judaism since Yeshua's time sought to gradually tighten divorce laws to protect the wife.[10] Neither Yeshua nor the rabbinic tradition is setting aside Moses; rather they are seeking to apply his teachings to the changing realities of life in the most consistent fashion. This entire realm of discussion is known in Judaism as *halakha*. Halakha recognizes the Scripture, particularly the Five Books of Moses, as divinely inspired but not divinely intended to cover every possible circumstance or application. Torah comes from above; its application rests with those here below.

> The divine truth had to be poured into human vessels; it had to be "humanized." Having left its heavenly abode, it had to be accommodated in the modest cottages of human uncertainty and inadequacy. This, in essence, is the task of Halakha. The "humanization" of the word of God requires that in applying the Torah to the human condition, one takes into consideration human nature and its needs, human character and its problems, the human condition in its ever-fluctuating dimension... [11]

Christians sometimes criticize Judaism as being legalistic, paying attention to minor details of law that don't really matter so much. They accuse the rabbis of replacing the words of Scripture with their own traditions. Yet anyone who seriously seeks to apply the teachings of Scripture has to admit that the details matter. For example, Rav Sha'ul teaches, in line with Yeshua's Torah from the Mount, "Do not repay anyone evil for evil, but take thought for what is noble in the sight of all" (Rom. 12:17). The words are inspiring enough, but honestly trying to obey them raises all kinds of questions and problems. Are we to practice total nonviolence; opposing war of any kind, the death penalty, and personal self-defense? Do we forgive everyone no matter what they have done and give them a chance to transgress again? In the very next verse, Sha'ul seems to recognize the challenges of actually carrying out this ideal, "If it is possible, so far as it depends on you, live peaceably with all" (Rom. 12:18). Even this more "realistic" verse, however, raises questions of exactly how we apply "so far as it depends on you" to getting along with other people. All of these questions lead to the sort of discussion that underlies halakha in the Jewish world.

Yeshua is engaging in just this kind of discussion with the Torah's instructions about marriage and divorce. He interprets the divine institution of marriage described in Genesis 2 to mean, "What God has joined together, let no one separate." This appears, however, to contradict Deuteronomy 24:1, which says that a man may separate from his wife as long as he provides her with a get. Halakha seeks to balance apparently competing principles of Torah and apply them in a realistic and humane fashion.

One principle of halakha that Yeshua seems to apply here is "… in case of a conflict between a specific law and another supervening concern of the Torah, one does the will of God by eliminating the specific law in the case at hand."[12] In other words, Yeshua "eliminates"—or limits—the law of Deuteronomy 24 to support the "supervening concern of the Torah" for the inviolability of marriage, which was expressed back in Genesis 2. This principle of halakha is essential if we are serious about actually putting Scripture into practice. If we cultivate a rigid adherence to every detail—even if we do so in the name of faithfulness to Scripture—we make Scripture unlivable and ultimately violate it. Author Garry Wills provides another example of this principle:

> At a time when slavery was accepted all through the United States—when even men like Jonathan Edwards and Benjamin Franklin and Benjamin Rush owned slaves because both the Jewish and the Christian Scriptures did not forbid slavery—men like Anthony Benezet and Jonathan Woolman said that all other scriptural defenses of the institution were abrogated by the Golden Rule. Do you wish others to make a slave of you? No? Then you must not make slaves of them.[13]

In other words, a rigid reading of Torah defended slavery, but the supervening concern of Torah, which Yeshua expressed in the Golden Rule, forbade it. In similar fashion, a narrow reading of Torah permits divorce at the discretion of the husband, but Yeshua limits divorce on the basis of Torah's more foundational teaching on the sanctity of marriage. As in all the passages in Matthew 5 introduced with the words, "you have heard … and I say to you," Yeshua continues in the direction set by Torah but goes further than other teachers in order to fulfill Torah's intent. And he also looks forward to the day when Torah will be fulfilled altogether. "Jesus appears to assume, in accordance with Jewish tradition, that the end will be like the beginning (where strict monogamy was the rule), and that, in the kingdom, at the end, God will no longer need to make concessions to sin (which is assumed to be the root cause of divorce). It follows not that Jesus contradicts Scripture, but that he rightly interprets it according to his eschatological outlook."[14]

Because Yeshua establishes his teaching on marriage "from the beginning," why does he provide an exception clause to his restriction on divorce? Both in his Torah from the Mount (Matt. 5:32), and later in Matthew 19:9, Yeshua says that divorce can be permitted because of "unchastity," or *porneia* in the original Greek. Porneia can refer to sexual immorality in a rather broad sense, but commentator Dale Allison argues that porneia refers in this context to adultery, citing the story of Yosef and Miriam. Matthew describes Yosef as a righteous man, and yet Yosef considers divorce to be a legitimate option. "When [Yeshua's] mother Miriam had been engaged to Yosef, but before they lived together, she was found to be with child from the Holy Spirit. Her husband Yosef, being a righteous man and unwilling to expose her to public disgrace, planned to dismiss her quietly" (Matt. 1:18–19a). Allison argues, "Now because Matthew elsewhere allows only one exception to the prohibition of divorce, and Joseph is a just [or righteous] man who decides to obtain a divorce, his circumstance must be covered by the exception clause. It is, if 'unchastity' means 'adultery.'"[15]

With this exception, Yeshua reconciles Deuteronomy 24 with Genesis 2. Deuteronomy says that a man might send away his wife because he finds something "objectionable" in her. Yeshua sides with those rabbis who limit this objectionable thing to sexual infidelity, specifically adultery. In a case like this, the one flesh of Genesis 2 has already been violated and divorce simply recognizes what has happened. Even such cases, however, do not *require* divorce. If the offending party admits his or her wrong and practices genuine repentance, reconciliation is still possible, especially between two partners who seek to follow Yeshua and practice the forgiveness of which he continually speaks.

Other Exceptions

Yeshua's example of setting aside one aspect of Torah to preserve a higher aspect might provide for other exceptions to the prohibition of divorce. Thus, Rav Sha'ul writes:

> To the rest I say—I and not the Lord—that if any be-
> liever has a wife who is an unbeliever, and she con-
> sents to live with him, he should not divorce her. And
> if any woman has a husband who is an unbeliever, and
> he consents to live with her, she should not divorce
> him. For the unbelieving husband is made holy
> through his wife, and the unbelieving wife is made
> holy through her husband. Otherwise, your children
> would be unclean, but as it is, they are holy. But if the
> unbelieving partner separates, let it be so; in such a
> case the brother or sister is not bound. It is to peace
> that God has called you. (1 Cor. 7:12–15)

Sha'ul's statement in verse 12, "to the rest I say—I and not the Lord
…" continues the kind of halakhic discussion we have been considering. He takes responsibility for applying Yeshua's teachings to the
conditions among the Corinthians, where some followers of Yeshua
are married to unbelievers. He argues from a broad Torah principle—
children are a fulfillment of God's holy purpose—to uphold the holiness of marriage even with an unbeliever. I have known of believers
in a similar situation who argued that they could divorce their unbelieving spouse because elsewhere Sha'ul says, "Do not be unequally
yoked… " Furthermore, they sometimes argue that Yeshua forbids
divorce because man shouldn't separate what God has brought together and God didn't bring together this marriage with an unbeliever.
Sha'ul counters both of those arguments and applies Yeshua's standards for divorce in such cases.

At the same time, he does envision an additional exception to the
one Yeshua stated. "But if the unbelieving partner separates, let it be
so; in such a case the brother or sister is not bound. It is to peace that
God has called you" (1 Cor. 7:15). The word translated as "separates"
here is the same as in Matthew 19:6—"Therefore what God has joined
together, let no one separate"—and 1 Corinthians 7:10–11—"To the
married I give this command—not I but the Lord—that the wife
should not separate from her husband (but if she does separate, let
her remain unmarried or else be reconciled to her husband)… " A
believer is not to separate from the marriage, but an unbeliever might.
Thus, when Rav Sha'ul says, "If the unbelieving partner separates,"
his point is not that it's permissible to separate because the partner is
an unbeliever; rather he can't imagine a believing husband or wife
departing from his or her partner. In applying this teaching today, the
relevant factor isn't whether the separating partner is a believer but
whether he or she has genuinely abandoned the marriage. Sha'ul protects the more vulnerable party, the abandoned believing partner,
who is called to "peace."

The meaning of this word *peace* remains controversial, but in context it is contrasted with the word *bound*. The one at peace is no longer *bound*, a term commonly used to describe the condition of slavery in which one person belongs to another. Hence, he or she is free to remarry. This exception is particularly important in the first-century world, where an unmarried woman was unlikely to be at peace at all but was highly vulnerable and dependent on others. Jewish custom, reflecting God's words from the beginning, "It is not good that the man should be alone" (Gen. 2:18), doesn't imagine a permanent state of ineligibility for marriage. Indeed, the whole point of the concession in Deuteronomy 24 is to make sure that if a husband divorces his wife, she has a certificate that will allow her to remarry. A state of permanent ineligibility would have been unjust and oppressive whether the marriage had been destroyed by adultery or abandonment. Thus, if a divorce is recognized as legitimate, it carries with it the right to remarry.

The best way to understand Sha'ul's teaching is as halakha that sets aside specific Torah restrictions on divorce because of a supervening concern of Torah. Each man and woman is made in the image of God and is to be treated with dignity and fairness. If an unbeliever departs from a spouse, the spouse is not to be held in bondage to a marriage that now exists on paper only, but is at peace to remarry. Of course, it would be the responsibility of the communal leadership to rule in such a case and establish the abandoned spouse's eligibility. We might apply the same principle to other possible exceptions to the ban on divorce, such as physical or mental abuse. Such abuse entails a threat to a person's immediate physical or mental well-being and, thus, violates the divine image within. Abuse, like sexual impurity, makes the other an object, instead of a divine image-bearer. Certainly such abuse falls within Yeshua's description of hardness of the heart. Divorce is never a good thing, but if the abuse is chronic and the abuser is unrepentant, divorce might be the lesser of two evils and a matter of setting aside one aspect of Torah to preserve a higher one.

This raises one of the most radical points in this whole discussion. Who decides whether a divorce is legitimate, whether circumstances necessitate it as the lesser of two evils? Scripture does not spell this out explicitly in Deuteronomy 24 or in the discussions on divorce in Matthew or Corinthians. But just as the wedding ceremony is conducted under the authority of the faith community, so there must be some communal authority to decide who may divorce. This is a radical claim in our day of extreme individualism, in which a person's right to privacy and autonomy trumps all other values. In the biblical world, however, the authority of the community bears on many questions. A follower of Yeshua who feels the need to seek divorce, based on principles such as we are discussing, should bring the issue to the congregational leaders rather than acting independently.

Thus, we can summarize the ethics of Messiah regarding divorce:

1. Marriage is a divine institution, normally unbreakable, and the right paperwork for divorce does not change this rule.
2. Yeshua spells out an exception to this rule—marital infidelity. Sha'ul spells out another—abandonment.
3. Other exceptions, such as physical or mental abuse, may be possible on the basis of Yeshua's example of setting aside one aspect of Torah to preserve a higher one.
4. The communal authority must be brought into the decision of when an exception might apply.
5. Divorce carries with it the right to remarry. Scripture does not envision a state of permanent disqualification from marriage.

It is ironic that conservative Christianity, which often insists that believers aren't "under the law," tends to read Yeshua's ban on divorce as a strict and incontrovertible law, disqualifying divorced people not only from remarriage, but also from important roles within the community. Pursuing the transformative ethics of Yeshua, however, is more than just going down a checklist of dos and don'ts. It might require us to make tough and complex decisions that balance one imperative of Scripture with another. Thus, we do well to remember that Yeshua is speaking Torah from the Mount, not a list of rules. "The issue is not a set of rules but a response from within. That response is not self-produced but is a reflection of a faith that trusts and follows in God's way."[16]

Following in God's way is not always a matter of black-and-white application of one particular verse of Scripture. Nevertheless, it's always the case that marriage involves covenant, a very high principle, and can only be ended for the most extreme and compelling reasons. And even then, divorce remains a concession for hardness of heart. "For I hate divorce, says the Lord, the God of Israel" (Mal. 2:16).

TORAH FROM THE MOUNT—TRUE SPEECH
Matthew 5:33–37

In late 2007, the sports world was shocked by the findings of a commission headed by former Senator George Mitchell investigating the use of steroids and other drugs in professional baseball. The commission listed numerous players who allegedly had used such substances, including star pitcher Roger Clemens. When Mike Wallace interviewed Clemens on the popular news program *60 Minutes*, Clemens admitted that his trainer did in fact give him injections, but only "with Lidocaine and B-12. It's for my joints, and B-12 I take still today."

> "And that's all?" Wallace asks.
> "That's it," Clemens says.

> When Clemens denies that he used any illegal drugs, Wallace asks, "Swear?" and Clemens answers, "Swear."

> Later, Wallace says, "If you were to testify before the Congress under oath, would you tell 'em exactly what you told me today?"[1]

Clearly, Mike Wallace places a different value on the ordinary words Clemens speaks to him than on the words that he might say under oath. The implication is that Clemens, like anyone else, would be honest if he swears to it, or is under oath especially before Congress, but in his ordinary speech he just might lie. Swearing, or using an oath, can serve to guarantee truth in special circumstances, but it ends up devaluing truth in other circumstances that are unprotected by an oath. Thus, Yeshua instructs us:

> "Again, you have heard that it was said to those of ancient times, 'You shall not swear falsely, but carry out the vows you have made to the Lord.' And I say to you, Do not swear at all, either by heaven, for it is the throne of God, or by the earth, for it is his footstool, or by Jerusalem, for it is the city of the great King. And do not swear by your head, for you cannot make one

hair white or black. Let your word be 'Yes, Yes' or 'No,
No'; anything more than this comes from the evil one."
(Matt. 5:33–37)

The Simple Truth

As in the previous section on divorce, Yeshua seems to overrule
Torah. Moses only requires that we carry out the vows made; Yeshua
forbids us from making vows at all. As with divorce, however, here
again Yeshua is not contradicting Torah, but bringing us back to its
original intent. The use of oaths is a concession, but certainly not an
ideal, as Rabbi Lapide notes:

> All swearing leads to an inflationary devaluation of all
> speech, which it unconsciously divides into two cate-
> gories: that which is confirmed by calling upon God
> and that which is asserted without such affirmation.
> But if only statements of the first type are uncondi-
> tionally true, then all others are seen as only relatively
> true or half-true or even as merely plausible. Not only
> is conscience unnecessarily strained, but the mutual
> trust of listener and speaker also is weakened, and the
> gate is opened to doubt, hypocrisy, and lies.[2]

A discussion in the Talmud reflects this perspective. Rabbi Eleazar
says,

> 'No' is an oath and 'Yes' is an oath. 'No' is an oath, as it
> is written: 'And the waters shall never again become
> a flood … ' (Gen. 9:15), and it is written: 'This is like
> the days of Noah to me: Just as I swore that the wa-
> ters of Noah would never again go over the earth …'
> (Isa. 54:9).

Eleazar claims that in Genesis, God doesn't take an oath or swear
not to flood the earth again, but in Isaiah he says that he did swear.
With God, a simple "no" concerning the flood is as binding as an
oath. God is committed to the truthfulness of every word that comes
out of his mouth. Eleazar continues, "How do we know that 'Yes' is
an oath? It is reasonable that, since 'No' is an oath, 'Yes' is also an
oath." Another rabbi adds, "Only if he said, 'No! No!' twice, or he
said, 'Yes! Yes!' twice, for it is written, 'Never again shall all flesh be
cut off by the waters of a flood (Gen. 9:11), and also, 'And the waters
shall never again become a flood [to destroy all flesh] (Gen. 9:15)." In
other words, because God must say no twice concerning the flood
for it to constitute an oath, so yes must also be said twice to constitute an oath.[3]

Yeshua, of course, puts it much more simply: "Let your word be 'Yes, Yes' or 'No, No'; anything more than this comes from the evil one." But the detailed interpretation in the Talmud reflects a perspective similar to Yeshua's. As in his teaching on divorce, Yeshua says that Torah may allow oaths, but from the beginning (or at least from the pre-Mosaic period of the flood), it was not so. Because God is utterly reliable, when he says, "No," (or "No, no"), it's as binding as an oath. Therefore the double no of a righteous person should be as binding as an oath.

A later rabbinic discussion on Ruth reflects this same simplicity:

> THEN SAID SHE: SIT STILL MY DAUGHTER ... FOR THE MAN WILL NOT REST UNTIL HE HAVE FINISHED THE THING (Ruth 3:18). R. Huna said in the name of R. Samuel b. Isaac: The yes of the righteous is yes, and their no, no, as it is said, FOR THE MAN WILL NOT REST UNTIL HE HAVE FINISHED THE THING THIS DAY.[4]

Thus, the rabbinic sources, which certainly allow for oath taking and regulate its use in great detail, seem to hold the simple answer of yes or no as the ideal. Oath taking can be necessary within the realities of life in this age, but it's not the ideal revealed in the earliest chapters of Scripture.

Christian commentators struggle with other questions that are raised by Yeshua's ban on oaths. The great Russian writer Leo Tolstoy "argued that Jesus' prohibition of oaths is absolute.... If one objects that a legal system cannot survive without demanding oaths from witnesses in court, then one has seen the truth. Matt. 5:33–37 is an implicit abolition of the legal system."[5] Tolstoy's perspective highlights a centuries-long discussion among Christian expositors on whether Yeshua intended to ban the use of oaths in legal or governmental settings. Indeed, common usage in the United States allows a person to say, "I swear," or, "I affirm," in many legal contexts. This seems to let the literalists off the hook—we don't have to swear an oath but simply affirm that we will tell the truth. But, of course, that still raises the issue: Why do we need to make a special affirmation at all? Why can't we just let our "yes" be yes and our "no" be no even in a court of law? And this is precisely Yeshua's bottom line: Be men and women of simple truthfulness. Speak the truth in all settings. Don't try to bolster your credibility by taking an oath but, "Let your word be 'Yes, Yes' or 'No, No'; anything more than this comes from the evil one" (Matt. 5:37).

Ya'akov, the brother of Yeshua, summarizes this principle even more forcefully toward the end of his letter. "Above all, my beloved, do not swear, either by heaven or by earth or by any other oath, but let your 'Yes' be yes and your 'No' be no, so that you may not fall under condemnation" (James 5:12). It is significant that Ya'akov's prohibition of swearing comes not long after his extended treatment of the tongue, "a small member" that "boasts of great exploits" (James 3:5). Ya'akov describes the tongue as a sort of bridle that controls the whole person. "Anyone who makes no mistakes in speaking is perfect, able to keep the whole body in check with a bridle" (James 3:2). Apparently, avoiding mistakes in speaking includes avoiding oaths, which can lead to condemnation because they are readily broken. If our word is unreliable, it can't be propped up by taking an oath. As in the Roger Clemens interview, if I'm not sure you're an inherently honest person, I'll ask you to take an oath. But, of course, a person who is inherently dishonest might well violate the oath.

We don't have to go far in Scripture to see how this potential for the abuse of oaths might play out. In Matthew's account of Yeshua's arrest and trial in Jerusalem, oath taking "leads, not to the uncovering of the truth and the doing of justice, but to falsehood and injustice."[6] First, the chief priests and the council seek false witnesses to bring a word of conviction against Yeshua (Matt. 26:59). Presumably, these witnesses take an oath before testifying, as was standard practice of that day. Then Peter employs oaths and swearing to deny that he even knows Yeshua (Matt. 26:72, 74).

> Thus Jesus is both abandoned and condemned to death through false oaths. But between these false oaths, Jesus is abjured to speak truthfully under oath by the high priest and say whether he is the "Messiah, the Son of God" (26:62–64). He responds truthfully but without taking an oath. He simply affirms that he is what the high priest has suggested ...[7]

Truth is foundational to ethical behavior. Oath taking, which is intended as a guardian of truthfulness, ends up weakening it. Instead of taking an oath to demonstrate reliability, a follower of Yeshua simply speaks the truth.

> Just as the intensified prohibition of killing, including slander, is concerned with the holiness of human life and human dignity, and just as the protection of marriage is concerned with the sanctification of the family as the basic unit of human society, so renunciation of swearing is concerned with the upholding of truth as a foundation of the Torah way of life.[8]

Lying—Is It Ever Justifiable?

This would seem to wrap up the case. Lying is never permitted for the follower of Yeshua; therefore, he or she should never even take an oath because that implies that words said outside the oath might be exempt from this strict truthfulness. End of discussion—or is it? Christian thinkers from Augustine to Immanuel Kant have held just this position. "Kant argued that if a would-be murderer inquires 'whether our friend who is pursued by him has taken refuge in our home,' we are forbidden to lie and mislead him."[9] Ironically, Kant, a German philosopher, would have made it impossible to rescue Jews from the German authorities during the Holocaust. Undoubtedly, even devout Christian rescuers had to tell lies, either explicit or implicit, to protect their Jewish wards, and surely, this was the right thing to do.

In the classic movie *The Sound of Music*, Nazi officials are trying to catch the Von Trapp family as they are fleeing to Switzerland. The Nazis run to their cars, which they have left parked near a convent, to pursue the Von Trapps, only to discover that the cars won't start. The Von Trapps have time to escape. The scene then switches to the convent's interior, where two nuns come to the Mother Superior, saying, "Mother, we have to confess our sins. We have stolen." In their hands they hold the ignition wires from the disabled cars. It's a light-hearted moment, but it raises a heavy issue. Would it have been better to remain outwardly sinless and permit the Nazis to catch up with the Von Trapps? Indeed, from a Jewish perspective, Kant's avoidance of lying in any circumstance looks like self-righteous self-absorption that is more intent on maintaining a personal sense of purity than on saving the life of another human being.

Accordingly, we can see in Scripture some incidents in which lying appears acceptable. In Exodus 1, Pharaoh commands two midwives, Shiphrah and Puah, to kill every male baby delivered among the Hebrews. Shiphrah and Puah defy this decree and let the babies live. When Pharaoh demands an explanation, they tell him, "Because the Hebrew women are not like the Egyptian women; for they are vigorous and give birth before the midwife comes to them." The story concludes, "So God dealt well with the midwives; and the people multiplied and became very strong" (Exod. 1:19–20). The midwives aren't rewarded for lying, of course, but for saving lives, but lying to Pharaoh to cover their deeds doesn't seem to diminish their reward.

Many years later, after the Israelites have left Egypt and are ready to enter the Promised Land, Joshua sends two spies to scout out the territory around Jericho, the first city they are to conquer. The spies stay in Jericho at the house of a prostitute named Rahab, but someone reports their presence to the king. He sends messengers to her house, demanding that she turn the men over to them.

> But the woman took the two men and hid them. Then
> she said, "True, the men came to me, but I did not
> know where they came from. And when it was time to
> close the gate at dark, the men went out. Where the
> men went I do not know. Pursue them quickly, for you
> can overtake them." She had, however, brought them
> up to the roof and hidden them with the stalks of flax
> that she had laid out on the roof. (Josh. 1:4–6)

The ruse is successful; the spies escape, and Rahab along with her whole family is spared when the Israelites conquer Jericho. Rahab is cited by the writers of the New Covenant as an example of faith, "By faith Rahab the prostitute did not perish with those who were disobedient, because she had received the spies in peace" (Heb. 11:31).

Again, the point isn't that lying is a good thing, but that it may sometimes be necessary to save life, which is always a good thing.[10] Conversely, Samson, who at first lies to Delilah to protect himself from betrayal, foolishly tells her the secret of his strength. She betrays him to the Philistines who shave his head, blind him, and lead him off in chains. Of course, the real point of his affair with Delilah is that he should have broken it off as soon as he suspected her of wanting to betray him. But telling her the truth in any event was foolish and unnecessary.

Real-life Ethics

As we consider the ethical implications of these biblical stories and of Yeshua's torah, which doesn't contradict but fulfills them, we can find ourselves agreeing, "It is hard to escape the fact that sometimes people are faced not with a choice between good and evil but with a choice between two evils … "[11] This reality leads in turn to three major points, which have bearing on our whole discussion of ethics.

1. It is impossible to live an ethical life if you are unwilling to make tough ethical decisions, including choosing between two evils. An ethical life isn't simply a matter of maintaining a sense of personal purity. "One is reminded of Dietrich Bonhoeffer, who after writing a book on the Sermon on the Mount participated in the conspiracy to overthrow Hitler," which included a plot to assassinate him.[12] Bonhoeffer had to set aside "turn the other cheek" and "love your enemy" to pursue an even higher obedience. He wrote, "The will of God may lie very deeply concealed beneath a great number of

available possibilities." Therefore, a person who follows Yeshua "must ever anew examine what the will of God may be."[13]

Biblical ethics, and especially the ethics of Yeshua, can never be reduced to a list of rules. As we have seen, the driving force of Yeshua's ethics is hesed, mercy or compassion, which sometimes must go beyond the letter of the law to accomplish God's purposes. This leads to a second foundational point:

2. All commandments are not equal. On the one hand, Yeshua warns us against breaking even the least commandment. On the other hand, Yeshua at times acts in accord with the Jewish understanding that it is sometimes necessary to break Torah in order to save Torah: "There are times when the suppression of the Torah may be the foundation of the Torah."[14] An ancient interpretation of Psalm 119:26 supports this idea. The verse reads, "It is time for the LORD to act, for your Torah has been broken." This interpretation reads this verse backwards: "Sometimes it is necessary to break the Torah in order to act for the LORD."[15]

3. Ultimately biblical ethics are embodied in Yeshua himself and fulfilled through following him. In Jewish thinking Torah is not a set of rules, but instruction from God that we must discuss, apply, and adapt, sometimes by making difficult choices. In the same way, when Yeshua gives us Torah from the Mount, it is not ultimately a set of rules but an ideal that he alone fully embodies. When we take responsibility to live according to this torah, it requires looking to him as an overall example and not just to his individual teachings.

An incident in Yeshua's life mentioned briefly in Chapter 2 illustrates these points.

> At that time Yeshua went through the grainfields on Shabbat; his disciples were hungry, and they began to pluck heads of grain and to eat. When the Pharisees saw it, they said to him, "Look, your disciples are doing what is not lawful to do on Shabbat." He said to them, "Have you not read what David did when he and his companions were hungry? He entered the house of God and ate the bread of the Presence, which it was not lawful for him or his companions to eat, but only for the priests. Or have you not read in the law that on Shabbat the priests in the temple break Shabbat and yet are guiltless? I tell you, something greater than the temple is here. But if you had known what this means, 'I desire hesed and not sacrifice,' you would not have

> condemned the guiltless. For the Son of Man is lord of
> Shabbat." (Matt. 12:1–8)

When David ate the bread of the Presence, his life was not in danger, but it was still permissible because of whom he was. He was the one who would provide the place for the Temple to be built, where the bread of the Presence would be kept for centuries to come. Hence, violating the bread one time enabled the bread to be kept holy for countless times. Likewise, the priests must break certain laws of Shabbat to maintain the service of the Temple. But "something greater than the Temple is here." We might understand this "something greater" as Yeshua himself. Because following him is the highest ethical pathway, it might be appropriate at times to overrule other aspects of Torah for his sake. Of course, we must be careful not to use following Yeshua as an excuse for ethical transgression; rather following Yeshua means practicing hesed, a principle of Torah that might at times supersede specific rules. This leads us to another, complementary, interpretation of this passage. Hesed itself is "something greater than the temple," something that might overrule other aspects of Torah. Under this interpretation, Yeshua's whole case rests on the claim for hesed made in Hosea 6:6, which Yeshua quotes in Matthew 12:7, "I desire hesed and not sacrifice." One aspect of Torah, hesed, overrules another, sacrifice.

Setting aside any aspect of Torah, including its command to tell the truth, requires more justification than just a subjective claim to be following Yeshua. It must be the pursuit of hesed, as defined in Torah and exemplified in the life of Messiah, which leads us to set aside another aspect of Torah. We might have to set aside a specific law at times to practice the overarching law of mercy. What one commentator says concerning Shabbat law also applies to our current topic of true speech.

> Matthew responds to human need, not by abrogating
> the law, but by arguing from the law and the prophets
> (5:17). The Sabbath is not overridden directly by hu-
> man need or decision, but by a correct understanding
> of the law of mercy contained in Hos. 6:6. … The
> Sabbath is overridden only in a limited and specific
> way for good reasons.[16]

In an extreme case, hesed might provide good reasons to overrule the commandment of honest speech. A follower of Immanuel Kant who insisted on telling the truth to the Nazi authorities even if it resulted in the deaths of Jewish people is not practicing hesed or keeping Torah. He might be maintaining his own sense of inner purity and holiness, but he is not following Yeshua. Divine reversal means that the inner sense of purity and holiness that the religious world values so highly may at times be worth far less than a crafty, hands-defiling act that saves a life, "so be wise as serpents and innocent as doves" (Matt. 10:16).

Ironically, however, the incident that Yeshua cites in Matthew 12 also illustrates the dangers of lying. In 1 Samuel 21, David lies to get the bread of the Presence, and the priests end up dead. The reasoning of the priests was sound—David is the promised king, so it is worth violating a law to save him. Furthermore, hesed decreed that a ritual restriction should be set aside to feed the hungry, but in this incident David acts out of calculating self-preservation. He doesn't trust Ahimelech the priest to help him out of simple compassion but lies to the priest, telling him that he is on a mission for King Saul. As a result, Ahimelech is deprived of the right to choose whether to supply bread to David under his real status as an outlaw. Furthermore, he is not on guard against being found out. Doeg, a servant of Saul, just happens to be in the area that day. Later, he betrays Ahimelech and the rest of the priests—who didn't realize they had done anything wrong—by reporting them to Saul, who orders him to execute them all (1 Sam. 21:1–7; 22:9–18).

Yeshua notes that David was guiltless when he ate the bread of the Presence because the law of hesed outweighed the normal restrictions on who can eat this bread. But David was not guiltless in manipulating the priests to give him the bread, as he realized later, "David said to Abiathar, 'I knew on that day, when Doeg the Edomite was there, that he would surely tell Saul. I am responsible for the lives of all your father's house'" (1 Sam. 22:22). If David realized that Doeg would report the priests to Saul, as he says, why didn't he warn them? Because that would have required him to admit that he had lied about being on a mission for Saul. If he had really been on assignment, then Doeg would have had nothing to report. David chose to preserve his lie rather than warn the priests, even though this might have saved their lives.

Surely, this story illustrates the dangers inherent in violating the instruction to let your "yes" be yes, and your "no" be no. The bottom line is that our word must be reliable and never compromised except when hesed necessitates it to aid another in a significant and unavoidable way. Lying for self-advancement or self-protection is never acceptable. As David himself writes:

> O LORD, who may abide in your tent? Who may dwell
> on your holy hill? Those who walk blamelessly, and
> do what is right, and speak the truth from their heart
> … who stand by their oath even to their hurt …
> (Ps. 15:1–2, 4b)

Yeshua, of course, says that the person who speaks truth from the heart doesn't even need to take an oath. The practical guideline on truth-telling remains: The person with integrity tells the truth even at his or her own expense and even when it hurts or costs something. This is a way that we can assess our own commitment to truth: Will we speak it even if it makes us look bad, or requires us to restore something or make amends with another person? In our era of abundant spin, including religious spin, will we speak the simple truth even if it includes an admission of our own error or weakness? The world is hungry for such honest men and women today, and it is right for those who claim to follow Yeshua to fill their ranks.

TORAH FROM THE MOUNT—RESISTANCE
Matthew 5:38–42

An eye for an eye will make the whole world blind.

This saying, which I first read on a bumper sticker, has been attributed to Gandhi, who was an avid student of the Sermon on the Mount. The saying reflects Yeshua's words, "You have heard that it was said, 'An eye for an eye and a tooth for a tooth.' And I say to you, do not resist an evildoer … " At the same time, it also reflects the common misunderstanding of the Torah principle of eye for eye and tooth for tooth, sometimes called *lex talionis* (Latin for "law of retaliation"). This common misunderstanding interprets the law as being all about revenge, requiring strict justice in every case, and ensuring that no one gets away with anything. This misunderstanding reinforces the idea that Yeshua is replacing the harsh, exacting old law with a new law of love. But is that really what he is saying here?

Eye for Eye

To understand Yeshua's teaching, we need to start with the passages of Torah that speak of "eye for eye and tooth for tooth." We also need to remember the realities of life in societies that pre-date the rule of law. We tend to worry about legalism, or too much law, but for most of human history a greater problem was lawlessness, or too little law. Author Jared Diamond describes a gathering of the Fayu, an isolated New Guinea tribe.

> To us, a few dozen people constitute a small, ordinary gathering, but to the Fayu it was a rare, frightening event. Murderers suddenly found themselves face-to-face with their victim's relatives. For example, one Fayu man spotted the man who had killed his father. The son raised his ax and rushed at the murderer but was wrestled to the ground by friends; then the murderer came at the prostrate son with an ax and was also wrestled down. Both men were held, screaming in rage, until they seemed sufficiently exhausted to be released.[1]

This is just one snapshot of life without a system of justice such as that commanded in Torah. It doesn't reveal an idyllic scene free from domination and strife but one filled with violence. Diamond goes on to describe a series of interviews with women in another primitive New Guinea tribe.[2]

> Woman after woman, when asked to name her husband, named several sequential husbands who had died violent deaths. A typical answer went like this: "My first husband was killed by Elopi raiders. My second husband was killed by a man who wanted me, and who became my third husband. That husband was killed by the brother of my second husband, seeking to avenge his murder." Such biographies prove common for so-called gentle tribespeople ...[3]

We might think of eye for eye as a harsh standard, but it is far milder than the sort of retribution that people seek without the restraint of Torah. The alternative to fair standards of justice is a cycle of brutality and violence. Indeed, the rabbis taught that establishing a system of justice was one of the essential laws given to all the nations in the covenant with Noah.[4] "Eye for eye and tooth for tooth" develops this basic universal law and applies it specifically to life under the Mosaic covenant. The phrase appears three times in the Torah, in Exodus 21:24, Leviticus 24:20, and Deuteronomy 19:21. We can detect several traits that bind the three passages together.

1. Communal responsibility for justice

In place of the cycle of personal revenge such as Diamond describes among some New Guinea tribes, Torah commands the Israelites as a community to administer justice fairly and consistently. Two passages in the Torah (Exod. 21:22; Deut. 19:18) specify that is the judges' responsibility to administer the application of eye for eye, so that it is not a matter of personal revenge. Judges by their very nature must be recognized and respected not just by scattered individuals, but also by the community as a whole.

2. Punishment that fits the crime

Eye for eye sounds brutal, but it prevents the victim or his family from damaging the perpetrator more than he damaged the victim—which is the natural tendency of human beings. Instead, the payment must fit the crime; retribution must be limited to the extent of the original damage. Even murder must be punished fairly and in a way that doesn't escalate the cycle of violence.

3. Compensation in place of retribution

Finally, at least in some cases, eye for eye involves monetary compensation rather than literally taking an eye or a tooth. Rabbinic discussions of eye for eye from ancient times emphasized setting a limit to retribution and setting fair monetary compensation for offenses. Israeli teacher and author Joseph Shulam points out that the idea of monetary compensation is based on Exodus 21:22–25.[5]

> If men fight, and hurt a woman with child, so that she gives birth prematurely, yet no harm follows, he shall surely be punished accordingly as the woman's husband imposes on him; and he shall pay as the judges determine. But if any harm follows, then you shall give life for life, eye for eye, tooth for tooth, hand for hand, foot for foot, burn for burn, wound for wound, stripe for stripe.[6]

The rabbinic commentaries seize on the statement, "he shall pay as the judges determine," and apply it to the statement about eye for eye that follows, concluding that monetary payment suffices in most cases and that the Torah is simply instructing that such payment be appropriate to the actual loss. This interpretation is reinforced by the verses that follow, in which a slave owner who destroys the eye or tooth of a slave must compensate the slave financially by letting him or her go free:

> When a slaveowner strikes the eye of a male or female slave, destroying it, the owner shall let the slave go, a free person, to compensate for the eye. If the owner knocks out a tooth of a male or female slave, the slave shall be let go, a free person, to compensate for the tooth. (Exod. 21:26–27)

The interpretation that "the law that an eye-for-an-eye refers to monetary compensation" is considered fundamental in Jewish thinking today.[7]

To summarize, in the Jewish understanding, which was probably already in place by the time of Yeshua, the eye-for-eye principle is not so much about retribution, as it is about the limits and alternatives to retribution. It helps maintain justice without unnecessary harshness or damage to the social fabric. When the instruction was first given in Torah, it was a great step in the direction of peace and equity in human society.

Beyond Eye for Eye

With this background, we can see how Yeshua's statement on nonresistance is an additional, and radical, step in the direction already set
by Torah:

> "You have heard that it was said, 'An eye for an eye
> and a tooth for a tooth.' And I say to you, do not resist
> an evildoer. But if anyone strikes you on the right
> cheek, turn the other also; and if anyone wants to sue
> you and take your coat, give your cloak as well; and if
> anyone forces you to go one mile, go also the second
> mile. Give to everyone who begs from you, and do not
> refuse anyone who wants to borrow from you."
> (Matt. 5:38–42)

The Torah instructed people to refrain from revenge and escalating
violence and to be satisfied with fair, equitable restitution. The Torah
says we can't demand an arm if someone knocked out a tooth. Yeshua
takes this instruction a step further, telling his followers not just to be
satisfied with fair restitution, but also to refrain from demanding restitution for themselves altogether. We might contrast this teaching
with the contemporary pursuit of outrageous lawsuits, which seek
imbalanced restitution. For example, in 2007, Washington D.C. admin-
istrative law judge Roy Pearson sued his neighborhood dry cleaners,
a Korean immigrant couple, for $54 million after they had misplaced
a favorite pair of dress slacks. The Torah would argue that you can
only sue for the real value of the slacks (these were part of a $1,000
Hickey-Freeman suit) plus whatever time you might have actually
spent in replacing them. Yeshua takes this a step further to say it is
better to write off the slacks altogether—which is what Pearson finally had to do after Judge Judith Bartnoff rejected his plea and ruled
that he was "not entitled to any relief whatsoever."[8]

In earlier chapters we saw how Yeshua corrects a common understanding of Torah by citing an earlier, more foundational passage. Deuteronomy permits divorce, for example, but from the
beginning, as revealed in Genesis 2, God's intention is lifelong monogamy. Torah permits oaths in several places, but God's own example from Genesis is to let our "Yes" be yes and "No" be no. Can we
find a similar basis in Genesis for Yeshua's teaching on going beyond
eye for eye?

One model for this teaching is Abraham. When Abraham responds
to God's call and leads his extended family to the land of Canaan, God
blesses him with great wealth in flocks and herds. Abraham's nephew
Lot, a member of his extended family, also grows wealthy. Indeed,
"the land could not support both of them living together; for their

possessions were so great that they could not live together, and there was strife between the herders of Abram's livestock and the herders of Lot's livestock" (Gen. 13:6–7). In response, Abraham goes beyond an eye-for-eye approach of trying to divide the land equitably. He simply gives Lot the choice of whatever land he desires, relinquishing the claim on the best land, which he could have reasonably made as Lot's patriarch and mentor.

Years later after Abraham's death, his son, Isaac, follows the same principle. He dwells among the Philistines, but when he prospers, they grow envious, stop up the wells that Abraham had dug to water his flocks, and drive him out of their land. When Isaac's servants re-open Abraham's wells in an adjoining territory, the local herdsmen quarrel with them. In response, Isaac "moved from there and dug another well, and they did not quarrel over it; so he called it Rehoboth, saying, 'Now the LORD has made room for us, and we shall be fruitful in the land.' From there he went up to Beer-sheba. And that very night the LORD appeared to him ..." (Gen. 26:22–24).

Abraham and Isaac go beyond eye for eye; instead of demanding fair treatment, they simply move on for the sake of peace. In Isaac's case he is dealing with those who could be called evil—Philistines who drive him out of their country because of envy (Gen. 26:14) and herdsmen who oppose his possession of wells that his father originally dug. Isaac carries his father's example even further in not resisting evil but simply moving to a place of peace. After that move, God appears to him and blesses him richly.

Yeshua may have these examples in mind when he tells us not to resist the evildoer. He doesn't negate Torah, so perhaps he is citing an earlier, more foundational Torah based on the example of the patriarchs. Furthermore, Yeshua's very words about turning the other cheek come from the Hebrew Scriptures, specifically Lamentations. A look at this phrase in its original context helps us further understand Yeshua's instructions:

> It is good that one should wait quietly for the salvation of the LORD.
> It is good for one to bear the yoke in youth,
> to sit alone in silence when the Lord has imposed it,
> to put one's mouth to the dust (there may yet be hope),
> to give one's cheek to the smiter, and be filled with insults.
> For the Lord will not reject forever. (Lam. 3:26–31)

Here, turning the other cheek, or "giving one's cheek to the smiter," is a sign of active hope in God's deliverance. It reflects the spirit of Abraham and Isaac, who felt little need to defend themselves because they relied upon God's abundant promises to them.

I suggest that Yeshua is carrying the Torah's mandate for justice instead of retaliation a step further and calling his followers to repudiate retaliation altogether.

> Yeshua says that when someone intentionally hurts or embarrasses us, we should not respond with evil against evil. Allowing that person to "hit us on the other cheek" is the strong thing, not the weak thing, to do. If someone intends to embarrass us publicly by striking us in the face, we must not give in to his evil and respond in kind because that would show him that he has affected us. Instead, we must prove to him that he cannot affect us. We must show him that we are proud and strong enough to stand another strike on the face.[9]

How do we put such a teaching into practice? In a moment we will consider whether this teaching applies on a public and general level, but it's clear that it applies personally, so here are some questions that can help us put it into practice:

- Do I have the inner strength and self-discipline to refrain from returning evil for evil or even rudeness for rudeness?
- Am I willing to walk away from a conflict even if it costs me to do so—and even if I would be likely to win if I didn't walk away?
- Am I willing to forego fairness in personal matters—to experience loss or suffer wrong—rather than to cause others to suffer? (Compare to 1 Corinthians 6:7, "In fact, to have lawsuits at all with one another is already a defeat for you. Why not rather be wronged? Why not rather be defrauded?")
- Am I willing to risk looking weak or foolish because of obeying this command?
- Can I trust God enough to defend me and drop my own self-defenses?

A Reality Check

Undoubtedly, Yeshua's instructions here, along with his even more radical teaching to love one's enemy in the next section, will be difficult for many of us to accept in their entirety. Is he telling us to forego fairness altogether? To never resist evil under any circumstances? In the context of recent Jewish history such words might seem to be unrealistic and even wrongheaded. Jews remember well the Holocaust, when actively resisting evil was the only right option, as Dietrich Bonhoeffer and other exceptional Christians demonstrated. Today, Jewish people can look at the situation of the state of Israel surrounded by enemies committed to its destruction. If the government of Israel ceased resisting the evildoers, the Jewish State would surely come to an end in a second Holocaust. We saw in our discussion of truth telling that it is sometimes necessary to set aside our personal desire for purity and get our hands dirty to save a life. Is Yeshua saying here that we are never to resist evil in any case, or is he saying something more complex? To answer this question, consider a few points:

1. Whatever Yeshua is saying about nonresistance, he said originally in a difficult context. We cannot say that these words no longer apply in the post-Holocaust, anti-Israel world of today because they were first given during the harsh Roman occupation of Israel. Indeed, some specific examples that Yeshua gives are based on conditions of Roman occupation, which allowed a Roman soldier to force a Jew to carry his pack for one mile. If Yeshua's teaching could work in the harsh conditions in which it was first given, it can work today. Therefore, our interpretation and application of Yeshua's words must also apply to today's practical realities.

2. Yeshua phrases his whole instruction in Matthew 5:38–42 in personal terms. In the plain sense he speaks of "you" being struck, being sued, or being forced to go a mile. It is one thing for me to turn my other cheek to the person who struck *me*; it is another thing to figuratively turn someone else's cheek by not resisting the evil perpetrated against *them*. It is one thing for me to relinquish my own demand for justice, but quite another to demand that someone else give up his or her demand for justice. The individual believer may practice something that corporate groups cannot or should not practice, given the realities of evil in our world.

   Yeshua's story of the forgiving king (Matt. 18:21–35) supports this interpretation. The king forgives the debt against himself, but rushes to defend the servant who is wronged by his fellow servant. "In this story the king lets himself suffer wrong, but when it is another who suffers, mercy gives way to justice."[10] Because the Torah incorporates the lex talionis as a basis for its system of justice, and Yeshua doesn't overthrow Torah, it is likely in this section of his Torah from the Mount that he is "speaking about interpersonal relations and declaring that it is illegitimate for his followers to apply the *lex talionis* to their personal problems. So he is not overthrowing the principle of equivalent compensation on an institutional level. The subject of what is appropriate for the legal process is just not addressed" in this passage.[11]

3. We also have indications in Yeshua's ministry itself that he isn't speaking of absolute pacifism. For example, the same Yeshua who says, "Do not resist an evildoer," later "entered the temple and

drove out all who were selling and buying in the temple, and he overturned the tables of the money changers and the seats of those who sold doves" (Matt. 21:12). Not long after, he advised his disciples, "But now, the one who has a purse must take it, and likewise a bag. And the one who has no sword must sell his cloak and buy one" (Luke 22:36). True, he doesn't allow his disciples to use their swords to protect him when he is being arrested, but he still speaks of them taking a more pragmatic and even aggressive stance.

At the same time, Yeshua's teachings do have implications for public policy. Thus, he might not require his followers to be pacifists because national defense may be a grim necessity in this world. The Scriptures, however, teach regard for the enemy as created in the image of God, and Yeshua expands that teaching to mean love for the enemy. His followers, therefore, must be hesitant about the extremity of war, cautious about collateral damage and harm to innocent civilians among the enemy, opposed to torture and any maltreatment of prisoners, respectful of the image of God present even among those on the other side, and so on.

4. A similar interpretation applies to the final instruction in this passage, "Give to everyone who begs from you, and do not refuse anyone who wants to borrow from you." Again, this is probably best understood in terms of personal practice rather than a blanket public policy, as evidenced by the regulations of public welfare in the Pauline letters. For example, Rav Sha'ul writes, "Anyone unwilling to work should not eat" (2 Thess. 3:10), or "Honor [with financial support] widows who are really widows. … But refuse to put younger widows on the list" (1 Tim. 5:3–11). In other words, the individual might "give to everyone who begs" him, but the community does not. It provides support only to the qualified. If Scripture clearly limits the application of this part of Yeshua's teaching, it's fair to limit the application of other parts of the teaching in the same way. At the same time, the underlying principle of respect and concern for those in need must shape the policy positions that followers of Yeshua take. They may not necessarily favor massive government intervention on behalf of the disadvantaged, but they certainly cannot advocate a form of social Darwinism that leaves every man to himself in the struggle for survival.

The implications of Yeshua's torah are manifold and sometimes complex, but clearly we are in the realm of divine reversal. In this world we look out for ourselves first; in Messiah's kingdom we don't look out for ourselves but only for others. In this world we learn to stand up for ourselves because no one else will; in the kingdom we learn to stand up for others and not worry about ourselves.

When to Resist

As with other points in Yeshua's ethical instruction, there is a limit to nonresistance. When the welfare of another is involved, hesed demands that we act on behalf of the weak and vulnerable. Thus, Abraham in Genesis 13 chooses to avoid strife by relinquishing any claim to fairness and passively allowing Lot to choose whatever land he wants. But in the next chapter, when Lot is threatened with violence, Abraham is anything but passive. He moves decisively to rescue him, arming 318 of his servants and leading them to attack the four kings who pillaged the city of Sodom.

This story illustrates the need to interpret and apply carefully the principle of nonresistance. Yeshua calls us to the higher Torah value of being peacemakers, even at personal expense, rather than following our human nature and entering the fray. But there are times when we must enter the fray. For example, the rabbinic literature portrays Aaron as the model peacemaker: "Be one of Aaron's students, loving peace and pursuing it, loving people and bringing them to the Torah."[12] But this desire for peace also explains Aaron's behavior at the incident of the Golden Calf when he cooperated with Israel's desire for an image of the divine rather than confronting that desire. His nonresistance of evil led to more evil.

As with Yeshua's teaching on forgiveness, we can create ethical confusion if we try to apply this teaching on nonresistance to areas that aren't our responsibility. I can only forgive an offense against myself, not someone else. In the same way, I can practice nonresistance in response to evil perpetrated or intended against me; it may not always be ethical to practice it on behalf of someone else. It might be right for me to turn the other cheek to the person who slaps me; it may not be right for me to figuratively turn the other cheek when someone slaps my mother or daughter.

The Kite Runner, the 2003 best-selling novel, explores the theme of courage, specifically the courage to stand up to evil. As a young boy, the protagonist, Amir, fails to defend his closest friend against evil and is haunted by guilt for years. He remembers his father, Baba, an exemplar of courage, who literally stood up to evil when the two of them were fleeing their home in Russian-occupied Afghanistan with a truckload of refugees. A Russian soldier stops the truck and demands a half-hour alone with a young Afghan mother among the refugees as the price for letting them pass.

That was when Baba stood up. It was my turn to clamp
a hand on his thigh, but Baba pried it loose, snatched
his leg away. When he stood he eclipsed the moon-
light. "I want you to ask this man something," Baba
said. He said to Karim [the driver and interpreter], but
looked directly at the Russian officer, "Ask him where
his shame is."

When the Russian answers with a threat to put a bullet into Baba if he
doesn't step aside, Baba says, "Tell him I'll take a thousand of his bul-
lets before I let this indecency take place." The Russian raises his gun
and Baba says, "Tell him he'd better kill me good with that first shot.
Because if I don't go down, I'm tearing him to pieces ..."[13]

Such resistance of evil on behalf of the vulnerable rings true and
reflects a biblical standard: "Like a muddied spring or a polluted foun-
tain are the righteous who give way before the wicked" (Prov. 25:26).
Baba demonstrates hesed toward the young Afghan mother in the
back of the truck through the courage to resist. Yeshua himself, as we
have seen, actively resists wrong when he drives the moneychangers
out of the Temple courts. When he does, "His disciples remembered
that it was written, 'Zeal for your house will consume me'" (John
2:17). Zeal for God's house, God's Name, leads to legitimate resistance; zeal for our own name and interests never does.

In the gospel story, however, Yeshua's triumph comes not in driving out the moneychangers, but in submitting to the cross. In his trial
and crucifixion, Yeshua demonstrates his own instruction to turn the
other cheek. As always, he fully walks out and embodies his own
teaching.

Throughout the Gospel he gives to those who ask
from him (8:5–13; 9:27–31; etc.). He does not retaliate
when struck (26:67–68). He does not defend himself
against false charges when accused before the authorities (26:57–68; 27:11–26). That Jesus is mostly
silent after his arrest is an eloquent illustration of
what it might mean not to resist or retaliate against
evildoers.[14]

This is the Yeshua who reminds his followers, "Do you think that I
cannot appeal to my Father, and he will at once send me more than
twelve legions of angels?" (Matt. 26:53). Nonresistance is not just an
ideal with Yeshua, but also his way of life; it is not a choice forced
upon him because of his weakness and vulnerability, but in the end a
stance of power that overcomes the powers of this world. He calls
his followers to practice such nonresistance as well, resisting evil

perpetrated against others but yielding to evil against themselves and trusting in God's ultimate protection. Thus, we follow him in demonstrating a power that reverses the powers of the world around us, gaining a triumph that mere competition or revenge can never afford us.

8

TORAH FROM THE MOUNT—LOVE
Matthew 5:43–48

A Jewish man survived a shipwreck only to find himself stranded for many years alone on a desert island. Finally, a passing ship spotted him and sent a rescue party ashore. They found the Jew living in a cave, but noticed two neat little huts that he had built near the shore. "What are those buildings?" the rescuers asked. The Jew pointed to one and said, "That's my synagogue, where I pray every morning." "And what about the other one?" asked the rescuers. "That one!? That's the synagogue I'd never set foot in!"

Religious people are famous, or infamous, for dividing the world into us and them, disdaining those who hold different views or practices, and holding out for differences that often seem petty to outsiders. Yeshua, however, gives us far more than an exhortation to just get along or even unify with like-minded folk; rather, he calls upon those who follow him to love their enemies. "You have heard that it was said, 'You shall love your neighbor and hate your enemy.' And I say to you, Love your enemies …" (Matt. 5:43ff.).

When nineteenth-century German Chancellor Otto von Bismarck declared, "No state can be ruled by the Sermon on the Mount," he may well have had these words in mind.[1] Those protecting a nation's interests can hardly be expected to practice love toward their enemies. Yet even those not concerned with statecraft might suspect this teaching to be pure idealism and impossible to follow in the real world. But is this the case? Or is this teaching an essential part of divine reversal, something we're to put into practice in our daily lives? Before answering these questions, we need to look at the teaching more closely.

Hate Your Enemy?

In this passage, Yeshua seems to treat his own words in the same way that he treated the words of Torah in earlier sections. It is as if he is saying here, "You have heard that it was said (by me!), 'Do not resist the evildoer,' and now I say to you, '*Love* the evildoer, your enemy.'" In a classic divine reversal, Yeshua turns normal standards on their head, calling us not just to nonresistance, but also to actual love for the enemy. But Bismarck isn't alone in doubting whether this standard can apply to public affairs, and many readers wonder if it is even valid for personal affairs. It's hard enough not to resist evil, but to *love* the evildoer...!

Furthermore, there is another problem with this radical statement. Yeshua introduces it with a command from Torah, "Love your neighbor," but he leaves out part of the command, reflected in the complete phrase in Leviticus 19:18, "Love your neighbor *as yourself*."[2] Then he adds a phrase that isn't in Torah at all, "and hate your enemy." Yeshua follows his reference from Torah with the words, "and I say to you," as he does throughout Matthew 5, to show that he isn't teaching something in contrast with Torah but in fulfillment. Here in Matthew 5:43, however, before he says, "and I say to you," he inserts the phrase, "hate your enemy," which only seems to heighten the contrast between Torah and his own teaching.

But does the Torah instruct us to hate our enemies? What teaching is Yeshua reacting to here? The Tanakh does include numerous passages that call down God's wrath upon our enemies, speak positively of hating their deeds, and even advocate hating the enemies of God themselves (e.g., Ps. 139:20–22). So perhaps Yeshua breaks with his normal usage in Matthew 5 to paraphrase the Tanakh here rather than to quote it directly. He did something similar in the very beginning of this section, "You have heard that it was said to those of ancient times, 'You shall not murder'; and 'whoever murders shall be liable to judgment'" (Matt. 5:21). The phrase "liable to judgment" is a summary of Torah rather than a direct quote. Likewise, "hate your enemy" summarizes at least one aspect of Torah. Still, it's a harsh summary, which doesn't reflect the understanding of later Jewish tradition, as an ancient story illustrates:

> There were once some highwaymen in the neighborhood of Rabbi Meir who caused him a great deal of trouble. R. Meir accordingly prayed that they should die. His wife Beruria said to him: "How can you pray like that!? Because you think it is written, 'Let *sinners* cease?' (Psalm 104:35). It actually means, 'Let *sins* cease.' Furthermore, look at the end of the verse: 'and let the wicked men be no more.' Since the sins will cease, there will be no more wicked men! Rather pray for them that they should repent, and there will be no more wicked men." He did pray for them, and they repented.[3]

Here, the illustrious Rabbi Meir must be corrected by his equally illustrious wife Beruria about the Tanakh's true teaching of love for the
evildoer. Surely, if this prominent teacher was able to pray for the
death of the obnoxious highwaymen, there may have been other
Jewish thinkers in Yeshua's day who thought that hating the enemy
was consistent with Torah. I am not implying that Judaism is more
prone to hate the enemy than other religious traditions, including
Christianity. Sadly, the evidence is that every religion tends to foster
disdain and discrimination against the other. In Yeshua's day, "You
shall love your neighbor and hate your enemy," may have been a popular saying that summarized the teachings in the Tanakh about keeping a distance from evildoers and hating those who hate the Lord.

Alternatively, Yeshua may be using "hate" here in the comparative
sense, as Scripture does in Malachi 1:2–3, "Jacob have I loved, but
Esau I have hated," or the statement about a man with two wives,
"one of whom he loves and one of whom he hates" (Deut. 21:15).[4] In
the same way, some might interpret the Torah to say that we are to
love our neighbor in contrast with our enemies whom we don't love.
This attitude can lead in turn to a narrow definition of who our neighbor is, of just who it is that we are required to love as we love ourselves. It's this narrow concept of neighbor that Yeshua addresses
and overturns.

Love Begins at Home

The first part of Yeshua's saying, "Love your neighbor," comes directly
from Leviticus, and a reading of the whole context hints at the second
part of the saying also—"hate your enemy." In Leviticus 19:17–18 we
read, "Do not go around spreading slander among *your people*, but
also don't stand idly by when *your neighbor's* life is at stake; I am
ADONAI. Do not hate *your brother* in your heart, but rebuke *your
neighbor* frankly, so that you won't carry sin because of him. You
shall not avenge, nor bear any grudge against *the children of your
people*, but you shall love *your neighbor* as yourself; I am ADONAI."[5]

In this context, "neighbor" is used as a synonym for "your people,"
"your brother," and "children of your people."[6] Yeshua expands the
definition of neighbor—and he does so, of course, in fulfillment of
Torah—but the discussion starts with neighbor as countryman, neighbor as fellow Jew. My colleague Dr. Stuart Dauermann writes, "When
the context is examined, it is incontrovertible that the Levitical command to love our neighbor as our self is speaking of our love for fellow Jews. This, after love of parents and family, is the foundation of
all later societal loves, and without this foundation, there is no proper
love to extend to others."[7] In its wisdom, Torah will not permit us to
think of love for our neighbor in some lofty, sentimental fashion,

which we could easily do if the command were first stated as "Love all of humanity." Instead, we have to learn to love our literal neighbor, the one who is close at hand, the one against whom we really may bear a grudge or desire vengeance. Only if this love for our neighbor is real can we begin to broaden it to include others.

Two of Yeshua's closest followers, Ya'akov and Yochanan, reflect on the truth that love must be expressed in concrete, everyday actions directed toward the real neighbor, rather than the abstraction of all mankind. First, Ya'akov asks, "If a brother or sister is naked and lacks daily food, and one of you says to them, 'Go in peace; keep warm and eat your fill,' and yet you do not supply their bodily needs, what is the good of that?" (James 2:15–16). In context, Ya'akov uses this example to argue that faith without works is dead. We must demonstrate our faith through works, but the point remains that love for our brother or sister—our neighbor in the most immediate sense—means responding to real material needs. Yochanan adds another point, "How does God's love abide in anyone who has the world's goods and sees a brother or sister in need and yet refuses help? Little children, let us love, not in word or speech, but in truth and action. ... Those who say, 'I love God,' and hate their brothers or sisters, are liars; for those who do not love a brother or sister whom they have seen, cannot love God whom they have not seen" (1 John 3:17–18; 4:20). Love in the biblical sense is never mere sentiment, but always expressed in deeds. Such love must begin right in the neighborhood, where people are hungry, lonely, and in need, but, of course, it doesn't end there.

Expanding the Neighborhood

The universal love that Yeshua commands begins with love for neighbor, with love for your fellow Jew, as the Torah states. But "love your fellow Jew," as Jewish tradition insists, must be expanded beyond your fellow Jew. One of the most famous sayings of rabbinic literature comes from the lips of the great Rabbi Hillel, "If I am not for myself, who will be for me? And, if I am for myself alone, then what am I?"[8] We might paraphrase Hillel, "If you do not love your fellow Jew, how can you claim to love humankind; but if you only love your fellow Jew, how can you claim to really love at all?" Or, as the religious joke goes, "I love the ministry—it's the people I can't stand."

But how do we arrive at this universal command to love from the words of Torah? When Yeshua tells us to love our enemies is he providing a new torah or revealing a truth from Torah itself? Leviticus 19:18 defines neighbor as the fellow Jew or the fellow Israelite, which forces us to love in practical and concrete ways, rather than as some sort of pious ideal that has little meaning in real life. Torah ensures that love for humanity begins with love for our neighbor, the person with whom we actually rub shoulders. Then it starts to expand the circle of love without abandoning those already within it. Yeshua continues this expansion in his Torah from the Mount. The rabbis not long after the time of Yeshua made a similar expansion of the rule to love your neighbor based on the Torah:

> In the generation after the destruction of the temple, rabbi Akiba declares "'Thou shalt love thy neighbour as thyself" is a fundamental rule in the Torah.' His contemporary, Ben Azzai agrees that this law of love is such a fundamental rule, provided it is read in conjunction with Gen. V, 1 ('This is the book of the generations of man. In the day that God created man, in the likeness of God made He him'); for this latter verse teaches reverence for the divine image in man, and proclaims the vital truth of the unity of mankind, and the consequent doctrine of the brotherhood of man. All men are created in the Divine image, says Ben Azzai; and, therefore, all are our fellow-men and entitled to human love.[9]

Leviticus 19 provides another step toward "Love your enemy."

> When an alien resides with you in your land, you shall not oppress the alien. The alien who resides with you shall be to you as the citizen among you; you shall love the alien as yourself, for you were aliens in the land of Egypt: I am the Lord your God. (Lev. 19:33–34)

Notice how this verse echoes the language of Leviticus 19:18—"love [the other] as yourself." Leviticus 19 commands us to love not only our neighbor, but also the alien, or stranger, as ourselves. And *alien* is defined in terms of Israel's experience as an alien in Egypt. *Alien* or *stranger* in this verse is sometimes translated as "proselyte" to interpret the verse as telling Israel to treat the convert in the same way as a native-born Jew.[10] This might be a positive ethical instruction, but it isn't an accurate translation. Torah goes well beyond this concern when it tells us to love the alien, "for you were aliens in the land of Egypt." The Israelites kept themselves separate from the Egyptians, maintained different values and customs, and proved to be strangers not just in origin, but also in their outlook and practice. They resisted assimilation into Egypt. Since you were aliens like this, Moses says, you are to love aliens, even aliens like this, as well. "You shall not oppress a resident alien; you know the heart of an alien, for you were aliens in the land of Egypt" (Exod. 23:9). In the same way, the alien whom we are to love might be different from us, not just the "good" outsider who is trying his best to be like us. The stranger might even turn out to be at enmity with us, as Israel was, or was perceived to be, during its sojourn in Egypt.

Whatever its origin, the saying, "You shall love your neighbor and hate your enemy," conceives of neighbor as the opposite of enemy, and tells us to treat the two in opposite ways. We tend to view the neighbor as the one like us and to favor him at the expense of the outsider. "Love the alien as yourself," however, forces the issue, as Yeshua recognized. Once, an expert in Torah asked Yeshua the inevitable question, "Who is my neighbor?" He responded with the famous story of the Good Samaritan (Luke 10:25–37). I discuss this story in my commentary on Leviticus 19–20 in *Creation to Completion* and conclude with a question, "My neighbor is the one who needs a neighbor. Holiness requires that I find such neighbors and provide the help they need. When I ask 'Who is my neighbor?' am I hoping to narrow my neighborhood or expand it? Am I ready to show mercy to a stranger?"[11]

Furthermore, the stranger whom we are to love, both in Leviticus 19 and in the Good Samaritan story, is "the stranger in your midst," who is actually right there under your nose, not the theoretical stranger who is far off. Lapide notes that this stranger is described as, or compared to, a brother in Leviticus 25:35[12] and takes this truth a step further in accord with rabbinic literature:

> That this brother can even be a pagan and an idolater is not infrequently stressed—as, for example, in the exegesis of Leviticus 19:13:

> You should not oppress your *reya'* [neighbor]! Your *reya'* is your brother; your brother is your *reya'*! From this it is learned that stealing from a pagan is theft. And one may not take "only your brother" in a narrow sense, for every human being is meant here [Seder Eliahu Rabba 49].[13]

Torah then starts with "love your neighbor as yourself" and takes the next step of "love the alien as yourself." Yeshua responds to that momentum and takes a third step in the same direction "love your enemy as yourself," thus fulfilling Torah. In Yeshua's torah, *neighbor* becomes so universal that it eliminates the contrast with *enemy* altogether. This is the teaching that he develops in the following verses, showing that this universal love characterizes the LORD himself.

In the concluding passage of Matthew 5, we are on familiar ground; Yeshua opens Torah to reveal its heart, which is often missed even by pious folk (like us). We are on familiar ground in another sense as well.

Here again Yeshua is countering the exclusiveness so common in the religious world, which is reflected in my opening story about building one synagogue in which to pray and another to avoid. Those most intent on serving God are quick to view those who don't believe or act like them as outsiders. Faith becomes the servant of prejudice and self-righteousness. Then Yeshua comes to bring the divine reversal that honors our creation in God's image above our particular affiliations or ethnicity. This reversal in no way diminishes the importance of biblical conviction; rather it forbids us from distorting our convictions into a pretense for self-righteousness and oppression—as has happened so often throughout history.

Perfection

If "love your enemy" is a lofty standard that forces many readers to ask whether Yeshua's Torah from the Mount is really meant to be a practical guide to living, the concluding statement seems even more challenging, "Be perfect, therefore, as your heavenly Father is perfect" (Matt. 5:48).

John Howard Yoder notes two common and opposite interpretations of this verse. "Perfectionist preachers saw there the promise of an accessible sinlessness; mainstream ethicists turned it around as proof that the Sermon's intent is not at all to be obeyed but to prepare people for grace by crushing them under the demand of an unattainable Godlikeness."[14] One interpretation, in other words, argues that "perfect" means perfectly without sin—and that this moral perfection is possible in this lifetime through the power of a transformed life. The other interpretation argues not only that such perfection is unattainable, but that Yeshua doesn't expect us to strive for it at all. Instead, he is trying to show us that God's standards are so high that all we can do is surrender to his grace and mercy. Yoder rightly disagrees with both interpretations. He argues that Yeshua's point is not sinless perfection, but being "indiscriminate" or "unconditional" in choosing whom we are to love, just as God is. The parallel teaching in Luke 6:32–36 makes this clear:

> "If you love those who love you, what credit is that to you? For even sinners love those who love them. If you do good to those who do good to you, what credit is that to you? For even sinners do the same. If you lend to those from whom you hope to receive, what credit is that to you? Even sinners lend to sinners, to receive as much again. But love your enemies, do good, and lend, expecting nothing in return. Your reward will be great, and you will be children of the Most High; for he is kind

to the ungrateful and the wicked. Be merciful, just as
your Father is merciful."

Love for enemy makes us perfect not because it frees us from ever
sinning again, but because it frees us from reacting to others and
from basing our pursuit of God and his ways on how others treat us.
The Hebrew word most likely underlying Matthew's use of "perfect"
is *tam* or *tamim*, which is used to describe a number of key characters in the Torah. Thus, Genesis 6:9 describes Noah as "a righteous
man, blameless [tamim] in his generation." The ancient Greek translation of this verse uses the same word, *teleios*, that appears in
Matthew 5:48 as "perfect." The Hebrew word tamim appears again in
Genesis, "When Abram was ninety-nine years old, the LORD appeared
to Abram, and said to him, 'I am God Almighty; walk before me, and
be blameless [tamim]. And I will make my covenant between me and
you ... " (Gen. 17:1–2). "When the boys grew up, Esau was a skillful
hunter, a man of the field, while Jacob was a quiet man [*ish tam*] who
stayed in camp" (Gen. 25:27). We know that Noah, Abraham, and
Jacob are not sinless or perfect in behavior. They all grow and develop as characters throughout the biblical narrative, but they all have
something in common—a wholehearted pursuit of God. They all
grow to increasingly reflect God's character and attributes. It is this
sort of wholehearted emulation of God's ways that Yeshua commends
in Matthew 5:48. And he reveals that the key to achieving it is to love
humankind without condition and without the usual barriers of eth-
nic, religious, and national exclusion.

With this background, we are ready to consider the practical implications of these verses—which many readers have concluded to
be altogether impractical! Is Yeshua really laying out a way to live, or
is this just a flowery, unrealistic vision of the way life ought to be? In
a moment we will consider two practical implications, one negative
and one positive. I am deliberately keeping these examples achiev-
able, feeling that it is better to discuss something we can actually do
than a higher ideal that we might never have the chance to apply.

Before we consider these applications, remember that readers of
the Sermon on the Mount continue to debate whether Yeshua is laying out principles for public policy or only for personal ethics. In
1940, for example, Gandhi misapplied Yeshua's teaching to preach
nonresistance to the British in the face of Nazi aggression:

> I want you to fight Nazism without arms or ... with
> non-violent arms. I would like you to lay down the
> arms you have as being useless for saving you or hu-
> manity. You will invite Herr Hitler and Signor Mussolini
> to take what they want of the countries you call your

possessions. Let them take possession of your beautiful island, with your many beautiful buildings. You will give all these but neither your souls, nor your minds. If these gentlemen choose to occupy your homes, you will vacate them. If they do not give you free passage out, you will allow yourself, man, woman and child, to be slaughtered, but you will refuse to owe allegiance to them ...[15]

As wicked as these words must have sounded to British ears in 1940, they sound even worse to Jewish ears. Surely, they do not represent the intent of Yeshua, whose teaching is so deeply informed by the Torah, which prizes human life and the protection of the innocent.

What is incontrovertible, however, is that Yeshua teaches and embodies nonresistance and love for the enemy as that applies to oneself. We need to practice such love for the enemy in our own lives before we consider its sociopolitical implications. As we consider some everyday applications of "love your enemy," we need to remember that "love" is not a feeling, because it would be unrealistic to command anyone to feel a certain way. Furthermore, the Bible isn't nearly as concerned with feelings in general as we are in the twenty-first century; rather the love commanded in Torah is always expressed in behavior toward the other. Our attitudes and feelings are important because they give rise to deeds, but the tree is known by its fruit—the deeds themselves. So consider two practical applications that aren't intended to be the highest expressions of this teaching, but which we might be able to pursue in our everyday lives.

First, a Negative Application: Don't Demonize the Opposition.

The commandment to love our enemies surely means that we should treat even those who are only opponents or adversaries with respect. I have sometimes been amazed, and disappointed, at how readily people who profess faith in Yeshua apply labels such as "heretic," "apostate," or "cult" to fellow believers with whom they disagree on various major and minor theological points. Rather than seeking understanding and common ground, we demonize the opposition to gain victory on some level.

In the 2008 presidential race, both Senator John McCain and Senator Barack Obama claimed to be Christians, and both seemed caught up in a struggle between religious conviction and political expediency in how they conducted their campaigns. My sense is that both men would have preferred to maintain a level of respect that reflected the collegiality of the Senate, if not their professed brotherhood in Christ. Early in the race, McCain stated, "My entire campaign

I have treated Senator Obama and Senator Clinton with respect. I will continue to do that throughout this campaign. ..."[16] Obama stated in his nomination acceptance speech, "The times are too serious, the stakes are too high for this same partisan playbook. So let us agree that patriotism has no party. I love this country, and so do you, and so does John McCain."[17]

But political pressures and conventional wisdom got the better of both candidates, even though both publicly stated that they were believers in Jesus. If the Jesus whom they serve told us to love our enemies, surely we should even more readily love our colleagues among the political, religious, or cultural opposition. Love for the enemy goes far beyond this concern, of course, but this is a good starting point. Sadly, as the weeks wore on, the campaign came to reflect the usual mud slinging and misrepresentation of most political campaigns. Only on election night when the results were clear, did McCain's concession speech and Obama's victory speech regain some of the tone that reflected a commitment to Yeshua.

Another example is even closer to home. I am a Zionist, committed to the existence and success of a Jewish state in the land of Israel, but I am often dismayed by the rhetoric that fellow supporters of Israel use against the Arabs. A ministry colleague once spoke in our synagogue, describing Muslims as "springing up everywhere like mushrooms, like fungus." I had to repudiate these remarks before the congregation. "Love your enemy" means that we recognize the divine image in every human being as Rabbi Ben Azzai noted many centuries ago. We must speak of them and treat them from that foundation of basic respect.

Second, a Positive Application:
Regard All People with Goodwill and Respect.

"Love your enemy" might not mean the end of military or police intervention or of law courts and punishment, but it certainly has an application to public policy. The rabbinic literature includes, "Even the criminal condemned to die has claim on our brotherly love, and we must spare him unnecessary suffering."[18] Closer to home, this principle means that we judge others—even those who seem alien or even in opposition to us—with fairness and charity. Rabbi Telushkin quotes an anonymous prayer that someone sent to him:

Heavenly Father,

Help us to remember that the "jerk" who cut us off
in traffic last night may be a single mother who worked
nine hours that day and who is now rushing home to

cook dinner, help with homework, do the laundry, and spend a few precious minutes with her children.

Help us to remember that the pierced, tattooed, disinterested young man who couldn't make change correctly at the register today is a worried nineteen-year-old student who is preoccupied with whether he passed his final exams and with his fear of not getting a student loan for next semester. ...[19]

"Love your neighbor" ultimately means love all humankind, but this universal regard doesn't invalidate particular loyalties. Rav Sha'ul captures the balance well, "So then, whenever we have an opportunity, let us work for the good of all, and especially for those of the family of faith" (Gal. 6:10). Some critics think Sha'ul is watering down Yeshua's teaching of universal love here, restoring that particularism that they thought Yeshua was eliminating. Once again, however, we have to read Yeshua's message through the lens of Matthew 5:17 and the lens of Torah. In reflecting the heart of Torah, Yeshua expands the particular love we are to show to the house of Israel to embrace all humankind, but he doesn't negate the particular love for Israel. Sha'ul does the same, applying the particular love not only to the house of Israel, but to the family of faith. He notes that the more universal love, "working for the good of all," is not always possible, but is still our ideal. Without grounding in a real community, our love is only theoretical and sentimental, but if we limit it to our home community, our love falls far short of the standard that Messiah demonstrates.

Summing It up

Yeshua summarizes his teaching of universal love—unconditional and unilateral positive intention toward all—in what we term the Golden Rule: "In everything do to others as you would have them do to you; for this is the law and the prophets" (Matt. 7:12). Yeshua's Golden Rule reflects not only Torah, as we would expect, but also traditional Jewish interpretations of the words of Torah, including "Love your neighbor as yourself" (*v'ahavata l're'echa k'mocha*):

> These three Hebrew words were early recognized as the most comprehensive rule of conduct, as containing the essence of religion and applicable in every human relation and towards all men. Even the criminal condemned to die, say the rabbis, has claim on our brotherly love, and we must spare him unnecessary suffering. Hillel paraphrased this rule into 'Whatever is hateful unto thee do it not unto thy fellow'; and

declared it to be the whole law, the remainder being
but a commentary on this fundamental principle of
the Torah.[20]

In the last chapter, we saw how Yeshua himself provided the fullest
illustration of his teaching on nonresistance in the way that he endured betrayal, arrest, beatings, and crucifixion. Now we see how at
the climax of the Passion, from the cross itself, he revealed what it
means to love your enemy. If we want to grasp how to bless those
who curse us and pray for those who despitefully use us, we need to
look upon Yeshua in his sufferings, who prayed, "Father, forgive
them; for they do not know what they are doing" (Luke 23:34). As always, Yeshua not only provides us with instructions that lead to life,
but also provides the example and goes before us. If he can so fully
embody love for the enemy amidst his unimaginable and undeserved
suffering, so can we begin to travel in that direction in the simple opportunities that we encounter in everyday life.

The Great Reversal

CLEANSING THE LEPER
Matthew 8:1–4

Throughout his Torah from the Mount, Yeshua unpacks the meaning of his brief statement, "Do not think that I have come to abolish the Torah or the prophets; I have come not to abolish but to fulfill." With this one sentence Yeshua upholds the continuing validity of the Hebrew Scriptures and at the same time places himself at the heart of Jewish messianic expectations as the one who fulfills Torah.

Yeshua demonstrates this fulfilled Torah in detail throughout his teachings in Matthew 5–7. When he finished, "the crowds were astounded at his teaching, for he taught them as one having authority, and not as their scribes" (Matt. 7:28–29). Yeshua's Torah-fulfilling work, however, doesn't end there, but continues as he descends the mount.

> There was a leper who came to him and knelt before him, saying, "Lord, if you choose, you can make me clean." He stretched out his hand and touched him, saying, "I do choose. Be made clean!" Immediately his leprosy was cleansed. Then Yeshua said to him, "See that you say nothing to anyone; but go, show yourself to the priest, and offer the gift that Moses commanded, as a testimony to them." (Matt 8:2–4)

Yeshua has just taught the fulfilled Torah. Now he demonstrates that fulfillment in action. He not only teaches the true, inward meaning of Torah, but he also restores the ideal conditions that Torah envisions. Looking at Yeshua's cleansing of the leper more closely gives us a greater understanding of what he means by fulfillment.

Garry Wills writes that "one of the main lessons" of Yeshua's miracles "is that people should not be separated into classes of the clean and unclean, the worthy and the unworthy, the respectable and the unrespectable."[1] Wills reminds us, "many of Jesus' miracles are worked for outsiders—for non-Jews like the centurion (Lk 7.9) or the woman from Tyre (Mk 7.29) or the leper from Samaria (Lk 17.16). But the greatest category has to do with people who are unclean, with whom observant Jews are to have no dealings ... to show that no person made in God's image should be treated as unclean." Ultimately Wills' Jesus is "willing to challenge the entire 'holiness code' of his time," which is largely synonymous with the book of Leviticus.[2]

The Laws of Leprosy

Wills' portrayal of Yeshua as a radical alternative to the proponents of religious formalism seems compelling, but he overlooks Yeshua's own words, "I have not come to abolish the Torah, but to fulfill." Yeshua does indeed transcend the leper's uncleanness by stretching out his hand to touch him, but then he removes the uncleanness. He doesn't just obliterate clean–unclean distinctions, as Wills claims, but he altogether removes uncleanness itself, thus fulfilling Torah. Then, just as dramatically, Yeshua upholds (and again fulfills) Torah by sending the cleansed leper to a priest, in obedience to the commandment, "This shall be the ritual for the leprous person at the time of his cleansing: He shall be brought to the priest; the priest shall go out of the camp, and the priest shall make an examination" (Lev. 14:2–3).

The Hebrew term for leprosy, *tzara'at*, actually signifies a number of different skin diseases, all of which threatened the holiness of Israel. This condition is covered extensively in Leviticus 13–14. The fate of someone struck with tzara'at was grave: Banned from the camp and assigned the clothing of a mourner, he was required to announce his own uncleanness wherever he went, crying *"Tamei, Tamei!"* ("Unclean, Unclean!"), so that no one would be polluted by his touch.

The priests, who were charged with maintaining the holiness of Israel, were responsible for examining those who showed any sign of tzara'at and declaring them afflicted or well. "It is a decree of Scripture," writes the great medieval commentator Rashi, "that there is neither impurity of afflictions of tzara'at nor their purification except by the word of a priest."[3] Even if a leper thought that he had become free of his disease, he wasn't to rejoin the people until a priest came to him "outside the camp" (Lev. 14:3) to declare him clean. The priest, however, could not cleanse him and certainly would not touch him if he were still unclean. His role was to examine and verify that the leper was cleansed and then to see that he offered a proper sacrifice to confirm his cleansing, but he had no authority to cleanse tzara'at himself.

Torah's description of tzara'at is puzzling if we see it as strictly a medical condition, because it doesn't exactly correspond to leprosy or any other condition known to medicine. Indeed, Leviticus portrays it attacking clothing and buildings as well as human bodies (Lev. 13:47ff. and 14:33ff.). The Jewish sages saw the levitical disease, therefore, as a unique symptom of sin, the visible outworking of inner disorder. The leper remained outside the camp morally as well as physically, suffering not only from disease, but also from disgrace. Another of the great medieval commentators, Nachmanides or Ramban, who was a practicing physician as well as a Torah scholar, summarizes this perspective. Tzara'at, writes the good doctor, "is not in the natural order of things, nor does it ever happen in the world outside Israel."

> But when Israel is wholly devoted to God, then His spirit is upon them always, to maintain their bodies, clothes, and houses in a good appearance. Thus as soon as one of them commits a sin or transgression, a deformity appears in his flesh, or on his garment, or in his house, revealing that God has turned aside from him.[4]

If we accept Ramban's claim that tzara'at will appear "as soon as one of them commits a sin or transgression," then we have to wonder why we are not all lepers.

> Do you not know that wrongdoers will not inherit the kingdom of God? Do not be deceived! Fornicators, idolaters, adulterers, male prostitutes, sodomites, thieves, the greedy, drunkards, revilers, robbers— none of these will inherit the kingdom of God. *And this is what some of you used to be.* But you were washed, you were sanctified, you were justified in the name of the Lord Yeshua the Messiah and in the Spirit of our God. (1 Cor. 6:9–11; emphasis added)

Fornicators, idolaters, adulterers, male prostitutes, sodomites, thieves, the greedy, drunkards, revilers, and robbers—Messiah cleanses lepers such as these. Yeshua healed a leper right after his foundational teaching of Torah from the Mount to remind us that we are all lepers, desperate for Messiah's healing touch. The leper's encounter with Yeshua is a paradigm for every person's transforming encounter with Yeshua, and a sign that his torah is not limited to words alone. It breaks into the human scene with redemptive power. Messiah has the authority not just to pronounce upon our leprosy as the priests can do, but to free us from it entirely as no priest can.

Two Authorities

Yeshua does not declare the clean–unclean distinction to be at an end as Wills claims, but he makes the leper clean again. And when he does so, he sends the leper to the priest. But if Messiah himself cleanses the leper, what need is there for a priest? Torah teaches that when a person is cleansed of leprosy, he is to stand outside the camp until the priest comes to verify that the leper is indeed cleansed, and then to see that he offers a proper sacrifice to confirm his cleansing. But the priest has no authority to cleanse; only Messiah possesses that.

Here are two different authorities. Messiah has kingly authority to change things: to heal, drive out evil spirits, and forgive sin. The priest has authority to maintain things: to teach, judge, and evaluate. The priest has powers for this age; the king for the Age to Come. These two roles are not necessarily in conflict—Yeshua sends the leper to the priest—but they are quite distinct. Priestly authority is needed to teach and apply Scripture, judge and make decisions, and maintain values and tradition. Without priestly authority, we have little sense of community and soon fall into religious anarchy. Kingly authority, however, is transformative.

Priestly authority can be wielded by a true or a false priesthood. A false priest serves the political or religious establishment. He will call the clean unclean and the unclean clean if it suits the powers of the day. The true priest discerns the underlying spiritual reality; he declares the leper clean only when he is indeed clean. Such a priesthood can work in harmony with the kingly authority of the Messiah. Thus, Yeshua tells the leper to report to the priest "as a testimony to them" to show that he is now clean and can return to the community.

"As a testimony to them," however, can mean something more—a declaration to the priest that he is encountering kingly authority. The cleansing of the leper demonstrates that one is here who has messianic powers. Such cleansing occurred only twice in the Tanakh: in the cases of Miriam (Numbers 12) and Naaman, the Syrian general (2 Kings 5). The rabbis, therefore, said it was as hard to cleanse a leper as to raise the dead. Accordingly, they wrote, "In this world the priest examines for leprosy, but in the World to Come—says the Holy One, blessed be he—'I will render you clean.' Thus it is written, *And I will sprinkle clean water upon you, and ye shall be clean* (Ezek. 36:25)."[5]

By cleansing a leper not in the World to Come, but in this world, Yeshua fulfills Torah. He doesn't bring Torah to an end or limit himself to teaching its true meaning and application, but he acts to restore the ideal that Torah envisions. He doesn't abolish laws of purity; instead, he exercises a kingly authority that restores us to purity in anticipation of the Age to Come in which all things will be restored.

The Two Authorities in Harmony

Priestly authority and kingly authority are both legitimate and can work together. In the religious world, however, priestly authority is far more common and readily attainable. The problem arises when it becomes satisfied with itself and even defends itself against

the kingly authority that can transform everything. Those who are in
spiritual authority may be able to judge fairly, but they can rarely
change things to match the standards by which they judge. Those
who exercise priestly authority need to do so with the constant
awareness of its limitations. Whenever we discipline or criticize another, we must do so knowing that we lack the power to change that
person for the better. We might be able to discern the effects of leprosy in others, and ourselves, but only Messiah can cleanse the leper—as he once cleansed us. And because he cleansed us, we need to
exercise priestly authority with humility.

Yeshua's story of the Good Samaritan ties these lessons together:

> A man was going down from Jerusalem to Jericho,
> and fell into the hands of robbers, who stripped him,
> beat him, and went away, leaving him half dead. Now
> by chance a priest was going down that road; and
> when he saw him, he passed by on the other side. So
> likewise a Levite, when he came to the place and saw
> him, passed by on the other side. But a Samaritan
> while traveling came near him; and when he saw him,
> he was moved with pity. He went to him and bandaged
> his wounds, having poured oil and wine on them.
> Then he put him on his own animal, brought him to an
> inn, and took care of him. The next day he took out
> two denarii, gave them to the innkeeper, and said,
> "Take care of him; and when I come back, I will repay
> you whatever more you spend." (Luke 10:30–35)

We are again witnessing divine reversal, where the marginalized and
despised Samaritan acts as the hero and the honored priest and Levite
act disgracefully. Yeshua is employing irony to drive home the priority of compassion and the need to translate compassion into action.
Wills points out, "[T]he injured man seemed almost dead, and the
Leviticus code said that touching a dead man made one unclean." I
want to interact with Wills here because he is a popular and insightful
writer, yet he remains tainted by the anti-Torah perspective of much
of Christianity. He writes that the priest and Levite are "avoiding con-
tamination. ... The story of the 'good Samaritan' is often told simply
to show goodness of heart in the rescuer. It also shows the inhuman
effects of the purity code of the Jewish priesthood. The story is a
powerful part of Jesus' attack on the formalisms of 'religion.'"[6]

Wills correctly notes that Yeshua does not oppose just Judaism,
but "the formalisms of 'religion'" per se: "All religious formalists have
reason to fear Jesus—a fact of Christian history as well as of Jewish."[7]
True enough, but Yeshua opposes the excesses of Jewish formalism

without destroying the foundation underlying it, which is Torah itself. To return to my terminology, the priest and the Levite exercise priestly authority to determine that the beaten traveler poses a risk, because helping him may entail a violation of some of Torah's standards. But they lack—or avoid—the kingly authority to restore him. Ironically, the Samaritan takes on kingly authority, which ultimately belongs to Messiah himself.

The Essence of Torah

The purity code can certainly be misapplied, and undoubtedly was in Yeshua's time, but it remains part of the Word of God, which Yeshua said couldn't be annulled (John 10:35). The purity code is within the domain of the priest and isn't to be abolished but to be exercised in harmony with the authority of the king. The story of the beaten traveler, then, does not contradict part of Torah but provides an example of Torah fulfilled.

In good Jewish style, Yeshua tells the story in response to a question on the ethical application of Torah. An expert on Torah asks Yeshua what he must do to inherit eternal life. Note that Yeshua doesn't respond by suggesting that he has brought in a new religion of love and grace in contrast with the old way of law; instead he responds by asking the expert what the Torah says. The lawyer rightly answers with a quote from the Shema, "You shall love the Lord your God with all your heart, and with all your soul, and with all your strength, and with all your mind" (Deut. 6:5). Then he adds a phrase from the same book of Leviticus that Wills finds so problematic— "and your neighbor as yourself" (Lev. 19:18). Yeshua again forgets to instruct the lawyer about the new religion of faith alone that transcends even the highest expressions of the law such as these. Instead, he simply says, "You have given the right answer; do this, and you will live" (Luke 10:28). When the Torah expert responds with a lawyerly question, "And who is my neighbor?"—in other words, "And who exactly is it that I must love as myself?"—Yeshua tells his story of the Samaritan. The expert knows what Torah says; Yeshua teaches him how to fulfill it.

The moral of the story isn't that the purity laws prevent religious people from doing good and so must be removed; instead it's that the lesser matters of Torah can distract us from the heart of Torah. The in-house preoccupations of religious practice can distract us from the issues of heart that matter most. "Woe to you, scribes and Pharisees, hypocrites! For you tithe mint, dill, and cummin, and have neglected the weightier matters of the Torah: justice and mercy and faith. It is these you ought to have practiced *without neglecting the others*" (Matt. 23:23, emphasis added).

The story also teaches us that the weightier matters of Torah, justice, mercy, and faith, are neither abstract concepts nor lofty ideals impossible to fulfill in real life. Yeshua tells the story to answer the expert's question, "And who is my neighbor?" At the end, he says, "'Which of these three, do you think, was a neighbor to the man who fell into the hands of the robbers?' The lawyer said, 'The one who showed him mercy [doubtless using the Hebrew word hesed, introduced in Chapter 2].' Yeshua said to him, 'Go and do likewise'" (Luke 10:36–37). Torah instructs us to love our neighbor; Yeshua fulfills Torah by revealing that the neighbor is the one to whom we show mercy, regardless of his standing. Moreover, he teaches us to fulfill Torah by expanding the category of neighbor to include the outsider, the risky, and the undesirable, and acting toward them accordingly.

I was once in San Francisco for a religious conference and had rented a car to travel to an early-morning speaking engagement in another city on one of the days of the conference. I rushed back to San Francisco to return the car on time and avoid paying an extra day's rental but discovered that gas stations were hard to find in the heart of the city. I finally found one, filled the tank so I wouldn't be charged the $6.99 a gallon the rental company would have charged me (which prior to 2008 sounded really expensive!), and arrived at their downtown office about a half-hour past my deadline. When I turned in the key, I asked the attendant to give me a break, and he did graciously enough. As I was walking the three or four blocks back to the conference hotel, I passed a man who appeared a bit deranged, begging on the street corner, crying out, "I just need $2.89 for a plate of spaghetti at Tommy's Joint [a local restaurant]!" I walked right by him; after all, I was hurrying back from an important assignment and had to get to another one at the hotel. I had hardly gotten across the street when I felt as if God spoke to me, "You wicked servant—the rental company just spared you thirty-five or forty dollars in late fees, and you can't give that guy a couple of bucks for lunch!" I went back and handed him a five-dollar bill. As I walked away, I thought, *but who knows if he really even* needs *the money?* Again, I felt a divine intervention, this time saying, "Right. Who knows if *he* needs the money? But *you* need to give it to him."[8]

I was the priest, the Levite intent on my religious assignment, and the crazy panhandler was my other, the beaten-up traveler or leper. Reaching out to touch him may have done more to fulfill Torah than the conference I had flown all the way to San Francisco to attend or the radio program to which I had driven another two hundred miles to speak. The crazy panhandler made me uncomfortable. Religious people, particularly when they take on the evaluative priestly role and forget its limitations, make others uncomfortable, too. But Yeshua met people, the ordinary Jewish people of his day, the religious authorities, and the outcasts as well, where they were. He did not just evaluate them, but he reached out to touch them. So should we.

Followers of Yeshua bear kingdom authority through him, but are not always willing to touch the lepers. We join the debate over issues such as homosexuality, abortion, or drug abuse to defend the perspective of Scripture. The secular community has enlisted false priests who say to various classes of sinners, "You are not unclean; you are not a leper." We might rightly object to such rulings, but we are called to go beyond this debate, to follow the one who fulfills Torah. We are to touch the leper, not to keep him at a distance with our pronouncements. We sometimes seem more interested in the priestly role of declaring the leper unclean than in the kingdom authority to touch him and see him transformed. If Messiah touched us, we can touch others.

[Portions of this chapter are excerpted from my book Gateways to Torah, *p. 119-121.]*

10

THE MESSIANIC SECRET
Mark 8:27–38; 9:30–37; 10:32–45

Yeshua, at least as Mark tells his story, appears more intent on hiding his messianic identity than on revealing it, and Mark seems eager to cooperate with this effort. He opens with the declaration that this is "the Good News of Yeshua the Messiah, the Son of God ..." (Mark 1:1), and goes on to record the testimony of Yochanan the Immerser (Mark 1:7–8), and then of a voice from heaven that says, "You are my Son, whom I love; I am well pleased with you" (Mark 1:11). But it soon becomes clear that this identity will be concealed. When the demons recognize Yeshua as the Son of God (Mark 1:24; 3:11; 5:7), Yeshua silences them and tells them not to make him known. He repeatedly instructs those he heals to tell no one about it (Mark 1:44; 3:12; 5:43; 7:36; 8:26). He refuses the Pharisees' request for a sign to prove that he is sent from God (Mark 8:11–12). When Yeshua visits his own hometown, the people ask, "Where did this man get all this? What is this wisdom he has been given? What are these miracles worked through him? Isn't he just the carpenter, the son of Miryam?" (Mark 6:2–3). Rather than recognizing him as Messiah, they take offense. His own disciples, when Yeshua performs the great miracle of calming a storm on the Sea of Galilee, ask, "Who can this be, that even the wind and the waves obey him?" (Mark 4:41).

In 2007, a book entitled *In Defense of Israel* created a stir in the Christian world. Author John Hagee interpreted Yeshua's practice of hiding his messianic identity to mean that he didn't come to be the Messiah to the Jewish people at all. Rather he came to be the Savior of the world and will be the Jewish Messiah only at his Second Coming. Pastor Hagee defended this thesis with statements like these:

- "If God intended for Jesus to be the Messiah of Israel, why didn't he authorize Jesus to use supernatural signs to prove he was God's Messiah, just as Moses had done?"[1]

- "Jesus refused to produce a sign ... because it was not the Father's will, nor his, to be Messiah."[2]

- "If Jesus wanted to be Messiah, why did he repeatedly tell his disciples and followers to 'tell no one' about his supernatural accomplishments? Think about it! If the man were trying to gain national attention to rally the support of the general public for the overthrow of mighty Rome, he would not go around the country saying, 'Tell no one!'"[3]

The book accurately notes that Yeshua made a point of concealing his identity, but reaches a false conclusion in explaining why he did so.

Garry Wills cites an influential book published a hundred years earlier that comes up with a different explanation. In *The Messianic Secret*, author William Wrede "argued that Jesus was not recognized as the Messiah in his lifetime." Mark "made an attempt to explain this by saying that Jesus *ordered* people to keep silent on the subject."[4] In other words, Mark pictures Yeshua hiding his Messiahship to explain why he wasn't more widely accepted in his own time. Wrede doesn't seem to provide any more help than Hagee in understanding Yeshua's story on its own terms. Can we find a better explanation for the messianic secret?

The Meaning of *Messiah*

Surely, Yeshua is not refusing to be Messiah. Rather he—and Mark after him—is confronting us with what it means to declare that he *is* Messiah. Yeshua suppresses the announcement that he is Messiah because he doesn't want the title to be applied to him before he can reveal what it really means. The first half of Mark's account begins to reveal the nature of Messiah through his miracles, his service, and his message. The turning point comes when Yeshua takes his disciples off to a retreat in the region of Caesarea Philippi, away from the bustle and exposure of the Galilean towns. On the way, he raises the question himself:

> "Who do people say that I am?" And they answered him, "John the Baptist; and others, Elijah; and still others, one of the prophets." He asked them, "But who do you say that I am?" Peter answered him, "You are the Messiah." And he sternly ordered them not to tell anyone about him. (Mark 8:27–30)

Obviously, the claim that Jesus did not come to be Messiah of Israel misses the whole point. He most definitely came to be Messiah—and to define who and what Messiah is for Israel. It isn't as if the Jews were incapable of grasping the sort of Messiah Yeshua came to be and can only wait for him to return as their kind of Messiah in the future. He has deliberately drawn the confession from the Jewish Peter, "You are the Messiah." Matthew records Yeshua's response, "Blessed are you, Simon son of Jonah! For flesh and blood has not revealed this to you, but my Father in heaven" (Matt. 16:17).[5]

But why does he continue to tell his disciples "not to tell anyone about him"? He must begin a process of unfolding, to them first, what it really means to declare him Messiah. This is the messianic secret that lies at the heart of the gospel itself. David Flusser, one of the great twentieth-century Jewish authorities on the life of Yeshua, comments on Mark's portrayal of the messianic secret. He notes that Yeshua was following the practice of charismatic holy men of his era, like Honi the Circle Drawer and Hanan the Hidden, in avoiding public accolades. "Nevertheless," Flusser notes, "it is true that Jesus did not say in so many words that he was the Messiah, because he had not yet fulfilled his messianic task."[6] In other words, as a Jewish holy man of the first century, Yeshua followed the habit of concealment established by miracle-working saints like Honi and Hanan, but he did so for his own deeper purpose.

The entire structure of Mark's account highlights the messianic secret. As we have seen, underlying the first half of Mark is the question of Yeshua's true identity and of real meaning of the term *Messiah*. The climax comes when Yeshua elicits the confession from his disciples that he is Messiah, but even then he instructs them to tell no one. First, Yeshua must teach them the meaning of Messiah, which he continues to do in word and deed until the end of the Gospel. "Then he began to teach them that the Son of Man must undergo great suffering, and be rejected by the elders, the chief priests, and the scribes, and be killed, and after three days rise again" (Mark 8:31).

As Yeshua leads his disciples from the Caesarea Philippi region on the northern fringe of the Galilee back toward Jerusalem, he repeats this statement about his upcoming betrayal, death, and resurrection two more times (Mark 9:31; 10:33–34). All three times the disciples make it painfully clear that they really do not understand the statement, and each time Yeshua responds with instruction on what it means to follow him as the crucified Messiah. As we examine these three incidents more closely, we will see that they are progressive. The disciples begin with a complete rejection of Yeshua's teaching about his suffering and resurrection and progress to an understanding that is distorted, but at least begins to respond to Yeshua's message. This whole sequence, which provides the transition from Yeshua's popular Galilean ministry to his final days on earth, culminates in a verse that defines his whole ministry: "For the Son of Man came not to be served but to serve, and to give his life a ransom for many" (Mark 10:45). Only after Yeshua announces this divine reversal that lies at the heart of his entire mission does the story move to

Jerusalem, where the messianic band has been headed all along and where Yeshua's threefold prediction soon comes to pass.

The messianic secret that Yeshua reveals, then, is not just a secret about him, but also about what it means to follow him. We can never fully understand who Messiah is apart from the question of who we must be in response to him. Every Christological debate has ethical implications.[7] These revelations all come on the road, as the messianic band makes its way toward Jerusalem. That journey with Yeshua and his disciples reveals his instructions and will help us consider how they will guide us today.

1. Caesarea Philippi

After Yeshua elicits Peter's confession that he is Messiah, he describes the sufferings that Messiah must endure to accomplish his mission. The same Yeshua who has told people and demons to say nothing about his powers and his stature as Son of God now speaks "quite openly" about his suffering (Mark 8:32). Ironically, Peter speaks up again, this time to rebuke Yeshua for saying that he must die. Peter not only misunderstands Yeshua's words about suffering, but rejects them altogether. He is saying to Yeshua, "This message is not for you and it is not for me." Yeshua puts Peter in his place: "Get behind me, Satan! For you are setting your mind not on divine things but on human things" (Mark 8:33).

Many readers have noted that the same Peter who is recognized a few verses back for being the first to acknowledge Yeshua as Messiah is now called "Satan." This term, however, is more than a nasty retort. Satan in Hebrew is literally the "adversary," the one who opposes God wherever he can. By objecting to Yeshua's imminent suffering and death at this critical moment, Peter becomes the adversary's instrument in opposing God's plan of redemption. But there is more, because Satan is also the tempter, who first appears in the Gospel when Yeshua is driven out to the wilderness to be "tempted by Satan" (Mark 1:13). Matthew and Luke reveal that this temptation in the wilderness has to do with the messianic secret.

In the temptation in the wilderness, Satan taunts Yeshua with suggestions to reveal himself and his Messiahship in powerful, undeniable, and suffering-free ways. First, "If you are the Son of God, command these stones to become loaves of bread" (Matt. 4:3). Satan is telling Yeshua to not just feed himself by creating one or two loaves, but to feed the multitudes with the transformed stones that surround him in the wilderness. Be like Moses, the tempter is saying, who provided manna in the desert for the entire house of Israel, and thus make it clear that you are Messiah. Then, "If you are the Son of God, throw yourself down" from the pinnacle of the Temple in the sight of all of Israel's worshipers (Matt. 4:6). When God miraculously rescues you, as his word says that he must do, says the tempter, everyone will see that you are Messiah. And finally, "[T]he devil took him to a very high mountain and showed him all the kingdoms of the world and their splendor; and he said to him, 'All these I will give you, if you will fall down and worship me'" (Matt. 4:8–9). You will be installed as the messianic king over the entire human race, thus accomplishing your mission in one stroke, and all you have to do is bow before me. Yeshua rejects all three temptations, not because he refuses to be Messiah, but because he refuses to be that kind of Messiah, one established "not on divine things but on human things," as he later states to Peter (Matt. 16:23).

Yeshua's victory over Satan in the wilderness is an early expression of the divine reversal that we are tracing throughout Yeshua's story. Natural ethics seek to preserve life, avoid suffering, and reach the goal as efficiently as possible. If Yeshua is Messiah, Peter says in line with the words of Satan in the wilderness, he has no business announcing his demise. When Yeshua responds, "Get behind me Satan!" he reveals that Peter's words represent a real temptation to him. He was, after all, tempted in all ways as we are, yet without sin (Heb. 4:15). Peter's words represent a real test for Yeshua, one he has already passed in the wilderness but which he continues to face until his final prayer in Gethsemane just before his betrayal (Mark 14:33ff.). To accomplish the will of God requires more than a one-time step of faith or moment of decision; rather it requires a disciplined, consistent acceptance of the divine reversal: God's way of victory is often the opposite of the way we would choose. It is often not the popular route, but the narrow, rigorous, and demanding way.

Peter rejects the way of Messiah that Yeshua outlines, saying, "This way is not for you and it is not for me." Yeshua responds by saying that he must walk the path of denial and sacrifice, and so must anyone who thinks himself a disciple. There is no carefree, low-impact, limited-risk Yeshua to follow:

> "If any want to become my followers, let them deny themselves and take up their cross and follow me. For those who want to save their life will lose it, and those who lose their life for my sake, and for the sake of the gospel, will save it. For what will it profit them to gain the whole world and forfeit their life? Indeed, what can they give in return for their life? Those who are ashamed of me and of my words in this adulterous and sinful generation, of them the Son of Man will also be ashamed when he comes in the glory of his Father with the holy angels." (Mark 8:34–38)

2. A House in Capernaum

Yeshua makes the second announcement of his death and resurrection on the road with his disciples as they are passing through Galilee, heading toward Jerusalem: "'The Son of Man is to be betrayed into human hands, and they will kill him, and three days after being killed, he will rise again.' But they did not understand what he was saying and were afraid to ask him." Later, when they come into the house in Capernaum that serves as home base, Yeshua asks, "'What were you discussing as we were traveling?' But they kept quiet; because on the way, they had been arguing with each other about who was the greatest" (Mark 9:31–34).

Why would Yeshua's grim announcement make the disciples start disputing about who was the greatest? Mark tells us that they didn't understand what Yeshua was saying. Perhaps they heard what Yeshua had said and then returned to their own preoccupations, which in a gathering of a dozen males would inevitably include matters of status and competition. Or they might have understood enough to catch Yeshua's mention of his resurrection. Surely this must mean that the Day of Judgment was at hand, the day when Messiah would be placed upon the throne of David. Indeed, were they not headed toward Jerusalem, the city of David? Yeshua had mentioned something about suffering and death, but surely the final victory was just ahead, and they were bound to have a share in it—but who would get the largest share? Who was the greatest among them? And off they went.

After Yeshua's first announcement of his suffering, Peter responded, "This way is not for you and it is not for us." After the second announcement, the disciples say, "This way is okay for you, but it is not for us." You do the suffering, and we will compete for the benefits. In response to their jockeying for status, Yeshua tells his twelve friends, "Whoever wants to be first must be last of all and servant of all." Then, to illustrate his point, "he took a little child and put it among them; and taking it in his arms, he said to them, 'Whoever welcomes one such child in my name welcomes me, and whoever welcomes me welcomes not me but the one who sent me'" (Mark 9:35–37).

The disciples have made two fundamental errors that have plagued those who profess faith in Yeshua throughout the ages, two fundamental errors that keep adherents from becoming followers. In place of these two fundamental errors, Yeshua teaches two points that are equally fundamental to following him.

The first fundamental mistake is implied in the story. The disciples hear Yeshua say, "The Son of Man is to be betrayed into human hands, and they will kill him, and three days after being killed, he will rise again," but they see the path of crucifixion as only instrumental, as a means to an end, namely the resurrection and all that it entails.

And they see it as something that only Yeshua will experience, so that he can bring them into resurrection and victory. They believe a doctrine that is still popular today: Yeshua suffered so we don't have to. Hence, they argue about their position in the victory parade. But Yeshua has already told them that to follow him they must take up their own cross. The crucifixion is not merely instrumental, but essential to following Yeshua.

The overemphasis on the crucifixion as instrumental is deeply engrained within today's Jesus-professing religious world. It's true that Jesus endured death on our behalf to give us life, and it's true that his story does not end in crucifixion but resurrection. The error is in seeing the cross as only a means to the glorious end and forgetting that it is also the symbol of a way of life. It represents divine reversal, in which apparent defeat holds the key to true life.

The second fundamental error is revealed in the argument over who is the greatest. The disciples imagine that the competition for status that characterizes every culture must also characterize the kingdom that Yeshua is about to establish. They imagine that it is a zero-sum kingdom, in which a person can only gain status at someone else's expense. This is certainly how the world works, and has always worked, so the disciples figure it must be the way that the kingdom will work as well. Indeed, we have all seen the spirit of competition at work in the religious world around us. When I attend meetings of pastors or rabbis, I'm always relieved when the competitive spirit is absent and we can interact with real freedom and effectiveness. All too often the competitive categories of size, image, and acquisition are imposed on work that is supposedly being done in God's name.

To counter the competitive spirit, Yeshua simply places a child in their midst. We might expect him to say something like he does a little later, "Whoever does not receive the kingdom of God as a little child will never enter it" (Mark 10:15). Rather than competing for positions in the kingdom, he might have exhorted his followers, just receive it in simplicity and gratitude. Instead, at this point, Yeshua talks to the disciples not about receiving the kingdom, but about receiving or welcoming him (the Greek word is the same in both places). "Whoever welcomes one such child in my name welcomes me, and whoever welcomes me welcomes not me but the one who sent me" (Mark 9:37). Not only is your competitiveness totally inappropriate for the kingdom, Yeshua says, but you must reverse it and start welcoming others in. The kingdom isn't a zero-sum system that will run out of resources if too many enter; rather it's the place of boundless welcome. Even a little child, having nothing to bring with him and able to lay no claim on admission, is to receive the same welcome as the master himself.

Yochanan apparently grasps the implications of Yeshua's message because he asks, "Rabbi, we saw someone casting out demons in your name, and we tried to stop him, because he was not following us." In other words, "We assumed the kingdom was a zero-sum system, and if he uses your miraculous powers in an unauthorized way, it might diminish us somehow." But Yeshua replies, "Do not stop him; for no one who does a deed of power in my name will be able soon afterward to speak evil of me. Whoever is not against us is for us" (Mark 9:38–40).

3. On the Way to Jerusalem

Yeshua and his band are approaching the holy city a few days before the joyous festival of Passover. The master pulls aside the Twelve to tell them for a third and final time how the story will unfold there. "See, we are going up to Jerusalem, and the Son of Man will be handed over to the chief priests and the scribes, and they will condemn him to death; then they will hand him over to the Gentiles; they will mock him, and spit upon him, and flog him, and kill him; and after three days he will rise again" (Mark 10:33–34).

As at Caesarea Philippi and Capernaum, the disciples don't know how to respond. As we watch them struggle with this information, we can picture ourselves and the sort of responses we might come up with. The response of Ya'akov and Yochanan is to come forward and make a request of Yeshua, "Rabbi, we want you to do for us whatever we ask of you." Like Yeshua's previous warnings, his statement about betrayal and death stirs a response in the disciples, but it's a response that misses the mark. Yeshua answers with a question that he might be asking us as well, "What is it you want me to do for you?" Ya'akov and Yochanan are ready with their answer, "Grant us to sit, one at your right hand and one at your left, in your glory" (Mark 10:36–37). As we follow Yeshua and gain a sense of his power, what do we want him to do for us? Will we seek to jockey our closeness to him into a position of advantage for ourselves? Will we try to import our old ideas of status and recognition into the kingdom of God?

These questions confront devoted, religious folk in every generation, and Jewish tradition is critical of anyone who makes his religious practice a source of personal advantage.

> Rabbi Tzadok said, … "Don't use [the words of the Torah] as a crown to build yourself up, nor as an adze to dig with, as Hillel said, 'The one who would make use of the crown [of the Torah] will pass away.' Thus you may learn that whoever [improperly] uses the word of Torah takes one's own life from this world."[8]

In Jewish tradition, *Torah* stands for the whole way of life based on Scripture. Improper use of the Torah involves using it to make a living or to enhance our reputation. The relevance of this tradition was highlighted early in the 2008 presidential election, as columnist Charles Krauthammer described it:

> Mitt Romney declares, "Freedom and religion endure together, or perish alone." Barack Obama opens his speech at his South Carolina Oprah rally with "Giving all praise and honor to God. Look at the day that the Lord has made." Mike Huckabee explains his surge in the polls thus: "There's only one explanation for it, and it's not a human one. It's the same power that helped a little boy with two fish and five loaves feed a crowd of 5,000 people."[9]

Krauthammer is concerned about the political implications of this approach, but I'm looking at it from a spiritual perspective. We have to wonder if some candidates were using religion "as a crown to build [themselves] up" or hoping it would leverage them a place in the glory come November.

After Yeshua's first announcement of suffering, Peter responded, "This way is not for you and it is not for me." After Yeshua's second announcement, the disciples responded, "This way is okay for you, but it is not for us." Now, after the third announcement, the disciples say, "This way is okay for you, and it is okay for us—so do for us whatever we ask!" They are beginning to understand that Yeshua's sufferings lead to resurrection and the glory to come. They are willing to pay the price, or so they think. And they want their share. How will Yeshua respond to this more complete but still deficient understanding?

> Yeshua answered, "You don't know what you're asking! Can you drink the cup that I am drinking, or be immersed with the immersion that I must undergo?" They said to him, "We can." Yeshua replied, "The cup that I am drinking, you will drink; and the immersion I am being immersed with, you will undergo. But to sit on my right and on my left is not mine to give. Rather, it is for those for whom it has been prepared."
>
> When the other ten heard about this, they became outraged at Ya'akov and Yochanan. (Mark 10:38–41, CJB)

Not only Ya'akov and Yochanan, but also the other ten disciples, are ready to compete for the prime spots at Yeshua's right and left, for the symbols of status and success, when he enters his glory. But none of them have considered the deeper question that Yeshua raises.

What Is Success?

Ya'akov and Yochanan brush aside Yeshua's warning about the suffering to come and look ahead to the glorious resurrection to follow. They want to register their request for special status ahead of the others. They are ready to turn Torah into a spade with which to dig. Even more fundamentally, they haven't answered the question of what real status is. Does it mean attaining the places of honor on Yeshua's right and left—or something far different?

A few years ago I was driving along the Ventura Freeway in Southern California on my way to visit my parents. The famous Los Angeles traffic was racing bumper to bumper at seventy-five miles per hour when a brand-new pearly white Mercedes with a gold-plated grill whizzed past on my left. I caught a glimpse of its prestige plate, "GT A JB," which struck me after a moment as "Get a Job." Obviously, the driver considered himself a success, with a pearly white Mercedes to prove it, and wanted to assure all those bums that he was passing that they could be a success, too, if they just got a job like his. But, of course, he hadn't answered the more fundamental question: What is success? The consumerism that he had bought into provided a way to find affirmation, some outward sign that his life meant something and that he was headed toward a good destination. His Mercedes was a way to keep score in the game of life, and he was winning. Ya'akov and Yochanan were beyond such materialistic scorekeeping, but they still sought an outward sign of success—positions on the right hand and on the left.

We likewise want success, but if we haven't worked on answering the question, "What is success?" we will settle for a default success—whatever the dominant culture labels as a worthwhile goal. The guy on the freeway is obviously a success because he is in the pearly white Mercedes. No one questions that, unless we ask what success is, or perhaps a better question: Who is genuinely successful? If we are seeking to follow Yeshua, we have already determined that he is the true success. The messianic secret is that the traveling rabbi from the lowly town of Nazareth is the Chosen One of God. Yet throughout his whole ministry, Yeshua displays his status not by flashing by in a white Mercedes, but by walking quietly with his disciples, doing good to all those around him, and shunning publicity. Hence, Yeshua responds to his disciples' request for special status, the kind of visible celebrity that he has avoided, "You do not know what you are asking!"

The disciples are still thinking in terms of default success, which defined itself 2000 years ago as it does today:

1. By what we amass in a zero-sum system, rather than by what we contribute, by what we gain, not what we give. Ya'akov and Yochanan open with "*Give* us" (or "Do us a favor"), and the other disciples become outraged because it means less for them.

2. In terms of comparison and competition: "Give us the *best* positions." It's impossible to have authentic discipleship or true community when this notion of success prevails.

3. Outwardly, with visible symbols that keep track of our score in the game of life but have never been examined or adequately questioned.

It was in defense of such success that Peter had taken Yeshua aside and rebuked him for speaking about his suffering and death. In defense of true success based on divine reversal, Yeshua rebuked Peter and pressed on toward Jerusalem. Real success is measured not by what we gain, but by what we give, not in comparison with others, but in benefit to others, and not by outward symbols, but in response to God's inward call. "The cup that I am drinking, you will drink; and the immersion I am being immersed with, you will undergo. But to sit on my right and on my left is not mine to give. Rather, it is for those for whom it has been prepared." You may suffer like me, Yeshua is saying, but still the goal isn't for you to become exalted.

We buy into default success because we don't recognize the kind of success involved in following Yeshua. After Yeshua's third announcement of his coming death and resurrection and his disciples' third indication that they just don't get it, he expands a third time on the implications of following him. This is his definition of genuine success:

> "You know that among the Gentiles those whom they recognize as their rulers lord it over them, and their great ones are tyrants over them. But it is not so among you; but whoever wishes to become great among you must be your servant, and whoever wishes to be first among you must be slave of all. For the Son of Man came not to be served but to serve, and to give his life a ransom for many." (Mark 10:42–45)

Real success, real status in God's kingdom, comes as we devote ourselves to serving others. It's a simple enough assignment, yet one that cuts at the heart of our egotism and the egotistic culture that we have built up around ourselves. It's a radical teaching that Yeshua repeats continually throughout his ministry.

Note that Yeshua defines true success by speaking of leaders, of those on the top, who become models to the rest Leaders are considered by definition to be successful, so leaders have the opportunity to reverse the definition of success. In *The Millennium Matrix*, an analysis of today's cultural shift, author Rex Miller speaks of the challenges that leaders face as they seek to apply Yeshua's teaching of servanthood:

> Current leadership models taught in seminaries and business schools emphasize that leaders should lead to serve. Those who lead to serve, however, often bring with them the baggage of being a loner, a need for achievement and recognition, the instincts for competition, a tendency toward political maneuvering, the quest for power or control, the fear of losing that control, and the insecurity of not being able to live up to their advertising.[10]

In other words, the true success that Yeshua describes can never come to leaders or anyone else through mere technique that uses servant leadership as a slogan, or worse, as a new marker of spiritual status. Rather, true success results from seeking Yeshua instead of status, denying self, and giving up our own lives to find real life. Such success is worth the effort, for the person who attains it and for those whom he or she serves.

> Congregants in the emerging digital culture are hungry for leaders who are approachable, touchable, accessible, transparent, and real. They want to connect with someone who is unscripted, unrehearsed, and not "on." They want a real person who walks among them, not someone who periodically comes down from the mountain to deliver a prescription for life or platitudes of hype.[11]

This model of leadership applies to the rest of us as well. We aren't to distort servanthood into a new form of religiosity or self-righteousness, but to practice it as real people with real relationships.

A common Greek word in the original gospel manuscript can help us to apply this lesson—*thelo*, meaning "to want or desire." Following Yeshua doesn't mean eliminating all our desires, so that we become super-pious, but redirecting our desires.

• At Caesarea Philippi, Yeshua says, "Whoever *desires* to come after me, let him deny himself, take up his cross, and follow me. For whoever *desires* to save his life will lose it, but whoever loses his life for my sake and the gospel's, will save it" (Mark 8:34–35).

- At Capernaum he says, "If anyone *desires* to be first, he or she will be last of all and servant of all" (Mark 9:35).

- On the way to Jerusalem, Ya'akov and Yochanan say, "Rabbi, we *desire* that you would do for us whatever we request." Yeshua responds simply "What do you *desire* that I should do for you?" (Mark 10:35–36). Then he continues with his instruction: "Whoever *desires* to be great among you will be your servant, and whoever *desires* to be the foremost will be slave of all" (Mark 10:43–44).

Success is defined by our desire to achieve whatever results we have decided we want the most. We could state it more simply: Success is getting what you desire. This is the problem that Miller points out with the lead-to-serve model. If the desire for self-advancement and recognition hasn't changed, then this model is just a front as it was for Ya'akov and Yochanan. What they were really after wasn't Yeshua-like servanthood but the status to which such servanthood might paradoxically lead.

Success, like money, is neutral—neither good nor bad in itself—but used in good or bad ways. The real value of success depends on the value of the goal, or *desire*, by which we measure it. This is why Yeshua zeroes in on desire in the passages above—to help us redirect our natural desires, which serve default success, toward the pursuit of true success. The goal is not elimination of self, as in eastern religions, but redirecting of self with its desires into selfless service toward others empowered by Messiah.

Just as Yeshua concealed his true identity throughout much of his ministry, he often remains concealed today except to the eyes of faith.

> Today the Messiah is hidden. … We live in hope of the coming of the Son of Man in his glory. Jesus' teaching, his ultimate instructions to his disciples, are for this time, the time of absence, in which his disciples must watch and wait, and for which Christ gives them the wisdom needed.[12]

Of course, Messiah is present through his spirit, by which he gives "the wisdom needed" to his followers. Nevertheless, he will only reveal himself fully at his return, and the way of faithfulness to a hidden Messiah is different from what we might choose for ourselves. It is certainly different from the way pointed out by today's religious consumerism. Yeshua draws us into the same question the disciples asked when they saw his awesome power over nature, "Who can this be?" (Mark 4:41). If we answer this question too quickly and with too much self-assurance, we may get it wrong. Yeshua doesn't seek to hide that he is Messiah, but he challenges us with what kind of Messiah he will be.

Here are signs of someone who has resisted the success offered by our consumerist culture to pursue true success, and some questions we might ask ourselves to determine what sort of success we are after. A person pursuing true success:

- **Overcomes the comparison trap**. Have I unthinkingly joined the competition for recognition and approval, acting like I'm in a zero-sum game in which someone else's gain means loss for me?

- **Forsakes external trappings of success**. Am I still working for a symbol, like the pearly-white Mercedes, a title, or a position, rather than working for goals that matter from the perspective of Messiah?

- **Expects to serve**. Am I ready—and do I seek out opportunities—to humbly place myself at the disposal of others?

- **Maintains healthy and growing relationships**. Do I have a community into which I give and from which I receive? Real community provides the alternative to the comparison-driven pursuit of success.

- **Practices perseverance**. Do I have an unwavering sense of purpose and commitment? When I operate out of an inward connection with God by pursuing what Yeshua has deemed important, I will not be easily discouraged.

As his story unfolds, Mark portrays divine reversal in a remarkable way. Ya'akov and Yochanan ask for positions, one on Yeshua's right hand and one on his left (Mark 10:37), and Yeshua responds that the positions on his right and left are not his to give (Mark 10:40). The phrase "on his right and on his left" appears just one more time in Mark's account—at the scene of crucifixion: "And with him they crucified two bandits, one on his right and one on his left" (Mark 15:27). In God's kingdom the position of status is one of sacrifice and the position of suffering is one of glory.

The messianic secret is revealed: God is glorified through Yeshua's obedience in suffering and death. And its corollary: Those who are close to him must follow the way of obedience and sacrifice as well. When Yeshua speaks of greatness among the pagans, he says to his followers, "But it is not so among you." In this simple phrase, Yeshua captures the divine reversal that turns the status markers of this world on their heads. This phrase also raises the unavoidable question, "Is it so among us?" Have we as followers of Yeshua taken seriously his instruction to put ourselves last and others first?

TRIUMPHAL ENTRY
Matthew 21:1–11; 27:20–25

The Jews rejected Jesus. This sentence is often stated as axiomatic, an unquestionable fact of religious history. But in the gospel accounts, when Yeshua comes to Jerusalem for his final Passover, he is welcomed to the city by multitudes of Jews before he is finally rejected. How do we explain this mixture of rejection and acceptance? What does it mean for us today?

Imagine yourself a Jewish pilgrim to the holy city among that Passover crowd in the days when the Temple still stood. You have journeyed for many days, and today you walked with thousands of others up the long grade from Jericho. You are about to make the final ascent to the Temple, but you're resting a moment near the Eastern Gate that leads into the city when you hear a mounting noise amid all the excitement. The crowd approaching the gate is singing, shouting, and waving palm branches; it reminds you of the time you had visited another city and a great Roman general had returned there after a military triumph.

The general was in a gleaming chariot, but before you even caught sight of him, there was a phalanx of soldiers in bronze and purple with their spear tips shining in the sun and banners flapping in the breeze. Then came the sleek horses pulling the chariot and the crunch of its iron wheels as it carried the great leader toward the city gates. A few people in that crowd cheered, and others seemed afraid or resentful, but all were impressed by the show of power.

Now, from this approaching crowd of pilgrims, you hear cheering interspersed with verses from the psalms, "Hosanna to the Son of David: Blessed is he that comes in the name of the Lord; Hosanna in the highest." And then, as the crowd flows by, you glimpse a young-ish-looking Jew in a plain robe with his feet almost touching the ground, riding on a donkey and jarring a bit with every step. *This is the Son of David—the king?* At first it seems like a joke, like a mockery of a Roman triumph. But when the man on the donkey gets closer, you see his face with its nobility and light, and you know he isn't mocking. It seems as if God himself is saying, "This is your king!"

The Chosen King

By entering the city in royal procession just before Passover, Yeshua is declaring his triumph, even though it is not yet clear what this triumph may be—he is poor, simply dressed, unrecognized. Within a few days he will be handed over to the powers that seem obviously triumphant and will end his life in disgrace and torture. But Yeshua makes it clear that triumph is at hand, a triumph altogether different from Rome's.

By riding into Jerusalem on a young donkey, Jesus enacted his message: the kingdom of God of which he spoke was a kingdom of peace, not violence.

> The meaning of Jesus' mode of entry is amplified by the realization that two processions entered Jerusalem that Passover. The other procession was the imperial one. On or about the same day, the Roman governor Pontius Pilate rode into the city from the opposite side, from the west, at the head of a very different kind of procession: imperial cavalry and foot soldiers arriving to reinforce the garrison on the Temple Mount. They did so each year at Passover, coming to Jerusalem from Caesaraea Maritima, the city on the Mediterranean coast from which the Roman governor administered Judea and Samaria.[1]

Yeshua has timed his entry into Jerusalem to provide another picture of divine reversal, a contrast between God's kingdom and the pomp of Rome. Pilate comes from the west; Yeshua from the east, the direction of the sunrise, light, and new hopes. His entry is a sort of ancient street theater, portraying the "central conflict of Jesus' last week: the kingdom of God or the kingdom of imperial domination. ... What we call Palm Sunday featured a choice of two kingdoms, two visions of life on earth."[2]

If you were among the pilgrims watching this drama, you probably would not know that this unlikely man has already fulfilled many of the words of the Prophets in the circumstances of his birth and early life. You might not realize right now that he's fulfilling the words of Zechariah:

> Rejoice greatly, O daughter Zion! Shout aloud, O daughter Jerusalem! Lo, your king comes to you; triumphant and victorious is he, humble and riding on a donkey, on a colt, the foal of a donkey. (Zech. 9:9)

Unlike the prophecies of his birth and early days, this prophecy has taken some initiative from Yeshua. Its fulfillment wasn't something that happened to him but something that he did, a statement that he made.

On his way to the city Yeshua had sent two disciples to the nearby village of Bethphage, telling them that they would find a donkey and her foal tied there. They would provide the way for him to ride into Jerusalem and fulfill the words of Zechariah. The foal was a beast upon which no one had ever before ridden, an animal suitable for a holy purpose. Whether by pre-arrangement or divine providence, his followers found the donkey and led it away with the simple explanation that their master needed it and brought it to Yeshua. He sat upon it and joined the throng of pilgrims.[3] Yeshua seized the opportunity afforded by Passover and its travelers to fulfill prophecy and create a scene that portrayed the essence of his ministry.

The announcement of *this* King in *this* manner is a divine response to the uncertainties and disappointments of the day. It remains God's response to our troubled day. Yeshua was making clear not only that he is the promised King, but also what kind of king he was, in contrast with the dominant values of the day. How did the people respond? Matthew chronicles it:

> A very large *crowd* spread their cloaks on the road, and others cut branches from the trees and spread them on the road. The *crowds* that went ahead of him and that followed were shouting, "Hosanna to the Son of David! Blessed is the one who comes in the name of the Lord! Hosanna in the highest heaven!" When he entered Jerusalem, the whole city was in turmoil, asking, "Who is this?" The *crowds* were saying, "This is the prophet Yeshua from Nazareth in Galilee." (Matt. 21:8–11; emphasis added)

Matthew uses the word *crowd(s)* three times in this brief passage, and it appears again later. For now, the crowds greet Yeshua as Son of David and call him a prophet.

The Chosen Lamb

When Yeshua entered the city, it was the tenth day of Nisan (see chart below), four days before Passover and the very day on which Torah commanded every household to select a lamb and hold it until the eve of Passover when it was to be sacrificed.

> Tell the whole congregation of Israel that on the tenth of this month they are to take a lamb for each family, a lamb for each household. … Your lamb shall be without blemish, a year-old male; you may take it from

the sheep or from the goats. You shall keep it until the fourteenth day of this month; then the whole assembled congregation of Israel shall slaughter it at twilight. (Exod. 12:3, 5–6)

Chronology of the Passion Week

Nisan			Matthew
10	Sunday	Triumphal Entry	21:1–11
11	Monday	Cleansing of the Temple	21:12–17
12	Tuesday	The Examination of Yeshua	21:23–22:46
		Yeshua's Verdict on Jerusalem	23:37-39
13	Wednesday	In Bethany	26:6–16
14	Thursday	(Evening) Last Supper	26:17–30
15	Friday	Arrest and Crucifixion	26:31–27:61
16	Saturday	In the Tomb	27:62–66
17	Sunday	Resurrection	28:1–20

For four days the family may observe the lamb and perhaps even grow fond of it. When the time of sacrifice comes, it isn't an impersonal act but the slaughter of a particular lamb that they have come to know.

When Yeshua enters the city as the triumphant king on the tenth of Nisan, he demonstrates that he is also the Passover lamb. Indeed, his quality as the lamb of sacrifice shapes who he is as king. He will reign with the lamblike qualities of humility, nonviolence, and self-sacrifice and call his followers to those same qualities. Yeshua's triumphal entry on the tenth of Nisan is ethical instruction as well as street theater.

Like the Passover lamb, Yeshua dwells within the household of Jerusalem for four days. There he undergoes repeated questioning by religious experts, who can find no blemish in him. Yeshua initiates this examination immediately after his triumphal entry by driving the moneychangers out of the Temple courts (Matt. 21:12ff.). This is a revolutionary act, which reveals another side of the lamb, his zeal for God's kingdom. The emphasis quickly returns, however, to Yeshua as the Passover lamb being prepared for sacrifice. Immediately after Yeshua cleanses the Temple, he is protected from the religious authorities by his popularity with the crowds (Matt. 21:26, 46), but he must undergo in-depth examination from various sorts of authorities:

- "The whole city"—Matthew 21:10
- Chief priests and scribes— Matthew 21:15
- Chief priests and elders— Matthew 21:23
- Pharisees and Herodians— Matthew 22:15–16
- Sadducees— Matthew 22:23
- A lawyer of the Pharisees— Matthew 22:34

None of these examiners can find a blemish in Yeshua, but the chief authorities agree that he is dangerous, decide to arrest him, and turn him over to the Romans for execution. They're still concerned about the crowds, however, fearing that Yeshua's arrest might cause "a riot among the people" (Matt. 26:5). Even after four days of examinations, the crowd is still with Yeshua. But the word *crowd* reappears a bit later in the story with a very different feel to it:

> Now at the festival the governor was accustomed to release a prisoner for the *crowd*, anyone whom they wanted. ... Now the chief priests and the elders persuaded the *crowds* to ask for Barabbas and to have Jesus killed. The governor again said to them, "Which of the two do you want me to release for you?" And they said, "Barabbas." Pilate said to them, "Then what should I do with Yeshua who is called the Messiah?" All of them said, "Let him be crucified!" Then he asked, "Why, what evil has he done?" But they shouted all the more, "Let him be crucified!" So when Pilate saw that he could do nothing, but rather that a riot was beginning, he took some water and washed his hands before the *crowd*, saying, "I am innocent of this man's blood; see to it yourselves." Then the people as a whole answered, "His blood be on us and on our children!" (Matthew 27:15, 20–25; emphasis added)

The Outside Crowd and the Inside Crowd

I have heard it preached more than once that the very same crowd that cried out to Yeshua, "Hosanna to the Son of David!" cries out a few days later, "Crucify him!" The same people who met him at the gates of Jerusalem with palm branches and shouts of praise now call for him to be cast out and killed. Thus, a preacher can picture the fickleness of the crowds and underscore the "Jews rejected Jesus" theme. The preacher can even read the final line—"His blood be on us and on our children"—as a curse that has remained upon the Jewish people ever since.

A more careful reading, however, suggests that there are two different crowds. The crowd that called for Yeshua's crucifixion "is a different crowd from the one that had listened to Jesus with delight during the week and whom the authorities feared. We have no reason to think that those in *that* crowd had changed their minds. Rather, *this* 'crowd' (presumably a small group) had access to the courtyard of Pilate's residence (Herod's palace). The authorities didn't let just anybody in."[4]

The outside crowd gathered in obedience to the Torah, which commands every man of Israel to appear before the Lord at three festivals each year; Passover, *Shavuot*, and *Sukkot* (Exod. 23:17; 34:23; Deut. 16:16). By the first century, Jews were living throughout the Roman Empire and beyond and had grown far too numerous to all appear at once before the Lord. Still, at each festival, pilgrims flocked to Jerusalem. The city swelled to three or four times its normal population; Jewish travelers stayed in homes within and around Jerusalem or camped on the hillsides surrounding the city. Jewish tradition later came to say of Passover, "On that night we were redeemed, and on that night we shall be redeemed,"[5] and the atmosphere in Yeshua's time would have been filled with rejoicing, excitement, and expectation. The custom at the festivals was to recite the *Hallel* Psalms, 113–118, including the words the crowd cried out when Yeshua approached. This crowd is made up of pious Jews from every nation under heaven, as Luke calls them in Acts 2:5.

Matthew himself draws a contrast between this outside crowd and those inside the city: "When he entered Jerusalem [from outside], the whole city [the inside crowd] was in turmoil, asking, 'Who is this?' The [outside] crowds were saying, 'This is the prophet Yeshua from Nazareth in Galilee'" (Matt. 21:10–11). From those inside the city, the religious leaders enlist a crowd to appear before Pilate a few days later. Indeed, as we have seen, the authorities are afraid of upsetting the outside crowd by arresting Yeshua openly and, therefore, develop a plot to arrest him secretly, which they can only accomplish when Judas offers to betray his master (Matt. 26:3). The inside crowd must have been a much smaller group, able to fit into Pilate's courtyard.

I have occasionally heard a preacher or commentator criticize the outside crowd because they answer the question, "Who is this?" by saying Yeshua is "the prophet from Nazareth of Galilee," instead of saying that he is Messiah. But the crowd has already greeted him as the Son of David, a messianic title. They are at least moving in the right direction by calling Yeshua a prophet. Remember that at this time no prophet had arisen in Israel in four hundred years, with the possible exception of Yochanan the Immerser. *Prophet* is a title of great holiness and power that evoked the memory of Elijah, Isaiah, and Jeremiah. The outsiders are on to something. The insiders, on the other hand, think they already know what the Messiah should look like and what he should do when he comes, and Yeshua doesn't fit the bill. The outside crowd speaks words of welcome—"*Baruch ha-ba.*" The inside crowd speaks words of condemnation.

Pilgrims, by definition, are on a journey. The phrase *spiritual journey* has become popular and probably overused today, but it fits in this context. The phrase implies that one is still in process, still seeking more of God, and still open and alert. Gatekeepers—again by definition—have arrived. They think they're already where they need to be.

Those of us who have had a life-changing encounter with the living Messiah feel that we have been brought out of darkness and alienation from God into a place in his household. We have arrived in that sense, but we haven't really arrived until the coming of the kingdom of God of which Yeshua continually speaks. Messianic Jews in particular haven't arrived until the Jewish people and the Jewish Messiah are reunited in the culmination of God's plan. Indeed, all believers should be awaiting this arrival, "For if their casting Yeshua aside means reconciliation for the world, what will their accepting him mean? It will be life from the dead!" (Rom. 11:15, CJB). Until then, we remain on a journey, aware of our incompleteness and that of the world around us, and open to what God might bring next.

Outsiders	Insiders
Pilgrims	Gatekeepers
On a journey	Already arrived
Aware of the times	Bound up in preconceptions
Speak welcome	Speak condemnation

Gatekeepers, on the other hand, are preoccupied with their arrival and have forgotten the journey. If we act like we have arrived, have all of the answers, and are charged with guarding the gates of truth, we can never reach those outside. We become the very sort of religious types who made us uncomfortable not so long ago. One of the great pitfalls in the spiritual journey is to forget where we started out. We encounter God, we are rescued from our rebellion and sin, and we forget from where we came. We enter the kingdom of God, and then we're not so sure anyone else should be allowed in. We leave the outside crowd of pilgrims to become gatekeepers.

We must ask ourselves, to which crowd do we belong? Are we pilgrims or gatekeepers? When I moved to New Mexico in 1970, I was amazed at the vast expanses of undeveloped land, the mountain villages that had hardly changed in a hundred years, and the reality of living in a state almost as physically large as my native California with about one-twentieth the population. Now that I was in, I wanted them to close the border behind me, so that no more outsiders could come in and ruin the scene. Some believers are like that with the kingdom of God. They enter in amazement and relief at their rescue from sin and alienation—and soon want to shut the door behind them so that no more sinners can come in and ruin the environment.

Yeshua, of course, modeled the opposite. He's the ultimate insider, but he continually reaches out in welcome to the outside crowd. He knows the heart, struggles, questions, and fears of his people. Congregations often envision outreach as getting people to come into their services and events, but that's a partial vision. Yeshua met people, often rather undesirable people, where they were, with no demand that they enter some kind of religious setting. And even in the religious setting of Passover, as multitudes of Jews are gathering at the great Temple in Jerusalem to prepare for the festival, Yeshua presents himself to the outsiders in terms that they can understand and to which they respond with the words of welcome, "*Baruch ha-ba b'shem Adonai*" (see Chapter 12 for more detail).

The Great Irony

This story has profound implications for Jewish–Christian relations. History records a tragic turnaround in the generations after Yeshua's entry into Jerusalem, a reversal that is the opposite of divine reversal. The great irony is that within a generation or two, the Yeshua believers, who are outsiders in the Gospels, turn into insiders and gatekeepers, and the rest of the Jewish people, including the gatekeepers of Yeshua's day, become the outsiders.

Most readers are familiar with the Jewish revolt against Rome that ended in the destruction of the Temple in 70 C.E. A couple of generations later, the Jews again rose up against Rome, under a messianic figure called Bar Kochba, or "Son of the Star," in reference to Numbers 24:17—"a star shall come out of Jacob"—which many took as a messianic prophecy. The Jews were defeated again, even more catastrophically than the first time. A hundred years after Yeshua's entry, the city of Jerusalem was utterly destroyed by Rome and its Jewish population sent into exile. A few years later, a church father, Justin Martyr, imagines himself discussing this tragedy with a Jew named Trypho:

> For the circumcision according to the flesh, which is
> from Abraham, was given for a sign; that you may be
> separated from other nations, *and from us*; and that
> *you alone* may suffer that which you justly suffer, and
> that you may be desolate, and your cities burned with
> fire; and that strangers may eat your fruit in your pres-
> ence and not one of you may go up to Jerusalem ...
> Accordingly, *these things have happened to you in
> fairness and justice.*[6]

Represented by Justin Martyr, the follower of Yeshua is now the insider, the religious expert, speaking words of condemnation to the
Jewish outsider. According to the new insiders, whatever misfortune
might befall the Jews was well-deserved punishment for their alleged
corporate rejection of Messiah. Indeed, as time went on and Rome
became a Christian empire, it seemed only right to ensure that hard
times would follow the Jews because of their supposed unbelief. The
pattern inaugurated by Justin only intensified in the following centuries, so that the Jews became the ultimate outsiders in the emerging
Christian world.

Yeshua's Triumph

A key to understanding this tragic reversal is the word *triumphal.*
Following a long-standing tradition, I used it to describe Yeshua's
entry into Jerusalem. *Triumph* is originally a Latin word describing,
"the entrance of a victorious commander with his army and spoils in
solemn procession into Rome, permission for which was granted by
the senate in honor of an important achievement in war."[7] The same
historical dictionary that provides that definition mentions the
phrase "the church triumphant"—"the portion of the church which
has overcome the world and entered into glory." In the quote above,
Justin Martyr displays an attitude of *triumphalism,* a belief that the
"church triumphant" was already on the scene. This belief grew as
the band of Yeshua's followers was gradually transformed into the
institutional Church of late antiquity. Instead of embracing Yeshua's
reversed triumph, which stood the values of power and domination
on their head, the Church came to emulate the Roman triumph. So
Justin sides with Rome in its treatment of the Jewish people and is
quick to separate "us"—the professed followers of Yeshua—from
"them"—the defeated Jews.

Religious triumphalism arises when one group perceives itself as
victorious, as rightfully dominant over another. Yeshua reversed the
very notion of triumph when he rode into Jerusalem, recognized neither by Roman Senate nor Jewish priesthood, but only by a crowd of

cheering pilgrims. He thereby created a model for his followers in all generations, but the Church largely abandoned Yeshua's model to grasp for visible triumph. Because it perceived itself to have been persecuted by Jewish authorities, it felt justified in turning the tables on them, a self-justification that is already evident in Justin Martyr's words. But, of course, paying back rejection and persecution in kind is exactly what Yeshua tells us *not* to do.

Yeshua's appearance in Jerusalem speaks against all forms of vengeance. This is the ethical lesson of the triumphal entry. Yeshua presents himself as the King who is also the Lamb. The book of Revelation speaks of the wrath of the Lamb (Rev. 6:16), and of the Lamb's conquest of the enemies of God (Rev. 17:14), but these events are by definition *apocalyptic*, part of the unique one-time revelation of God's justice at the end of the age. In the meantime, the followers of the Lamb triumph over the adversary "by the blood of the Lamb and by the word of their testimony, for they did not cling to life even in the face of death" (Rev. 12:11). In divine reversal, the sacrificial death of Messiah proves more effective than the power and domination of the dragon. The followers of Messiah prevail through bearing active, costly testimony (the word in Greek is *martyria*) of his death. Like Messiah, they are ready to enact the opposite of triumph even to the point of relinquishing their own lives—which is the true triumph.

This picture provides the standard for victory for Yeshua's followers in all conditions, one by which we can assess ourselves. Are we willing to relinquish domination and outward success even when we might attain it? Do we insist that the spiritual community of which we are members does the same?

Author Garry Wills summarizes Yeshua's critique of religious triumphalism:

> What is the kind of religion Jesus opposed? Any religion that is proud of its virtue, like the boastful Pharisee [in Luke 18:10ff.]. Any that is self-righteous, quick to judge and condemn, ready to impose burdens rather than share or lift them. Any that exalts its own officers, proud of its trappings, building expensive monuments to itself. Any that neglects the poor and cultivates the rich, any that scorns outcasts and flatters the rulers of this world.[8]

This is a powerful portrayal of triumphalism that we can use to measure our own spiritual practice. Wills, however, concludes his description with a sentence that reveals a degree of triumphalism itself. "If that sounds like just about every form of religion we know, then we can see how far off from religion Jesus stood."[9] As we saw in Chapter 9, Wills sees Yeshua as "opposed to all formalisms in worship—ritual purifications, sacrifice, external prayer and fasting norms, the Sabbath and eating codes, priesthoods, the Temple, and the rules of Sadducees, Pharisees, and Scribes. He called authentic only the religion of the heart, the inner purity and union with the Father the he had achieved and was able to share with his followers ..."[10] Wills interprets Yeshua as criticizing religion itself, not Judaism per se, but he sees Judaism as superseded by the faith of Yeshua. For Wills, Judaism, at least in Yeshua's day, represented a religious barrier that stood against the true teachings of the Master. This view is close to the sort of anti-Judaism that has been all-too-common in Christendom. Furthermore, this "religion of the heart" that is the only authentic religion sounds a bit too twenty-first century, too compatible with the subjectivism and individualism of our day. Yeshua always returns to the text of Scripture and calls us to return there as well. He overturns false interpretations and false applications, but he does so to reveal not "the religion of the heart" but the heart of the divine text. As we saw when he cleansed the lepers, Yeshua continued to recognize the authority of the priests established in Torah. He kept the Passover in accord with Torah and largely followed Jewish tradition of his day (see Chapter 12 for more detail). He certainly debated with the "Sadducees, Pharisees, and Scribes" over their rules and interpretations, but did not reject the Torah upon which they based their interpretations, or reject them wholesale either.

This nuance is vital because the view of Yeshua as opposing all religion actually feeds into the very triumphalism that Wills would surely decry. If Yeshua rejects Judaism as a religion, it is easy for his followers to take a triumphal attitude toward the Jewish people, who have been shaped and preserved by that religion for millennia. How can the followers of the Jewish Messiah appoint themselves as religious gatekeepers and declare the Jewish people to be the outsiders?

Yeshua had seized the stage afforded by Passover and its throngs of pilgrims to announce himself as the true king of the Jews. But he is a marginal, paradoxical king—and remains so to this day. In this role he is particularly relevant to Jewish people, who despite our acceptance in modern America, remain outsiders. We have had enough of religious triumphalism, of religion as a means of establishing one party's superiority and oppressing and excluding others. We can embrace an outsider king like this.

In the end, Messiah bridges this outsider–insider gap altogether. At his final visit to Jerusalem, the crowd greeted Yeshua with, *"Baruch ha-ba bashem Adonai"* ("Blessed is the one who comes in the name of the Lord"), words of welcome in the Hebrew language even to this

day. A few days later, Yeshua said that these same words must someday arise from within the city walls.

> "Jerusalem, Jerusalem, the city that kills the prophets
> and stones those who are sent to it! How often have I
> desired to gather your children together as a hen gath-
> ers her brood under her wings, and you were not will-
> ing! See, your house is left to you, desolate. For I tell
> you, you will not see me again until you say, 'Blessed
> is the one who comes in the name of the Lord.'"
> (Matt. 23:37–39)

Even today hundreds and perhaps thousands of Jewish followers of
Yeshua dwelling within Jerusalem are speaking those words of welcome. They are joined by thousands of Jewish followers of Yeshua
around the world, who stand within Jewish community and tradition
to welcome him. And they are supported and strengthened by numerous friends in the Christian world, who join in welcoming Messiah
back to his people.

The Talmud records that Rabbi Joshua compared two verses concerning the coming of Messiah: "Behold, the Son of Man comes 'on
the clouds of heaven' (Dan. 7:13) and 'lowly and riding on an ass'
(Zech. 9:9). If they are worthy 'with the clouds of heaven'; if they are
not worthy, 'lowly and riding on an ass.'"[11] I will take the liberty to
modify the rabbi's comment: If we receive the king who is "lowly and
riding on an ass" in a worthy manner, reflecting the values of his kingdom, then we will be worthy to see him come "with the clouds of
heaven."

CHAPTER
12
THE LAST PASSOVER
Luke 22:7–30

Leonardo Da Vinci's painting of the Last Supper is an artistic masterpiece, but its biblical and historical credentials are less clear. First, how did those fluffy Italian loaves get on the table during the Feast of Unleavened Bread? And what about that table? Jewish tradition in Yeshua's day decreed reclining at Passover, lying on floor cushions around a low table, not sitting upright in chairs. Finally, why is it that the only guest in Leonardo's painting who looks really Jewish is Judas?

The Last Supper, of course, was also the last Passover—a Jewish holiday—that Yeshua spent with his disciples. From this perspective, we see more clearly why the Master did what he did on this occasion, and what he was teaching us through it. In particular, we see that the last Passover is another expression of divine reversal, one that is to continue in the life of the community brought together by Messiah.

At Messiah's Table

As Yeshua's story progresses, he travels inexorably toward Jerusalem. It becomes clear that he intends to be there for Passover, one of the three festivals on which the Torah ordains that every Jew must gather at the place where the Lord is worshiped (Exod. 23:14–17; Deut. 16:16). Early in Luke's account, Yeshua had hinted at another reason for his journey to Jerusalem: "Yet today, tomorrow, and the next day I must be on my way, because it is impossible for a prophet to be killed outside of Jerusalem" (Luke 13:33).

Finally, a few days before the festival, Yeshua arrives at the holy city, although he spends his nights in a nearby village on the Mount of Olives. When the time comes, Yeshua sends Peter and John into the city to prepare the Passover meal. He tells them that they will encounter a man carrying a pitcher of water who will lead them to a guest room prepared for the feast (Luke 22:7–12). That evening, Yeshua reclines there with his disciples, and says, "I have eagerly desired to eat this Passover with you before I suffer; for I tell you, I will not eat it until it is fulfilled in the kingdom of God" (Luke 22:15–16).

163

Yeshua eagerly desires to share Passover with his followers because Passover is a time of great rejoicing, termed in Jewish tradition *z'man cherutenu,* "the season of our redemption." This term raises some questions for us: What is redemption? How do we obtain it? What do we do with it? The first two questions can be handled as abstract theology, and have occupied the Christian mind since the earliest days. The last question is more of a Jewish question, the sort of ethical question that underlies this entire book. What does Passover teach us about how to live as redeemed people? Yeshua's last Passover meal is the basis of what became known in Christianity as *communion,* or the *Eucharist.* Christians famously have debated the nature of communion for centuries. What exactly happens? Do the bread and wine actually become the body and blood of Messiah anew? Yeshua, on the other hand, as soon as he institutes this memorial meal, turns to a discussion of its lessons for how to live. He doesn't dwell so much upon the nature of the meal as he does on its ethical implications.

The Jewish celebration of Passover is based on the *haggadah,* a collection of songs, prayers, and Scripture readings that recount the story of the Exodus at a festive meal around the family table. Elements of the haggadah, and the Passover meal called the *seder,* which it frames, go back to the time of Yeshua.

At the original Passover, God lifted the Jewish people out of slavery and helplessness in Egypt and brought us into an intimate relationship with himself. But Passover is not just about this past deliverance; it is also about the present and the future. It's not only a past and national event, but also an immediate and personal event. The haggadah says:

> In every generation it is one's duty to regard himself as though he personally had gone out from Egypt, as it written (Exod. 13.8): "It was because of this that [the Lord] did for 'me' when I went out of Egypt." It was not only our fathers whom the Holy One redeemed from slavery; we, too, were redeemed with them, as it is written (Deut. 6:23): "He brought 'us' out from there so that He might take us to the land which He had promised to our fathers."[1]

At the time of the last Passover, Yeshua and his Jewish people were living under Roman occupation. As in the days of Pharaoh, the state was laying claim to the lives, and often the bodies, of God's chosen people—but they still considered themselves as redeemed and celebrated their redemption each year. The Roman occupiers had a custom of reclining around low tables at their feasts, and the Jews decided that this was the way they would celebrate Passover, to signify that they were free, indeed freer than their occupiers. Jewish men, women, and even children reclined around the table to declare that they belonged to the Lord alone and were free people, despite the designs of any government.

As a good Jew, Yeshua looked forward to Passover each year as a time to relive and celebrate this redemption—not just as a past, but also as a present reality. But there is more: Passover is also the season in which the Jewish people look ahead to redemption still to come. As we have seen, Jewish tradition says that on this night we were redeemed and on this night we shall be redeemed. The Passover seder reflects this twofold view of redemption, as one modern rabbi writes, "[T]he Haggadah is divided into two parts; the first half, which is concerned with the redemption from [Egypt], and the second half, which centers around our hope for the ultimate redemption."[2]

When Yeshua says of the Passover feast, "I will not eat it until it is fulfilled in the kingdom of God" (Luke 22:16), he is looking ahead to this Passover to come, the future season of our redemption. *Fulfilled* is a key word in this sentence and often misunderstood. As we have seen, Christian commentators sometimes think of the word as completing or bringing to an end. So when they read that Messiah fulfills the Torah, they think that he brings it to an end. But the word in Greek is *plero'o*, which comes from a word meaning "full." It means to fill up, to abound, or to be "given its full meaning" as David Stern translates this verse in the *Complete Jewish Bible*. Thus, later on in the Passover meal, Yeshua distributes the cup among his disciples and says, "I tell you, I will never again drink of this fruit of the vine until that day when I drink it new with you in my Father's kingdom" (Matt. 26:29). There is a past and present Passover, and also a Passover to come, which will be celebrated in the kingdom of God. Every Passover, in Yeshua's time as well as our own, looks forward to this fulfilled Passover. On that night we were redeemed and on that night we shall be redeemed.

In his opening words, Yeshua also hints at something that he will soon make clear, perhaps all too clear, to his disciples, "I have eagerly desired to eat this Passover with you before I *suffer*." The future Passover is somehow linked to his suffering, which will take place at this present Passover.

In light of Passover's hope and immediacy and the nearness of his suffering and death, we can understand why Yeshua is eager to eat this Passover with his disciples. Nevertheless, there is still something unusual here. Normally Passover is shared within the family—young and old, male and female—with one lamb per household as the Scripture decrees (Exod. 12:3, 46). But Yeshua eats the Passover with his disciples, apparently without their families present at all. He has

formed a new household, brought together not by birth and proximi-
ty, but through connection with him. Yeshua is going to demonstrate
through the seder that in this household there is no division or need
because Yeshua himself supplies it. Ultimately, this household will
not be confined to this one room or gathered around this one table,
but will be open to all.

Passover is the festival of redemption, and in the simple act of
reclining for Passover with his followers, Yeshua pictures one essential meaning of redemption: inclusion in the household of God. Each
person is to celebrate Passover as if he personally has gone forth
from Egypt, but the meal celebrates far more than just individual redemption, as vital as that is. Redemption entails a transfer into the
household of God. Under Rome, as in Egypt, Israel was God's son
(Exod. 4:23), but was serving Pharaoh. God brought Israel out of
Pharaoh's household and back into his own household to serve him
alone. This was redemption. Centuries later, Rav Sha'ul writes to believers in Yeshua, "He has rescued us from the power of darkness and
transferred us into the kingdom of his beloved Son, in whom we have
redemption, the forgiveness of sins" (Col. 1:13–14). Redemption is
the rescue from one domain and inclusion in another, the domain of
Messiah. It entails forgiveness of sins because only as forgiven people
can we enter God's household.

Simply by gathering his followers around himself to recline in
freedom at the Passover table, Yeshua is picturing this redemption,
but he goes much further as he continues through the seder.

> Then he took a cup, and after giving thanks he said,
> "Take this and divide it among yourselves; for I tell
> you that from now on I will not drink of the fruit of the
> vine until the kingdom of God comes." (Luke
> 22:17–18)

This is the normal beginning of the seder. Jewish tradition mandates
four cups, a tradition going back to earliest times, which Yeshua appears to have followed.[3] In Jewish thinking, the cup of wine symbolizes joy. Each week, the Sabbath meal is inaugurated with a blessing
over the cup, "Blessed are you, O Lord our God, king of the universe,
creator of the fruit of the vine." The Passover meal, because of the
great joy of the season of redemption, includes four cups, each with
a distinct function and name. The first is called the Cup of
Sanctification, or the Cup of Holiness, for it sets apart Passover and
the festive meal from the ordinary days and meals of the week.
Over this cup Yeshua recites the blessing before passing it to his disciples. As he does, he again hints at his departure and links it to the

redemption to come: "I will not drink of the fruit of the vine until the kingdom of God comes."

The Bread of Affliction

After he passes the cup to his disciples, Yeshua moves ahead through the seder to reveal a mystery about the promised redemption:

> Then he took a loaf of bread, and when he had given thanks, he broke it and gave it to them, saying, "This is my body, which is given for you. Do this in remembrance of me." (Luke 22:19)

The "loaf of bread," of course, is the matzah, the distinctive flat, unadorned, and unleavened bread of Passover. David Stern translates this verse:

> Also, taking a piece of *matzah*, he made the *b'rakhah* [the traditional blessing], broke it, gave it to them and said, "This is my body, which is being given for you; do this in memory of me." (Luke 22:19, CJB)

Matzah is called the bread of affliction in the Torah (Deut. 16:3), a reminder that we had to flee from Egypt in haste before our dough had time to rise. When we taste the matzah each year, we relive the story of divine rescue. Centuries after Yeshua's time, Jewish tradition added a reading to the haggadah based on this verse in Deuteronomy. Before the father recites the blessing over the matzah and breaks it, he lifts it up and says:

> This is the bread of affliction that our fathers ate in the land of Egypt. Whoever is hungry—let him come and eat! Whoever is needy—let him come and celebrate Passover! Now, we are here; next year may we be in the Land of Israel! Now, we are slaves; next year may we be free men![4]

At the heart of the festival is radical welcome, especially to those most vulnerable. Passover is personal and immediate—"In every generation one must see oneself as if he had personally gone forth from Egypt"—but it is also communal, the festival of redemption for all Israel and ultimately for all humanity. As we celebrate our freedom, we cannot ignore those who are still bound by hunger and need.

This reading had not yet become part of the seder in Yeshua's day, but it was already the custom for him as leader to take the matzah, make the blessing, break it, and distribute it to all those at the table. Then Yeshua said something altogether new, something hinted at by Scripture and the Jewish tradition based upon it, but unheard of at

that time. He said of the Passover bread, "This is my body, which is
given for you." Thus, Yeshua revealed himself at the center of the
whole story. It is Yeshua who offers himself in sacrifice as the way
into the household. We are not born into it or included through some
legal transaction or religious ceremony; rather we become part of
the household of God because we share in the life of the Son of God.
Redemption is inclusion in the household of God with a place guar-
anteed by the blood, the very life, of Messiah himself. Yeshua under-
scores this reality with the next part of the Passover meal: "He did the
same with the cup after supper, saying, 'This cup that is poured out
for you is the new covenant in my blood'" (Luke 22:20).

A New Covenant

The matzah symbolizes the whole festival. When Yeshua says, "This is
my body," he is signifying that he himself is the Passover. The red
wine is a reminder of the blood of the Passover lamb, which pur-
chased our redemption from Egypt. God provided this redemption
because he had made a covenant with Israel's ancestors, a solemn
pact that constitutes and guarantees a familial relationship between
two parties.

Exodus opens with the early years of Moses, including his premature attempt to liberate the Israelites. He kills an Egyptian slave driver, incurs the wrath of Pharaoh, and must flee Egypt. Forty long years
pass until finally Pharaoh dies, and "the Israelites groaned under their
slavery, and cried out. Out of the slavery their cry for help rose up to
God. God heard their groaning, and God *remembered his covenant*
with Abraham, Isaac, and Jacob. God looked upon the Israelites, and
God took notice of them" (Exod. 2:23–25). Because of his covenant
with Israel's ancestors, God calls their descendants collectively "my
son" (Exod. 4:23), and is compelled to act on their behalf. Later, God
renews and expands this covenant with all the Israelites at Mount
Sinai and commands them to keep it for all generations. When the
Israelites accept the covenant and commit themselves to it, Moses
seals it with blood, saying, "See the blood of the covenant that the LORD
has made with you in accordance with all these words" (Exod. 24:8).

The covenant at Sinai answers the question we raised earlier:
What do we do with our redemption? Israel is set free from service to
Pharaoh to enter service to Adonai. The original Hebrew text of the
Torah uses the same word to describe service, or bondage, to Pharaoh
and service, or worship, to the Lord. Israel is not set free just to be
free, but to become God's instruments and representatives. "Now
therefore, if you obey my voice and keep my covenant, you shall be
my treasured possession out of all the peoples. Indeed, the whole
earth is mine, but you shall be for me a priestly kingdom and a holy

nation" (Exod. 19:5–6). Only now at Mount Sinai is the exodus from Egypt complete, for here God makes Israel into a kingdom of priests, a nation serving him on behalf of all the nations.

The ceremony at Mount Sinai is like a wedding, signifying that God and his people are bound together in unbreakable union. The instructions of Torah guide this union. If Israel keeps these instructions, they are able to serve as priests for all the nations, but even if the people wander from Torah, God remembers the covenant, just as he did when they were still in bondage. Centuries after the Sinai covenant was made, the prophet Jeremiah speaks of a renewal of this covenant, or a new covenant to be made with Israel:

> It will not be like the covenant that I made with their ancestors when I took them by the hand to bring them out of the land of Egypt—a covenant that they broke, though I was their husband, says the LORD. But this is the covenant that I will make with the house of Israel after those days, says the LORD: I will put my law within them, and I will write it on their hearts; and I will be their God, and they shall be my people. (Jer. 31:32–33)

Centuries later, when Yeshua speaks of a new covenant, he is surely citing the words of Jeremiah. Just as the covenant at Mount Sinai was ratified with blood, so will this covenant be—but with a stunning difference. Yeshua points to the cup that he is about to pass among his disciples and says that this is the blood of the covenant. In this new covenant the disciples partake of the very life of Messiah. They are included in the household of God by sharing in the life of the Son of God himself. Thus, as Jeremiah foretold, the Lord puts his Torah within them and writes it on their hearts, and they indeed are his people. As he celebrates his last Passover, Yeshua reveals that the way of redemption into the household of God is through his own body and blood.

Yeshua as the Passover lamb brings us into covenant with God. Covenant has rules and regulations, but at its heart is really about two parties becoming one—a family. One of the only types of covenant that remains in our lawless society is marriage, and even that seems threatened by extinction. Through covenant, Israel is married to God. He rescues us from Egypt by marrying us, binding us to himself, and carrying us out. Now Yeshua retells the Passover story to offer that marriage to all humankind through his own blood.

At the original Passover, God redeemed Israel from bondage by his own power; we were helpless to redeem ourselves. In this day of advanced technology and material abundance, we are still helpless to save ourselves and in need of God's rescue. God rescues us by providing a sacrifice, the Passover lamb. Every house in Egypt that was marked by the blood of the lamb was spared the death of the firstborn. Those within the house that was marked by the blood of the sacrificed lamb were led forth out of Egypt and into the service of God. It is the lamb provided by God that brings redemption.

Yeshua speaks of a new, expanded redemption that he brings to those who are helpless to save themselves and in need of God's rescue. But we have to recognize that we need to be rescued and that "those who are helpless" describes the whole human race, including us. We need to end our state of denial, which says that we're doing just fine, even if we need a little tweaking. Then we have to partake of the bread and cup, the very life of Yeshua. Thus, we enter into covenant with him. Redemption, which is central to the whole biblical story, is not just a repair or reformation of our former state; rather it involves new life, a beginning that only God can bring.

The Reason behind Redemption

At his last Passover, Yeshua enacts the meaning of redemption in a way that continues to guide and challenge those who follow him today. Scripture reveals much more about redemption in its pages, but the last Passover is particularly relevant to our discussion of divine reversal. It teaches us that:

- Redemption is inclusion in the household of God. This defines the *what* of redemption.
- Redemption is accomplished and sealed through the death of Messiah—the *how* and the *who* of redemption.
- Redemption is continually expanding the household of God to welcome those outside—the *why*, or *what for*, of redemption.

Yeshua doesn't redeem us from bondage to do our own thing or create a new religious elite that looks down upon the unredeemed masses; he redeems us from bondage to become bound to him and share in his work of expanding the household of God. If we claim to partake of Messiah's Passover, are we saying, "All who are hungry, let them come and eat. All who are needy, let them come and celebrate Passover with us"?

I am tempted to conclude this chapter with that question, because it is a great example of divine reversal. At Passover those who are outside and hungry are brought into God's household and fed abundantly upon his provisions. The story of the last Passover, however, doesn't end there. Instead, it goes on to challenge us further to follow Yeshua's example.

When Yeshua spoke of the blood of the covenant, he implied that it was his own blood. But for blood to be shed there must be a death, and immediately Yeshua goes on to describe how this death will come to pass. "But see, the one who betrays me is with me, and his hand is on the table" (Luke 22:21). The disciples begin to ask each other who among them could possibly do such a deed, and this quickly becomes an argument "as to which one of them was to be regarded as the greatest" (Luke 22:24).

Imagine this. Yeshua has just invited his closest followers to the table of redemption, which is to be supplied without limit from his own body and blood, and they start arguing about who among them is the greatest! In John's account of the same meal, the disciples are reclining around the table, ready for the Passover feast but without anyone to serve. Yeshua himself rises up from the head of the table and takes on the most menial of tasks, washing the disciples' feet from the dust and grime of the street. He tells them:

> "So if I, your Lord and Rabbi, have washed your feet, you also ought to wash one another's feet. For I have set you an example, that you also should do as I have done to you. Very truly, I tell you, servants are not greater than their master, nor are messengers greater than the one who sent them. If you know these things, you are blessed if you do them." (John 13:14–17)

We might imagine that God rescued us from Egypt to set us free to do our own thing, but in reality God delivered us from serving Pharaoh so that we would serve him. On this night of Passover, Yeshua is showing his followers what serving him looks like. Foot washing isn't a religious ceremony but an ordinary task that needs to get done. We can imagine the disciples gathered around the table, ready to eat, nervously eyeing each other, and wondering whom will be assigned the task of serving. Yeshua takes on the task willingly, but the disciples don't quite get the message. At the end of the meal, they are not just wondering about status, but arguing about it openly. So Yeshua again teaches them about genuine greatness, "The kings of the Gentiles lord it over them; and those in authority over them are called benefactors. *But not so with you*; rather the greatest among you must become like the youngest, and the leader like one who serves" (Luke 22:25–26; emphasis added).

Can we say it is not so with *us*? We have heard this message of servanthood numerous times already, and it lies at the heart of divine reversal. Have we begun to take it seriously enough to change the way we live day by day?

Sacred Community

The message of servanthood has particular impact in the context of
Passover, when we consider our God-purchased freedom and how to
use it. For those of us who live in America or other nations of the
developed West, this is anything but a theoretical question. We have
been given a level of political and social freedom that is unheard of in
most times and places of human history. What are we doing with this
freedom? It's obvious that much of it goes to choosing what to buy,
which mode of entertainment to enjoy, and how to spend our time in
the most convenient, stimulating, and trouble-free way. The political
freedom that has been won at such a great price in the western de-
mocracies seems to be unappreciated and misused by those who pos-
sess it today.

In the religious world, the situation doesn't look any better. We
use our freedom to choose which church or synagogue to try out
next, which one offers the most abundant programs at the lowest
cost. We have been redeemed from our sins, perhaps, but not from
our self-absorption. One contemporary rabbi contrasts what he calls
sacred community with the market community, the consumerist culture, so dominant in our times. He writes:

> The everyday is what we use as means to ends. The
> sacred exists as its own end. … Sacred community…
> is devoted to certain tasks, but these can be realized
> only in a sacred ambience, not in a market community
> where people weigh value by the list of limited liability
> deliverables that they think their dues are buying.[5]

Much good may proceed from a sacred community, but it isn't consti-
tuted just to get a job done; rather congregations represent community for its own sake. Thus, our congregations aren't means to an
end—a collection of programs, projects, and benefits—but gatherings of individuals in a shared calling. Once a member begins to ask,
"What's in it for me?" he or she has left sacred community and returned to consumerism.

The rabbi continues, "The synagogue is a place for pursuing
Torah, worshiping God, sacralizing relationships, healing the sick,
and feeding the poor. It is a place where we know the presence of
God among us and honor each other as made in God's image."[6] This
rabbi isn't a believer in Yeshua, but his vision of community is re-
markably close to what Yeshua pictures at the Passover table. I
would only add two points: First, that creating such a community
ultimately requires redeemed people, those who are freed by the
power of Messiah from the selfishness, greed, and competitiveness
that destroy community. Second, that Yeshua defines *sacralizing*

relationships as "serving one another." Sacralizing relationships means recognizing the holy image of God in others and treating them accordingly. Yeshua teaches that this recognition leads us to forsake competition and status seeking and serve one another. Self-giving service makes our relationships holy and transforms our gatherings into sacred communities.

Yeshua frees us from bondage to transform us into servants of God. We freely give this service to him, primarily through renouncing the competition for status, which dominates every culture, and becoming servants to others: "The greatest among you must become like the youngest, and the leader like one who serves." This atmosphere of service sustains the community created through Yeshua's sacrifice and modeled at his last Passover. We must recognize, however, how deeply the competition for status has penetrated our souls and the ways that we treat each other. Without thinking, we import this competition into our religious world, thereby creating religious hierarchies in place of spiritual community.

The New Testament deals repeatedly with this problem. In Rav Sha'ul's first letter to the Yeshua believers in Corinth, for example, we get the impression that Messiah's remembrance meal was enacted as prelude to a larger meal shared by the community. To this day in the Jewish world we inaugurate the meal on Shabbat or other festive occasions with *Kiddush*, meaning "holiness" or "setting apart" of the special dinner. Kiddush in its simplest form is a prayer of blessing to God for creating the fruit of the vine and bringing forth bread from the earth. The father, or other leader, recites the blessings, all those around the table respond with amen to share in the blessings, and then all partake of the bread and cup, signifying their participation in community brought together by the Lord. Usually a meal follows the breaking of bread, a meal that has been made holy through the Kiddush. Sha'ul's exhortation to the Corinthians seems to picture a similar practice:

> When you come together, it is not really to eat the Lord's supper. For when the time comes to eat, each of you goes ahead with your own supper, and one goes hungry and another becomes drunk. What! Do you not have homes to eat and drink in? Or do you show contempt for the community of God and humiliate those who have nothing?
>
> For I received from the Lord what I also handed on to you, that the Lord Yeshua on the night when he was betrayed took the matzah, and when he had given

> thanks, he broke it and said, "This is my body that is for
> you. Do this in remembrance of me." (1 Cor. 11:20–24)

Notice that the remembrance of the Lord's supper was not confined
to a symbolic wafer and a sip of wine, but was shared in the context
of a meal. "The implication is that the Lord's Supper is eaten in conjunction with a communal meal. ... [Paul's] point is that in eating
what is supposed to be a meal consecrated to the Lord, some by their
actions are actually eating their own private meals."[7]

The believers in Corinth opened the meal with the remembrance
of Yeshua's sacrifice and then ate the rest of the meal in their cliques,
even to the point of dividing between the haves and the have-nots.
Some overindulged, and some went home hungry and humiliated.
This was pretty outrageous behavior, but Sha'ul's indictment reached
beyond Corinth and even beyond the tradition of the Lord's supper
itself to the whole matter of following Yeshua, "When you come together, it is not really to eat the Lord's supper." We can go through the
motions that recall Yeshua's last Passover, but it cannot be the Lord's
supper if it distorts the meaning of his Passover redemption. We are
redeemed from the bondage of sin, competition, and status seeking
and brought into the household of God, where there is unlimited acceptance for all. We are set free from Pharaoh's enslavement to serve
the living God through serving one another, not by infecting the sacred community with the social distinctions and tensions of Egypt. If
we miss this point when we come together, we cannot really eat the
Lord's supper at all.

Those in spiritual leadership must be particularly watchful in this
matter. We tend to categorize newcomers to our community in terms
of their potential contribution to the cause, whether financially, so-
cially, or physically. We tend to become more excited when a well-
groomed couple with one or two well-behaved children shows up
some morning than when a lone street person comes through the
door. We need to remember the warning of Ya'akov, the leader of the
early Jerusalem congregation:

> My brothers, practice the faith of our Lord Yeshua,
> the glorious Messiah, without showing favoritism.
> Suppose a man comes into your synagogue wearing
> gold rings and fancy clothes, and also a poor man
> comes in dressed in rags. If you show more respect
> to the man wearing the fancy clothes and say to him,
> "Have this good seat here," while to the poor man
> you say, "You, stand over there," or, "Sit down on the
> floor by my feet," then aren't you creating distinc-
> tions among yourselves, and haven't you made

yourselves into judges with evil motives? Listen, my
dear brothers, hasn't God chosen the poor of the
world to be rich in faith and to receive the Kingdom
which he promised to those who love him? But you
despise the poor! (James 2:1–6a, CJB)

In Messiah's Passover the door of welcome is open to all. We recline
like royalty and feast before the Lord, and we open the royal feast to
the hungry, poor, and enslaved. This is not a one-time event, or even
an annual event, but the abiding quality of our community. But this
is only part of the picture. Indeed, framing the discussion in terms
of how we welcome those who come through our doors serves to
highlight our problem. As long as we think of the congregation primarily as a place where people come or a service that people attend,
we're missing the full impact of Yeshua's message. Congregation
isn't just a location, service, or offering of programs, but sacred
community. Yeshua shapes the sacred community as outgoing, dynamic, and expanding. Our spiritual communities today are to be
agents of divine reversal. Instead of competing for consumer loyalty
with all of the institutions, events, and entertainment offerings that
crowd upon us, our congregations are to actively gather people into
a wholly different realm, supplied without measure from Messiah's
table. Our willingness to draw upon that supply instead of society's
offerings, and to open it to others, is the test of true community.

THE ULTIMATE REVERSAL

The crucifixion and resurrection of Messiah are the ultimate divine reversal.

Yeshua hinted at this reversal when he said, "And I, when I am lifted up from the earth, will draw all people to myself" (John 12:32). Contemporary Christians often speak of lifting up Yeshua in the sense of giving him praise and honor, which then draws people to accept him. I remember a chorus that says:

> Lift Jesus higher, lift Jesus higher.
> Lift him up for the world to see.
> He said if I be lifted up from the earth.
> I will draw all men unto me.

If we read the phrase *lifted up* in context, however, this song might sound odd, or even sinister, for "He said this to indicate the kind of death he was to die" (John 12:33). Yeshua indeed is lifted up—on to a Roman cross! And yet the misuse of the phrase in the pop Christian world isn't entirely misguided. Yeshua is basing his "lifted up" terminology on Isaiah 52:13. "See, my servant shall prosper; he shall be exalted and *lifted up*, and shall be very high." With these words Isaiah introduces his famous chapter 53, which speaks of the Suffering Servant and has been recognized as a messianic text from the earliest centuries by Jews as well as Christians.[1] John makes the connection with Isaiah 53 explicit a few verses down: "Although he had performed so many signs in their presence, they did not believe in him. This was to fulfill the word spoken by the prophet Isaiah: 'Lord, who has believed our message, and to whom has the arm of the Lord been revealed?'" (John 12:37–38, referencing Isa. 53:1). Yeshua's death, which appears shameful and tragic to men and women, is a sign of his exaltation before God.

The *lifted up* wording appears three times in John's Gospel to refer to the crucifixion: John 12:32–33, which I quoted above; John 3:14–15, "And just as Moses lifted up the serpent in the wilderness, so must the Son of Man be lifted up, that whoever believes in him may have eternal life;" and John 8:28, "When you have lifted up the Son of Man, then you will realize that I am he … "

> [This phrase] refers both literally to the crucifixion as a lifting up of Jesus above the earth and figuratively to the same event as Jesus' elevation to the status of divine sovereignty over the cosmos. The cross is already his exaltation. … The literal elevation, which Jesus' executioners intended as humiliation, an exhibition of his disgrace for all to see, John's readers see … as the event in which Jesus' divine identity is manifested for all to see, thereby drawing all people to himself.[2]

In the crucifixion, Yeshua is lifted up to reveal God—the God of self-sacrificing love. God, acting in Yeshua, gains victory over the religious–political powers of this world not through force and domination, but through the divine reversal of apparent weakness and defeat, which is really power and victory.

Mark also highlights the divine reversal of the cross and its implications for those who would follow Yeshua. As we saw in the Prologue, Mark opens his Gospel with the words, "The beginning of the good news of Yeshua the Messiah, the Son of God." Some ancient manuscripts, and, therefore, some English translations, exclude *Son of God* here, but "There is good presumptive reason for judging that 'Son of God' in Ch. 1:1 is an integral part of the text since Mark's [opening line] affords an indication of the general plan of his work. …"[3] In other words, the phrase *Son of God* sets up a theme that will run throughout Mark. We can follow this theme through a series of statements about Yeshua as Son of God that reach their climax at the cross.

Soon after Mark's opening line, Yeshua is immersed in the Jordan and a voice speaks to him from heaven, saying, "You are my Son, the Beloved; with you I am well pleased" (Mark 1:11). God gives testimony to Yeshua as his own Son, but the men and women in Mark's account do not seem to grasp it. Ironically though, the demons understand who Yeshua is (Mark 3:11; 5:7). Later, at the turning point of the whole story, Yeshua appears before his disciples in dazzling white with Moses and Elijah at his side. The disciples still don't seem to realize who Yeshua is, and so Peter makes the helpful suggestion, "Rabbi, it is good for us to be here; let us make three dwellings, one for you, one for Moses, and one for Elijah." God responds by echoing the words he spoke from heaven at the beginning, "This is my Son, the Beloved; listen to him!" (Mark 9:2–7).

As we saw in Chapter 10 on the messianic secret, the question "Who is Yeshua?" underlies Mark's entire account. The Father knows, the demonic powers know, but the humans don't know. When Yeshua is arrested and brought before the high priest, the priest asks the same question, "Are you the Messiah, the Son of the Blessed?" Yeshua answers, "I am; and 'you will see the Son of Man seated at the right hand of the Power,' and 'coming with the clouds of heaven'" (Mark 14:61–62). The high priest and all in attendance, however, reject this answer and use it as a pretext to turn Yeshua over to the Roman authorities for crucifixion. They reject the answer to the question "Who is Yeshua?" because the answer is that he is Son of God. Only at the end of the story, in the shadow of the cross, will a human being finally answer the question of Yeshua's divine identity.

> Then Yeshua gave a loud cry and breathed his last. And the curtain of the temple was torn in two, from top to bottom. Now when the centurion, who stood facing him, saw that in this way he breathed his last, he said, "Truly this man was the Son of God!" (Mark 15:37–39)

Only now does a human being recognize Yeshua as Son of God, thus closing the theme initiated at the beginning. Despite the voice from heaven and the anguished cries of recognition wrested from the mouths of demons, Yeshua's closest followers don't seem to grasp who he is, nor do the highest religious authorities among the Jewish people. A Gentile, an officer of the hated Roman occupation in charge of the cruel deed of crucifixion, is the first human to recognize Yeshua as Son of God. Scholars argue whether his words should be translated, "Truly this man was the Son of God!" or "Truly this man was a son of God!" or even "a son of the gods." But the point remains. The Roman officer might not have fully grasped what he was saying, but he knew he was in the presence of the divine and, whether he knew it or not, his words fulfilled the opening theme of Mark.

The divine reversal of the cross applies not only to Yeshua, but also to those who follow him. When Mark describes the crucifixion, he includes a detail that we might easily miss, "And with him they crucified two bandits, one on his right and one on his left" (Mark 15:27). These words echo an earlier passage in Mark, which we considered in Chapter 10, when Yeshua was on his way to Jerusalem with his disciples for his final Passover.

> Ya'akov and Yochanan, the sons of Zavdai, came forward to him and said to him, "Rabbi, we want you to do for us whatever we ask of you."
>
> And he said to them, "What is it you want me to do for you?"

> And they said to him, "Grant us to sit, *one at your right hand and one at your left*, in your glory."
>
> But Yeshua said to them, "You do not know what you are asking. ..." (Mark 10:35–38, emphasis added.)

In the divine reversal of the cross, the places of honor at the right and at the left are redefined as places of co-crucifixion. Yeshua calls us not to positions of privilege and recognition, but to the death of privilege and recognition. I am rankled by the popular Christian terminology that speaks of Jesus as our "personal Savior," because it just sounds too much like "personal trainer" to me. Ironically, such terminology tends to portray the cross of Messiah as the means of personal fulfillment, when in reality the cross is about transcending the personal. Following Yeshua is not a means of fulfillment but a means of obedience to God that might be most costly. Therefore, Yeshua tells us repeatedly to take up our own cross and follow him.[4] Just as Yeshua displayed divine reversal in his body upon the cross, so his followers are called to display divine reversal in their own lives. For this reason, I have included throughout this book practical issues that we might encounter every day.

Yeshua's death is followed, of course, by his resurrection, the greatest of all divine reversals. Crucifixion is the verdict upon Yeshua reached by all humankind, both Jews as represented by the religious elite, and Gentiles as represented by the Roman imperial authority. Resurrection is the verdict of God. It reverses the human assessment and overturns the apparent victory of sin and death. The Messiah who dies in defeat and disgrace rises up three days later in power and glory. When he does, he bestows the same kind of power upon his followers, so that they do not follow him on their strength but his.

Messiah's death and resurrection remain the source of hope from God in a world that holds little real hope apart from him. "For Jews demand signs and Greeks desire wisdom, but we proclaim Messiah crucified, a stumbling block to Jews and foolishness to Gentiles, but to those who are the called, both Jews and Greeks, Messiah the power of God and the wisdom of God" (1 Cor. 1:22–24). May the power and wisdom revealed in the divine reversal enable us to live by the transforming ethics of Yeshua.

NOTES

Introduction

1. Pinchas Lapide, *The Sermon on the Mount: Utopia or Program for Action?* Translated from the German by Arlene Swidler (Maryknoll, NY: Orbis Books, 1986), p. 3.
2. N. Thomas Wright, "Jesus and the Identity of God," *Ex Auditu* 14 (1998), 42–56.
3. Brad H. Young, *Jesus the Jewish Theologian* (Peabody, MA: Hendrickson Pub. 1995), p. xxiv.
4. Lapide, p. 31.
5. Garry Wills, *What Jesus Meant* (New York: Viking, 2006), p. *xviii*.
6. Luke Timothy Johnson, *Living Jesus: Learning the Heart of the Gospel* (San Francisco: Harper, 1999), p. 196.
7. I generally replace *law* in the New Revised Standard Version with Torah. This term and its usage will be explained later in the introduction.
8. Rabbi Joseph Telushkin, *A Code of Jewish Ethics*, vol. 1 (New York: Bell Tower, 2006), pp. 10–25.
9. Telushkin, pp. 12–13, citing Rabbi Shubert Spero.
10. Telushkin, p.14.
11. Telushkin, p. 18.
12. 1 Samuel 17:13.
13. For a more detailed treatment of Jewish interpretation, see the introduction to my book *Creation to Completion* (Clarksville, MD: Lederer Books, 2006).
14. For Jews, the Scriptures include the Torah; Prophets, or *Nevi'im*; and Writings, or *K'tuvim*, and are often called the *Tanakh*, an acronym for these three chapters. Christians read the same exact books in a different arrangement and call it the Old Testament.
15. Resnik, *Creation*, p. 30 f.n.
16. Joseph Shulam, *Hidden Treasures: The First Century Jewish Way of Understanding the Scriptures* (Jerusalem: Netivyah Bible Instruction Ministry, 2008), p. 88.
17. Eugene H. Peterson, *The Jesus Way: A Conversation on the Ways that Jesus is the Way* (Grand Rapids, MI: Eerdmans, 2007), p. 240.

Prologue

1. Hebrew for the body of water also known as the Sea of Galilee or the Lake of Genneseret.
2. See my discussion in *Gateways to Torah*, pp. 61–64 (Shemot) and *Creation to Completion*, pp. 64–66 (B'shallach).
3. William L. Lane, *The Gospel according to Mark: The English Text with an Introduction, Exposition, and Notes* (Grand Rapids, MI: Eerdmans, 1974), p. 55.
4. Lane, pp. 56–57.

Chapter 1

1. Lane, p. 43 (emphasis original).
2. Our system of chapters and verses is a fairly recent addition to the Bible, originating about five hundred years ago. The Jewish and Christian chapter and verse divisions are almost identical but with a few exceptions that we will note. In such cases, the Jewish chapter and verse will be noted with the Christian chapter and verse in brackets.
3. Hyam Maccoby, *Judaism on Trial* (Rutherford, Madison, Teaneck, NJ: Farleigh Dickinson University Press, 1982), p. 120.
4. Some details in this and the next email exchange are changed to protect the identity of my correspondents.
5. Telushkin, p. 19.
6. Sotah 14a.
7. Pirke Avot 1.2.
8. Eugene H. Peterson, *The Jesus Way: A Conversation on the Ways that Jesus is the Way* (Grand Rapids, MI: Eerdmans, 2007), p. 240.
9. Midrash Rabbah, Ruth 2.14.
10. Peterson, p. 8.
11. Peterson, p. 15.
12. Peterson, pp. 125–126.
13. I'm happy to report that Terry encountered Messiah on a hitchhiking journey across North America a year or two later and has been a devoted follower ever since.
14. Johnson, p. 150.
15. Johnson, p. 5, 195.

Chapter 2

1. Marcus J. Borg. *Jesus: Uncovering the Life, Teachings, and Relevance of a Religious Revolutionary.* (San Francisco: HarperSanFrancisco, 2006), p. 159.
2. Geza Vermes, *Jesus the Jew: A Historian's Reading of the Gospels*, (Philadelphia: Fortress Press, 1973), p. 224.
3. Borg, p. 159.
4. Borg, p. 160.
5. *The Jewish Study Bible* (New York: Oxford University Press, 2004), p. 1148 fn.

6. Telushkin, p. 17.

7. *The Complete Artscroll Siddur.* Rabbi Nosson Scherman, trans. (Brooklyn: Mesorah Publications, 1999), p. 17.

8. *Artscroll Siddur*, p. 17.

9. Johnson, p. 165.

Chapter 3

1. Lapide, Pinchas, *The Sermon on the Mount: Utopia or Program for Action?* Translated from the German by Arlene Swidler (Maryknoll, NY: Orbis Books, 1986), p. 12.

2. Lapide, p. 28.

3. Lapide, p. 30.

4. This Greek translation is called the Septuagint and is the source of many of the quotations of the *Tanakh* that appear in the New Covenant Scriptures.

5. Psalm 2:12; 34:9 [34:8]; 40:5 [40:4]; 84:6 [84:5], 84:13 [84:12]; 146:5.

6. Psalm 112:1; 119:1–2.

7. Psalm 41:1; 128:1.

8. Lapide, p. 15.

9. The ceremonial trumpet made of a ram's horn.

10. The exception is Exodus 30:23, where *dror* is an adjective modifying myrrh. The other uses are Leviticus 25:10; Isaiah 61:1; Jeremiah 34:8, 15, 17 (twice); and Ezekiel 46:17.

11. Dale C. Allison, *The Sermon on the Mount: Inspiring the Moral Imagination* (New York: Crossroad, 1999), p. 16.

12. Darrell L. Bock. *Jesus According to Scripture: Restoring the Portrait from the Gospels.* (Grand Rapids, MI: Baker Academic, 2002), p. 128.

13. Bock, p. 128.

14. Allison, p. 16.

15. Bock, pp. 128–129.

16. By Joe Hill. Accessed 11/8/2008. http://www.ciscohouston.com/lyrics/pie_in_the_sky.shtml.

17. In his *Critique of Hegel's Philosophy of Right*, referenced at http://www.quotationspage.com/quote/31765.html. Accessed 11/8/2008. The entire quote reads, "Religion is the sigh of the oppressed creature, the heart of a heartless world, just as it is the spirit of a spiritless situation. It is the opium of the people."

18. *Webster's New Universal Unabridged Dictionary* (New York: Simon & Schuster, 1979.)

19. This term is taken from M. Rex Miller, *The Millennium Matrix* (San Francisco: Jossey-Bass, 2004).

20. Miller, p. 159.

21. Lapide, p. 14.

22. Matthew 5:21, 27, 31 [with a slight variation], 33, 38, 43.

23. David H. Stern, *Jewish New Testament Commentary* (Clarksville, MD: Jewish New Testament Publications, 1992), p. 26.

24. David Daube, *The New Testament and Rabbinic Judaism* (Peabody, MA: Hendrickson Publishers, 1956), pp. 55–62.
25. Lapide, p. 44.
26. Accordingly, when I quote Yeshua's teachings in the following chapters, I will replace the "but" in the translation with "and."
27. This body of discussion leads to what later is called *halakha* in the Jewish world. See further discussion in Chapter 5.
28. Jacob Neusner, *A Rabbi Talks with Jesus: An Intermillennial, Interfaith Exchange* (New York, Doubleday, 1993), pp. 18–36.
29. Neusner, p. 31.
30. Lapide, p. 141.

Chapter 4

1. Name has been changed for privacy.
2. Allison, p. 70.
3. Lapide, pp. 459–50.
4. Telushkin, pp. 248–258.
5. Telushkin, p. 259.
6. Paul is often called Rav Sha'ul in Messianic Jewish circles, attaching the honorific title *Rav* to his original Hebrew name, and this will be my practice henceforth. Acts 13:9 says that Saul (or Sha'ul) was *also* known as Paul, indicating that he didn't altogether change his name but used different names depending on the context of his ministry.
7. R.T. Kendall, *Total Forgiveness* (Lake Mary, FL: Charisma House, 2002). p. 67.
8. *Yalkut Shimoni* on Leviticus 19:18, cited in Yitzchak Buxbaum, *Jewish Spiritual Practices* (Northvale, NJ; Jason Aronson, 1990), p. 221.
9. Buxbaum, p. 222.
10. Simon Wiesenthal, *The Sunflower* (New York: Schocken Books, 1997), p. 98.
11. Ibid. p. 182.
12. *The Mishnah, a new translation.* Jacob Neusner, ed. (New Haven, CT: Yale University Press, 1988), Yoma 8:9.
13. Fred Luskin, *Forgive for Good: A PROVEN Prescription for Health and Happiness* (New York: Harper One, 2003), p. 105ff.
14. Ibid. p. 69.
15. Luskin, p. 65.
16. Telushkin, p. 195, referencing Rosh Hashana 17a.
17. Ibid. p. 199.
18. Ibid. p. 201.
19. Luskin, p. 105.
20. Ibid. p. 33ff.
21. John Howard Yoder, *The Politics of Jesus* (Grand Rapids, MI: Eerdmans, 1994), p. 62–63.

Chapter 5

1. Robert Scheer, "Jimmy Carter: The Playboy Interview." *Playboy.* November 1976. Accessed 4/20/2008, http://www.arts.mcgill.ca/history/faculty/TROYWEB/Courseweb/JimmyCarterThePlayboyInterview.htm.
2. Ibid.
3. David Flusser with R. Steven Notley, *The Sage from Galilee: Rediscovering Jesus' Genius* (Grand Rapids, MI: Eerdmans, 2007), p. 64.
4. Joseph Shulam, *Hidden Treasures: The First Century Jewish Way of Understanding the Scriptures* (Jerusalem: Netivyah Bible Instruction Ministry, 2008), p. 65–66.
5. Bock, p. 134.
6. Gittin, 90a.
7. Gittin 90b.
8. Lapide p. 68.
9. Ibid. p. 68.
10. Ibid. pp. 64–66
11. Eliezer Berkovits, *Not in Heaven: The Nature and Function of Halakha.* (New York: Ktav Publishing House, 1983), p. 73.
12. Ibid. p. 78.
13. Wills, p. 91.
14. Lapide, p. 61.
15. Allison, pp. 77–78.
16. Bock, pp. 131–132.

Chapter 6

1. "Clemens Vehemently Denies Steroid Use," 60 Minutes. Video of Jan. 6, 2008 interview with Mike Wallace. Accessed 6/30/2009 <www.cbsnews.com>.
2. Lapide, p. 72.
3. Author's paraphrase of Shevuot 36a.
4. Midrash Rabbah, Ruth 7:6.
5. Allison, p. 2.
6. Anthony J. Saldarini, *Matthew's Christian-Jewish Community*, (Chicago: The University of Chicago Press, 1994), p. 154
7. Saldarini, p. 154.
8. Lapide, p. 73.
9. Cited in Telushkin, p. 423 from Kant's *Critique of Practical Reason.*
10. See also 1 Samuel 16:1–3 and Jeremiah 38:24–28 as examples of lying to save life.
11. Allison, p. 90.
12. Ibid. p. 91.
13. Ibid. p. 91, citing Bonhoeffer's Ethics.
14. Menachoth 99a–b.
15. Berachot 63a.
16. Saldarini, p. 131.

Chapter 7

1. Jared Diamond, *Guns, Germs, and Steel: The Fates of Human Societies*, (New York: WW Norton, 1999), p. 265.
2. I use the term primitive not as a value judgment but simply to designate a tribe lacking an impersonal justice system.
3. Diamond, p. 227.
4. Sanhedrin 56a.
5. Shulam, pp. 67–70.
6. I use the NKJV here instead of the NRSV as in most Bible references because of a translation issue with major ethical implications. The NKJV says that the fighting men cause the woman to "give birth prematurely"; NRSV that they cause her to miscarry. Kaiser argues that such translations and commentaries "are all in gross error in referring to a miscarriage here" (170). The fighting causes a premature birth, not an abortion.
7. The *Complete Artscroll Siddur*.   Rabbi Nosson Scherman, trans., (Brooklyn: Mesorah Publications, 1999), 49 fn. The Siddur's commentary mentions this as an example of the laws that "were handed down for many centuries from teacher to student" and that "were well known without a need to search for their Scriptural sources."
8. "Court Rules for Cleaners in $54 Million Pants Suit," Henri E. Cauvin. Washington Post, June 26, 2007. Accessed on   www.washingtonpost. com 6/27/2009.
9. Shulam, p. 70.
10. Allison, p. 96.
11. Ibid. p. 93.
12. *Pirke Avot* 1:12.
13. Khaled Hosseini, *The Kite Runner* (New York: Riverhead Books, 2003), pp. 100–101.
14. Allison, pp. 94–95.

Chapter 8

1. Cited in Lapide, p. 96.
2. Emphasis added. Lapide notes that Matthew also leaves out the rest of the verse, "I am the Lord," but it seems natural that in a summary of the verse, Yeshua might leave out this concluding phrase.
3. Berachot, p. 10a.
4. Lapide, p. 85ff.
5. *Complete Jewish Bible* [CJB]. David H. Stern, trans., (Clarksville, MD: Jewish New Testament Publications, 1998), emphasis added.
6. I'm indebted to my colleague Dr. Stuart Dauermann for pointing out this exegesis of Leviticus 19:17–18 in email communication dated 8/7/08.
7. This exegesis also supports the Jewish concept of *ahavat Yisrael*, or "love for the whole people of Israel." This traditional value is sometimes criticized as being narrow or ethnocentric, but it has clear biblical roots and, as we shall see, is seen in Jewish tradition as part of a broader love for humanity.
8. *Pirke Avot* 1:14.

9. *The Pentateuch and Haftorahs*, J. H. Hertz, ed., (London: Soncino Press, 1971), p. 563. I am indebted to my colleague Benzi Sherry for pointing out the references in Hertz.
10. See for example, *The Chumash* throughout, including Leviticus 19, pp. 657–667. *The Chumash, Stone Edition*, Nosson Scherman, ed., (Brooklyn: Mesorah Publications, 1994).
11. Resnik 2006, pp. 114–117.
12. Translations of this verse vary. NKJV reads, "If one of your brethren becomes poor, and falls into poverty among you, then you shall help him, like a stranger or a sojourner, that he may live with you."
13. Lapide, p. 82.
14. Yoder, p. 116.
15. "To every Briton, 1940." Accessed on September, 5, 2008, http://en.wikiquote.org/wiki/Mahatma_Gandhi.
16. "McCain Repudiates Hussein Obama Remarks." Accessed August 30, 2008, http://thecaucus.blogs.nytimes.com.
17. "Prepared text of Obama's nomination speech." Accessed August 31, 2008, http://www.necn.com/Boston/Politics.
18. Hertz, p. 502.
19. Telushkin, p. 74.
20. Telushkin, p. 74. Hillel lived a generation before Yeshua and was active about 30 B.C.E. to 10 C.E.

Chapter 9

1. Wills, p. 29.
2. Ibid. pp. 31–32.
3. *The Torah: with Rashi's Commentary*. Yisrael Isser Zvi Herczeg, trans., (Brooklyn: Mesorah Publications, 1997), Leviticus 13:2.
4. Charles B. Chavel, trans. *Ramban: Commentary on the Torah*. (New York: Shilo Publishing House, 1971) Leviticus p. 183.
5. *Midrash Rabbah*, Leviticus 15.9.
6. Wills, p. 72.
7. Ibid. p. 67.
8. I tell a shorter version of this story in my book, *Creation to Completion*, p. 181.

Chapter 10

1. John Hagee, *In Defense of Israel: The Bible's Mandate for Supporting the Jewish State*, (Lake Mary, FL: FrontLine, 2007), p. 137.
2. Ibid. p. 138.
3. Ibid. p. 139.
4. Wills p. 39.
5. Ironically, *In Defense of Israel* only touches on this crucial passage to make the claim that "Simon son of Jonah" doesn't refer to Simon's father but to the prophet Jonah. Like Jonah, Simon will be forced to go to the Gentiles with God's message (Hagee, p. 138).

6. Flusser, pp. 98–99.
7. Christology refers to the doctrine of the character and work of Christ, or Messiah.
8. Pirke Avot 4:5.
9. Charles Krauthammer, "Redundance on Religion: The proper role of faith in the presidency still eludes candidates." *National Review.* Accessed December 14, 2007. www.nationalreview.com.
10. M. Rex Miller, *The Millennium Matrix*, (San Francisco: Jossey-Bass, 2004), p. 154.
11. Ibid. p. 155. The "emerging digital culture" Miller refers to is the new culture shaped by the digital communications of the computer and the Internet, which is succeeding the "broadcast culture" of the past fifty or sixty years shaped by mass media such as radio, TV, and motion pictures.
12. Cardinal Jean-Marie Lustiger, *The Promise*, (Grand Rapids, MI: Eerdmans, 2007), p. 42.

Chapter 11

1. Borg, pp. 231–232.
2. Ibid. pp. 231–232.
3. Matthew mentions both donkeys at this point, the mother and its foal, leading some commentators to believe that Matthew has Yeshua seated on both of them when he rides into Jerusalem, but see David Stern's discussion in *Jewish New Testament Commentary*, (Clarksville, MD: Jewish New Testament Publications, 1992), pp. 62–63.
4. Borg, pp. 264–265.
5. *Midrash Rabbah* Exodus 18:12.
6. Quoted in David Rausch, *A Legacy of Hatred*, (Chicago: Moody Press, 1984), 21, emphasis added.
7. *The Oxford Universal Dictionary on Historical Principles, third ed.*, (London: Oxford University Press, 1955), p. 2250.
8. Wills, p. 77.
9. Ibid.
10. Ibid. p. 59.
11. *Talmud, Soncino edition*, (Brooklyn: Judaica Press, 1990). Electronic version, Davka Corp. 1995. Sanhedrin, p. 98a.

Chapter 12

1. Rabbi Nosson Scherman, trans., *The Family Haggadah*, (Brooklyn: Mesorah Publications, 2002), p. 45.
2. Rabbi Yitzchak Sender, *The Commentators' Haggadah*, (Jerusalem: Feldheim Pub., 1991), p. 250.
3. *Mishnah, Pesahim*, p. 10.
4. Scherman, p. 25.
5. Rabbi Lawrence Hoffman, *Rethinking Synagogues, A New Vocabulary for Congregational Life*, (Woodstock, VT: Jewish Lights, 2006), pp. 140–141.

6. Ibid. p. 141.
7. Gordon Fee, The First Epistle to the Corinthians, in the *New International Commentary on the New Testament*, (Grand Rapids, MI: Eerdmans, 1987), p. 541.

Epilogue

1. See, for example, Sanhedrin 98a–b.
2. Bauckham 1998, p. 65.
3. Lane, p. 41fn.
4. Matthew 10:38, 16:24; Mark 8:34; Luke 9:23, 14:27; cf. Galatians 6:14.196 *Mishnah, Pesahim*, p. 10.

BIBLIOGRAPHY

Allison, Dale. *The Sermon on the Mount: Inspiring the Moral Imagination.* New York: Crossroad Publishing, 1999.

Bauckham, Richard. *God Crucified: Monotheism and Christology in the New Testament.* Grand Rapids: Eerdmans, 1998.

Berkovits, Eliezer. *Not in Heaven: The Nature and Function of Halakha.* New York: Ktav Publishing House, 1983.

Bock, Darrell L. *Jesus According to Scripture: Restoring the Portrait from the Gospels.* Grand Rapids: Baker Academic, 2002.

Borg, Marcus J. *Jesus: Uncovering the Life, Teachings, and Relevance of a Religious Revolutionary.* San Francisco: HarperSanFrancisco, 2006.

Buxbaum, Yitzchak. *Jewish Spiritual Practices.* London: Jason Aronson, 1990.

The Chumash, Stone Edition. Nosson Scherman, ed. Brooklyn: Mesorah Publications, 1994.

"Clemens Vehemently Denies Steroid Use," *60 Minutes.* Video of Jan. 6, 2008 interview with Mike Wallace. <www.cbsnews.com> Accessed 6/30/2009.

The Complete Artscroll Siddur. Rabbi Nosson Scherman, trans. Brooklyn: Mesorah Publications, 1999.

Complete Jewish Bible [CJB]. David H. Stern, trans. Clarksville: Jewish New Testament Publications, 1998.

"Court Rules for Cleaners in $54 Million Pants Suit," Henri E. Cauvin. *Washington Post,* June 26, 2007. <www.washingtonpost.com> Accessed 6/27/2009.

Daube, David. *The New Testament and Rabbinic Judaism.* Peabody: Hendrickson Publishers, 1956.

Diamond, Jared. *Guns, Germs, and Steel: The Fates of Human Societies.* New York and London: WW Norton, 1999.

Fee, Gordon. *The First Epistle to the Corinthians,* in *The New International Commentary on the New Testament.* Grand Rapids: Eerdmans, 1987.

The Five Books of Moses: A Translation with Commentary. Robert Alter, trans. New York: W. W. Norton & Company, 2004.

Flusser, David, with R. Steven Notley. *The Sage from Galilee: Rediscovering Jesus' Genius.* Grand Rapids: Eerdmans, 2007.

Hagee, John. *In Defense of Israel: The Bible's Mandate for Supporting the Jewish State.* Lake Mary: FrontLine, 2007.

191

Harris, R. Laird, Gleason L. Archer, Bruce K. Waltke, eds. *Theological Wordbook of the Old Testament*. Chicago: Moody Press, 1981.

Hertz, J. H., ed. *The Pentateuch and Haftorahs*. London: Soncino Press, 1971.

Hoffman, Rabbi Lawrence. *Rethinking Synagogues: A New Vocabulary for Congregational Life*. Woodstock: Jewish Lights, 2006.

Hosseini, Khaled. *The Kite Runner*. New York: Riverhead Books, 2003.

The Jewish Study Bible. Adele Berlin and Marc Zvi Brettler, eds. New York: Oxford University Press, 2004.

"Jimmy Carter: The Playboy Interview–Excerpt November 1976." <http://www.arts.mcgill.ca/history/> Accessed 4/20/2008.

Johnson, Luke Timothy. *Living Jesus: Learning the Heart of the Gospel*. San Francisco: Harper, 1999.

JPS Hebrew-English Tanakh: The Traditional Hebrew Text and the New JPS Translation, Scholar PDF Edition [NJPS]. Skokie,: Varda Books, 2001.

Kaiser, Walter. *Toward an Old Testament Ethics*, Grand Rapids: Academie Books, 1983.

Kendall, R.T. *Total Forgiveness*. Lake Mary: Charisma House, 2002.

Krauthammer, Charles. "Redundance on Religion: The proper role of faith in the presidency still eludes candidates." *National Review* <www.nationalreview.com> Accessed December 14, 2007.

Lane, William L. *The Gospel according to Mark: The English Text with an Introduction, Exposition, and Notes*. Grand Rapids: Eerdmans, 1974.

Lapide, Pinchas. *The Sermon on the Mount: Utopia or Program for Action?*. Arlene Swidler, trans. Maryknoll, NY: Orbis Books, 1986.

"Lift Jesus Higher." <www.michael-thomas.com>, Accessed 9/27/08.

Luskin, Dr. Fred. *Forgive for Good: A PROVEN Prescription for Health and Happiness*. New York: Harper One, 2003.

Lustiger, Cardinal Jean-Marie. *The Promise*. Grand Rapids: Eerdmans, 2007.

Maccoby, Hyam. *Judaism on Trial*. Rutherford, Madison, Teaneck: Farleigh Dickinson University Press, 1982

"McCain Repudiates Hussein Obama Remarks." <http://thecaucus.blogs.nytimes.com> Accessed 8/30/08.

Midrash Rabbah, 10 Volumes. H. Freedman and Simon Maurice, eds. and trans. London, New York: Soncino Press, 1983.

Miller, M. Rex. *The Millennium Matrix*. San Francisco: Jossey-Bass, 2004.

The Mishnah, A new translation. Jacob Neusner, ed. New Haven and London: Yale University Press, 1988.

Neusner, Jacob. *A Rabbi Talks with Jesus: an Intermillennial, Interfaith Exchange*. New York: Doubleday, 1993.

New King James Version [NKJV], copyright © 1988 Thomas Nelson, Inc. Electronic Version, Online Bible 2.20.02.

New Revised Standard Version Bible, [NRSV] copyright © 1989 National Council of the Churches of Christ in the United States of America. Electronic Version, Online Bible 2.20.02.

The Oxford Universal Dictionary on Historical Principles, third edition.
    London: Oxford University Press, 1955.
The Pentateuch and Haftorahs, J.H. Hertz, ed., London: Soncino Press,
    1971.
Peterson, Eugene H. *The Jesus Way: A Conversation on the Ways that
    Jesus is the Way*. Grand Rapids: Eerdmans, 2007.
Pirke Avot: A Modern Commentary on Jewish Ethics. Leonard Kravitz, and
    Kerry M. Olitzky, eds. and trans. New York: UAHC Press, 1993.
"Prepared text of Obama's nomination speech." <http://www.necn.com/
    Boston/Politics> Accessed 8/31/08.
Ramban: Commentary on the Torah. Charles B. Chavel, trans. New York:
    Shilo Publishing House, 1971.
Rausch, David. *A Legacy of Hatred*. Chicago: Moody Press, 1984.
Resnik, Russell. *Creation to Completion: A Guide to Life's Journey from
    the Five Books of Moses*. Clarksville: Lederer Books, 2006.
————. *Gateways to Torah: Joining the Ancient Conversation on the
    Weekly Portion*. Clarksville: Lederer Books, 2000.
Saldarini, Anthony J. *Matthew's Christian-Jewish Community*. Chicago and
    London: The University of Chicago Press, 1994.
Scherman, Rabbi Nosson, trans. *The Family Haggadah*. Brooklyn: Mesorah
    Publications, 2002.
Sender, Rabbi Yitzchak. *The Commentators' Haggadah*. Jerusalem: Feldheim
    Pub., 1991.
Shulam, Joseph. *Hidden Treasures: The First Century Jewish Way of
    Understanding the Scriptures*. Jerusalem: Netivyah Bible Instruction
    Ministry, 2008.
Stern, David H. *Jewish New Testament Commentary*. Clarksville: Jewish
    New Testament Publications, 1992.
Talmud, Soncino edition. Brooklyn: Judaica Press, 1990. Electronic
    version, Davka Corp. 1995.
Telushkin, Rabbi Joseph. *A Code of Jewish Ethics, Volume 1*. New York:
    Bell Tower, 2006.
"To every Briton, 1940." Cited at <http://en.wikiquote.org/wiki/Mahatma_
    Gandhi> Accessed 9/5/2008.
The Torah: with Rashi's Commentary. Yisrael Isser Zvi Herczeg, trans.
    Brooklyn: Mesorah Publications, 1997.
Vermes, Geza. *Jesus the Jew: A Historian's Reading of the Gospels*.
    Philadelphia: Fortress Press, 1973.
Wiesenthal, Simon. *The Sunflower*. New York: Schocken Books, 1997.
Wills, Garry. *What Jesus Meant*. New York: Viking, 2006.
Wright, N. Thomas. "Jesus and the Identity of God." *Ex Auditu* 1998.
Yoder, John Howard. *The Politics of Jesus*. Grand Rapids: Eerdmans, 1994.
Young, Brad H. *Jesus the Jewish Theologian*. Peabody: Hendrickson Pub.,
    1995.

OTHER RELATED RESOURCES
Available at Messianic Jewish Resources Int'l
www.messianicjewish.net
1-800-410-7367

Complete Jewish Bible *David H. Stern, Ph.D., translator*
Presenting the Word of God as a unified Jewish book, the Complete Jewish Bible is a new versioan for Jews and non-Jews alike. It connects Jews with the Jewishness of the Messiah, and non-Jews with their Jewish roots. Names and key terms are returned to their original Hebrew and presented in easy-to-understand transliterations, enabling the reader to say them the way Yeshua (Jesus) did!

| Hardback JB12 | $34.99 | Paperback JB13 | $29.99 |
| Leather Cover JB15 | $59.99 | Large Print JB16 | $49.99 |

Gateways to Torah *Russell Resnik*
Joining the Ancient Conversation on the Weekly Portion
From before the days of Messiah until today, Jewish people have read from and discussed a prescribed portion of the Pentateuch each week. Russ Resnik has written an excellent commentary on each of the weekly portions, bringing another perspective on the Torah, that of a Messianic Jew.
LB42 $15.99

Creation to Completion *Russell Resnik*
A Guide to Life's Journey from the Five books of Moses
Paul urged Timothy to study the Scriptures (2 Tim. 3:16), advising him to apply its teaching to all aspects of his life. Given first to the nation of Israel, God intended the Torah to be useful for all people, Jewish or non-Jewish. Now, Russ Resnik has written a warm devotional commentary that will help you understand and apply the Law of Moses to your life in a practical way.
LB61 $14.99

The World To Come *Derek Leman*
A Portal to Heaven on Earth
People want to know the future. They want to know about Heaven and Hell. Who isn't concerned about issues beyond to-day's news? We want to know what the Bible teaches about "the World to Come," and expression used by Jewish people. Derek Leman has written an insightful book, exposing fallacies and false teachings that surround this extremely important subject.
LB67 $9.99

In Search of the Silver Lining   *Jerry Gramckow*
Where is God in the Midst of Life's Storms?

When faced with suffering, what are your choices? Answers to the problem of pain and tragedy often elude the people of God. This sensitive book attempts to answer one of life's toughest questions. For those going through difficult circumstances, this book offers a hopeful, scriptural approach that can help you through the storms of life.

LB39 $10.99

Proverbial Wisdom & Common Sense *Derek Leman*
A Messianic Jewish Approach to Today's Issues from the Proverbs

Unique in style and scope, this commentary on the book of Proverbs, written in devotional style, is divided into chapters suitable for daily reading. A virtual encyclopedia of practical advice on family, sex, finances, gossip, honesty, love, humility, and discipline.

LB35 $14.99

Blessing the King of the Universe   *Irene Lipson*
Transforming Your Life Through the Practice of Biblical Praise

Insights into the ancient biblical practice of blessing God are offered clearly and practically. With examples from Scripture and Jewish tradition, this book teaches the biblical formula used by men and women of the bible, including the Messiah; points to new ways to praise the Lord; and explains more about the Jewish roots of the faith.

LB53 $11.99

The Greatest Commandment   *Irene Lipson*
How the Sh'ma Leads to More Love in Your Life

"What is the greatest commandment?" Yeshua was asked. His reply – Hear O Israel, the Lord our God, the Lord is one, and you are to love the Lord your God with all your heart, with all your soul, with all your understanding, and all your strength. Irene Lipson has written a superb book explaining each word of this lofty statement, so it can be fully grasped. Her depth of understanding of Hebrew opens up new insight into The Greatest Commandment.

LB65 $12.99